Lecture Notes in Computer Science

Edited by G. Goos, J. Hartmanis and J. van Leeu

T0237755

Springer

Berlin
Heidelberg
New York
Barcelona
Hong Kong
London
Milan
Paris
Singapore
Tokyo

Klaus R. Dittrich   Giovanna Guerrini
Isabella Merlo   Marta Oliva
M. Elena Rodríguez (Eds.)

Objects
and Databases

International Symposium
Sophia Antipolis, France, June 13, 2000
Revised Papers

Springer

Volume Editors

Klaus R. Dittrich
University of Zurich, Department of Computer Science
Winterthurerstrasse 190, 8057 Zurich, Switzerland
E-mail: dittrich@ifi.unizh.ch

Giovanna Guerrini
Isabella Merlo
Università di Genova, Dipartimento di Informatica e Scienze dell'Informazione
via Dodecaneso 35, 16146 Genova, Italy
E-mail: E-mail: {guerrini/merloisa}@disi.unige.it

Marta Oliva
Universitat de Lleida, Departament d'Informàtica i Enginyeria Industrial
C. Jaume II, 69, 25001 Lleida, Spain
E-mail: oliva@eup.udl.es

M. Elena Rodríguez
Universitat Politècnica de Catalunya
Departament de Llenguatges i Sistemes Informàtics
Mòdul C 6, C. Jordi Girona Salgado 1-3, 08034 Barcelona, Spain
E-mail: malena@lsi.upc.es

Cataloging-in-Publication Data applied for

Die Deutsche Bibliothek - CIP-Einheitsaufnahme

Objects and databases : international symposium, Sophia Antipolis,
France, June 13, 2000 ; revised papers / Klaus R. Dittrich ... (ed.).
- Berlin ; Heidelberg ; New York ; Barcelona ; Hong Kong ; London ;
Milan ; Paris ; Singapore ; Tokyo : Springer, 2001
   (Lecture notes in computer science ; Vol. 1944)
   ISBN 3-540-41664-1

CR Subject Classification (1998): H.2.4, H.2, D.1.5, D.3

ISSN 0302-9743
ISBN 3-540-41664-1 Springer-Verlag Berlin Heidelberg New York

Springer-Verlag Berlin Heidelberg New York
a member of BertelsmannSpringer Science+Business Media GmbH
© Springer-Verlag Berlin Heidelberg 2001
Printed in Germany

Typesetting: Camera-ready by author, data conversion by PTP-Berlin, Stefan Sossna
Printed on acid-free paper   SPIN: 10781349   06/3142   5 4 3 2 1 0

Preface

These post-proceedings contain the revised versions of the papers presented at the "Symposium on Objects and Databases" which was held in Sophia-Antipolis, France, June 13, 2000, in conjunction with the Fourteenth European Conference on Object-Oriented Programming, ECOOP 2000. This event continued the tradition established the year before in Lisbon (Portugal) with the First Workshop on Object-Oriented Databases.

The goal of the symposium was to bring together researchers working in various corners of the field of objects and databases, to discuss the current state of research in the field and to critically evaluate existing solutions in terms of their current usage, their successes and limitations, and their potential for new applications.

The organizing committee received 21 papers which were reviewed by a program committee of people active in the field of objects and databases. There were 3 reviews for each paper, and finally the organizing committee selected 9 long papers, 2 short papers, and a demonstration to be presented and discussed at the symposium. The selected papers cover a wide spectrum of topics, including data modeling concepts, persistent object languages, consistency and integrity of persistent data, storage structures, class versioning and schema evolution, query languages, and temporal object-oriented databases.

In addition to the regular papers, the symposium included an invited presentation, given by Prof. Malcolm Atkinson from the University of Glasgow (Scotland) where he heads the Persistence and Distribution Group.

We wish to express our gratitude to all those individuals and institutions who made this symposium and the proceedings possible: to the authors of papers; to the members of the program committee and the external reviewers for carefully reviewing the papers; to Malcolm Atkinson for accepting our invitation to give a talk and to prepare a paper for this volume; and to the publisher for the pleasant co-operation. In addition we wish to thank the Organizing Chairs of ECOOP 2000, Denis Caromel and Jean-Paul Rigault for the economic support for inviting Malcolm Atkinson, and the workshop chairs of ECOOP 2000, Sabine Moisan and Jacques Malenfant, for their efforts in scheduling and local arrangements. Finally, we thank all the participants, without whom the symposium would not have been possible.

January 2001

Klaus R. Dittrich
Giovanna Guerrini
Isabella Merlo
Marta Oliva
M. Elena Rodríguez

Program Committee

Suad Alagić	Wichita State University, USA
Akmal Chaudhri	Computer Associates Plc, UK
Christine Collet	INPG-Ensimag Grenoble, France
Philippe Collet	University of Nice Sophia Antipolis, France
Óscar Díaz	University of Basque Country, Spain
Leonidas Fegaras	University of Texas at Arlington, USA
Elena Ferrari	University of Milano, Italy
Jesús García Molina	University of Murcia, Spain
Giorgio Ghelli	University of Pisa, Italy
Antony Hosking	Purdue University, USA
Gerti Kappel	Johannes Kepler University of Linz, Austria
Alfons Kemper	University of Passau, Germany
Paloma Martínez	University Carlos III of Madrid, Spain
Bernd Mathiske	Sun Microsystems Laboratories, USA
Adoración de Miguel	University Carlos III of Madrid, Spain
Moira Norrie	ETH Zürich, Switzerland
Tamer Özsu	University of Alberta, Canada
Tony Printezis	University of Glasgow, UK
Awais Rashid	Lancaster University, UK
Tore Risch	Uppsala University, Sweden
Elke Rundensteiner	Worcester Polytechnic Institute, USA
Gunter Saake	Otto-von-Guericke University of Magdeburg, Germany
Markku Sakkinen	Tampere University of Technology, Finland
José Samos	University of Granada, Spain
Roberto Zicari	Johann Wolfgang Goethe-University, Frankfurt/Main, Germany

Additional Referees

Edgard Benítez-Guerrero	Iqbal Goralwalla
Kajal Claypool	Svetlana Kouznetsova
Stephan Dassow	Genoveva Vargas-Solar

Organizing Committee

Klaus R. Dittrich	University of Zürich, Switzerland
Giovanna Guerrini	University of Genova, Italy
Isabella Merlo	University of Genova, Italy
Marta Oliva	University of Lleida, Spain
M. Elena Rodríguez	Technical University of Catalonia, Spain

Table of Contents

Data Mining and Data Warehouse

Miscellaneous

Pannel Discussion

Persistence and Java — A Balancing Act

Malcolm Atkinson

Department of Computing Science, University of Glasgow, Scotland.
mpa@dcs.gla.ac.uk

Abstract. Large scale and long-lived application systems, *enterprise applications*, require persistence, that is provision of storage for many of their data structures. The Java[TM] programming language is a typical example of a strongly-typed, object-oriented programming language that is becoming popular for building enterprise applications. It therefore needs persistence.

The present options for obtaining this persistence are reviewed. We conclude that the *Orthogonal Persistence Hypothesis*, OPH, is still persuasive. It states that the universal and automated provision of longevity or brevity for all data will significantly enhance developer productivity and improve applications.

This position paper reports on the *PJama* project with particular reference to its test of the OPH. We review why orthogonal persistence has not been taken up widely, and why the OPH is *still* incompletely tested. This leads to a more general challenge of how to conduct experiments which reveal large-scale and long-term effects and some thoughts on how that challenge might be addressed by the software research community.

1 Introduction

One attempt to describe engineers says "An engineer can do for five pence what ordinary folk can do for five pounds". Our industry is dominated by the task of building, maintaining, deploying and operating very large and very many application systems. I call these large and long-lived applications *Enterprise Applications* in accord with the current fashion.[1] They become progressively larger and more complex. More and more skilled application developers are involved in this work every year. There is currently a serious shortage of the relevant skilled labour and forecasts of greater shortages. The growth in cheap and ubiquitous computing, and the expanding ambitions of organisations, whose appetite has been whetted by initial enterprise applications, will surely reinforce these trends.

Revisiting the engineers' *modus operandi*, we ask "How do they do it?" Generally, the answers are: "By automation", "By using better materials or better technology" and "By clever design". Given the skill shortages and hence dramatically increasing costs of enterprise-application development and maintenance, you would expect to see all three of these engineering strategies strongly to the fore. And there are some encouraging examples. For example, the automated

---

[1] In [8] these were termed "Persistent Application Systems" (PAS).

K.R. Dittrich et al. (Eds.): Objects and Databases 2000, LNCS 1944, pp. 1–31, 2001.
© Springer-Verlag Berlin Heidelberg 2001

main-memory management in Java, and the automated detection of many errors through strong typing are believed to be increasing productivity. The better automation of migration between platforms, is perhaps another example. Once we consider the provision of persistence for all of Java's data structures, there is not much sign of progress.

Progress in engineering depends on a fairly formal (often codified and well-tested) process for adopting new technology. Engineers cannot take unreasonable risks. For example, they cannot use the production of a product to test a hypothesis about a new way of making it. The cost of failure, would make this unprofessional conduct. Instead, the engineering process proceeds incrementally. It establishes new models and hypotheses, by conducting experiments to establish their validity, parameters and properties. It then develops "established" theory based on these experiments, that can be used with much lower risk. Still, early use is accompanied by more errors and problems, and so a prototype or pioneering project has to be properly and honestly resourced.

By these standards, even the "good practice" that we take for granted, such as: type safety, automated memory management, object orientation and relational storage, may not have been properly evaluated and measured to verify their benefits to software engineering productivity before they were deployed [65]. The reasons seem to include:

Overconfidence — researchers and practioners feel comfortable with depending on hunches, fashion, anecdote and belief.

Distraction — they focus on measuring things that are easy to measure, such as performance and main-memory footprint.

Difficulty — measuring such things as the *long-term* effect on productivity is difficult.

Due to these three factors, we sometimes use arguments based on loud assertion (I'll admit to this myself with respect to the value of orthogonal persistence) rather than following the preferred engineering process.

Aware of these deficiencies, and positing that they might be the cause of the lack of take up of orthogonal persistence, the PJama project was conceived[2]. This project met with mixed success and it is worth reviewing a little of its history and then trying to understand the causes of its limited influence. A more complete and detailed review is available as [5], and some aspects of this paper derive from that report.

1.1   Definition of Orthogonal Persistence

The history, rationale and definition of orthogonal persistence are presented in [8]. The earliest implementations appeared in 1980. The crucial concept is that the management of long-term storage should be automated in much the same

---

[2] Originally called the 'PJava project', but that name was commandeered by Sun to refer to Personal Java, for mobile devices.

way as it should for main-memory data, in order that developers can focus on the logic of their application and not be distracted by having to implement their own persistence, e.g., via a mapping to some other technology. For this to work, three properties must apply.

Orthogonality — The persistence facilities must be available for all data, irrespective of their type, class, size or any other property. This is essential. If this is not the case, then application programmers quickly encounter data structures for which longevity is not available and they are forced to resort to hand crafting facilities to make that data persist. This resurrects the distraction and source of errors, and may mean that they have to deal with everything, because their own code has to coordinate, e.g. in transactions, with the persistence of other data. Furthermore, lack of orthogonality makes the next two requirements hard to meet.

Completeness or Transitivity — If some data structure is preserved, then everything that is needed to use that data correctly must be preserved with it, for the same lifetime. A common example is that when an object contains references to other objects, the transitive closure of such references must be preserved. Otherwise dangling reference errors will occur when those data are later used. In the case of an object-oriented language, data are described in terms of classes which associate behaviour with state. *That behaviour must also be preserved, in order that the data are correctly interpreted in the future.*

Persistence Independence — The source and byte codes should not require any changes to operate on long-lived data. Furthermore, the semantics of the language must not change as the result of using persistence. For example, evaluation order, type safety, security and object-identity, must be exactly the same for code that operates on long-lived objects as it is for code that operates on transient objects. If this requirement is not met, we lose reliability and code re-usability; imported code has to be changed to work with persistent data, and often multiple versions are required to deal with different persistence mechanisms. Persistence independence minimises the amount application developers have to learn before they can use persistence to create long-lived data. It is much simpler than using files and databases.

This leaves as an issue, how to identify the roots of persistence, analogous to the roots for retention known to the garbage collector in main-memory management, and how to deal with long-term issues, such as class evolution. It also poses a challenge as to how to implement it well.

1.2   Organisation of This Paper

This paper addresses three topics: a brief review of the available mechanisms for persistence that can be used with Java, an analysis of the PJama project and an attempt to justify and characterise the requirements for large-scale, cooperative experimental computing science research. The first topic is likely to date rapidly;

it corresponds to an assessment made in June 2000 for the talk at the Symposium on Objects and Databases in Sophia Antipolis, France. The second topic may be a biased interpretation as the author is still closely involved in that work. The third topic is an initial foray into the issues of how experimental evidence for the value of foundation software may be gathered and it requires much further development.

The options for achieving persistence in Java are summarised in Section 2 and the initial experimental plan is reviewed in Section 3. The technical progress and final achievements of the PJama project are sketched in Section 4. The limited impact is analysed in Section 5. This leads to the identification of a general challenge, and a suggestion that this should be met through the introduction of new approaches to experimental computing science in Section 6.

2   Current Persistence Options for Java

Initially the standard core classes for Java [35] offered only connection to an external file system and *ad hoc* support for encoding and decoding a property table (`java.util.Properties`).

The JDK 1.1 release added Java Object Serialization (JOS) and Java Database Connectivity (JDBC) [37]. JOS is a mechanism that supports the encoding of an object to an output stream and the subsequent decoding from an input stream. JOS is used both for persistence and for communicating copies of objects in the support for distributed programming.

2.1   Java Object Serialization

JOS is *the standard* means of providing persistence for the Java programming language. It uses a binary encoding, which makes a copy of all of a specified object's fields (instance variables) and all of those objects transitively reachable from it. It is customisable, and a common idiom for customising it misuses the keyword **transient** [42,58]. Though close to orthogonal persistence, JOS has several problems.

It is not orthogonal. For reasons of security, it requires that an object implement the **interface Serializable** before it can be serialised. Therefore, many core classes and classes imported in byte code form cannot be preserved using JOS. A consequence is that transitivity also fails.

It fails to implement completeness. The class information defining behaviour, primarily the byte codes, is not preserved with the state of objects. Consequently it has a harsh regime, which can be over-ridden, to ensure that objects are re-used by exactly the same class. It does not have enough information to support class evolution that includes instance reformatting [4]. Indeed, **class Class** is an example of a failure of orthogonality ( ) — even if an instance of it is referenced directly, its behaviour will not be preserved.

It fails to implement persistence independence on several counts. For example, as it copies objects, object identity is lost. When two different objects (and their dependant data structures) are preserved in two separate serialisations, then when they are deserialised, previously common sub-structures are duplicated, with an obvious change in semantics. Similar discrepancies occur if a program re-reads a data structure from a serialisation while it still holds parts of the original data structure. Associated with this loss of identity is a failure to preserve the value of the `identityHashCode` of serialised objects.

The relationship between **static** variables, and instance variables is not preserved. For example, the following class should guarantee that each of its instances had a different `id`.

```java
public class UniqueInstanceId implements Serializable {
    private static int nextId = 0;       // The next id to issue
    private int id;                      // Each inst. different value
    public UniqueInstanceId() {          // The only constructor
        id = nextId; nextId++;           // Issue next id
    }
    public int getId() {
        return id;                       // Each instance should
                                         // return a different value
    }
    ...
}
```

But, if it was preserved using JOS and then reloaded, `nextId` would be reset to zero. Consequently, it would re-issue identies already issued, so that, if instances of `UniqueInstanceId` still exist or were reloaded via this or another JOS deserialisation, there would be duplicate identities, *in contradiction of the explicitly programmed invariant.*

It doesn't scale very well. It suffers from the *big inhale* and *big exhale* problem. That is transfers to and from disk are not incremental. In consequence, if a small proportion of a data structure is to be traversed or updated, the whole of it has to read first and the whole write has to take place afterwards. Programmers try to overcome this, by breaking up their data structure, but they then find themselves engaged in much complexity.

It is hard to make it provide transactional, recoverable and concurrently usable persistence. This can be done, for example, by storing separate JOS serialisations in files (and using renaming, etc.) or in tuples in a database. Care has to be taken to prevent this collection of separate serialisations from suffering the other problems listed above.

2.2   Links to Relational Databases

The JDBC API provides a mechanism for accessing and updating RDBs from Java programs. Although in principle it will link with any DBMS, in practice it is almost always used to connect with relational databases. This means that it is well designed for interworking with legacy RDB applications and data collections. The emerging standard SQL/J [19] provides added convenience, by automating some aspects of the interface between Java objects and SQL. In particular, it uses Java's type system well, to help programmers use cursors correctly. It also allows **static** methods to be used in SQL and as database procedures, and supports the storage of subgraphs of objects via JOS ($\rightsquigarrow$2.1).

Both of these suffer from the significant *impedence mismatch* between Java and the relational model, and therefore leave the programmer handling a complex mapping. They require explicit code which may obscure application logic and hinder maintenance. They do not attempt orthogonality, i.e. they cannot handle all objects ($\rightsquigarrow$2.1). These are not issues when legacy interaction is considered; this Java-to-RDB API, and its packaging via SQL/J, are well adapted to that task.

2.3   Automated Object-Relational Mappings

When application developers are creating new Java data structures which they want to persist, the JDBC or SQL/J interface technology is, at best, cumbersome. The developers have to define a relational schema and then create, operate and maintain a complex mapping from the instances of Java classes and references to that schema. One strategy to assist such developers in such circumstances has been to automatically generate and maintain the Object-Relational (OR) mapping[3]. The JavaBlend^{TM} system [64] is an example. Reflection over the Java class definitions is used to extract a schema, generate its SQL definition, and to generate the SQL and JDBC code that will automatically save instances and restore them. In principle, this is a good idea, but it has several practical limitations at present. Complex networks of class definitions and complex object usage patterns may defeat the automatic generation. Once generated, the code can be slow and awkward to use. Experience shows that tuning these systems requires modifications to the generated schema, which in turn requires extensive knowledge of the mapping, and so proves very difficult. It has also proved difficult to change applications that are operating using such mappings.

The inverse generation, from relations to objects, can also automated. This is somewhat easier to manage, but produces collections of classes rather close to the original relations. This is helpful if a new application is to be written based on a legacy data definition, but it does not address the issue of how to provide persistence for the results of object-oriented design and development. In particular, behaviour is not preserved and there is little basis for supporting class evolution.

2.4   Object-Database Mappings

The Object Database Management Group (ODMG) has defined a binding of its object model to the Java programming language [16]. This *definition* has

---

[3] No doubt motivated by the investment in, trust in and availability of RDBMS.

adopted the principles of orthogonality and transitivity. So Java data structures can be simply mapped from class definitions to ODB schemata, and simply preserved and recovered by incremental and transactional mechanisms. Other permitted operations in the Java language binding, such as explicit delete, and various controls for transactions, etc. rather defeat the persistence independence of this ideal. Many of the actual implementations have other problems, such as being a long way from orthogonal, requiring extra steps in program production, such as post-processing byte codes, and requiring extra operations on objects, which takes them much further from the orthogonally persistent ideal of not distracting the developer from the logic of the application. Gemstone/J stands out as providing the closest approximation to orthogonal persistence [34].

2.5 Java Data Objects

At the time of writing ODMG has suspended development of the ODMG Java binding pending completion of the Java Data Objects (JDO) specification that is being developed under the Java Community Process [60]. JDO is an ambitious attempt to define a standard API that provides access to a wide variety of heterogeneous data sources. The intent is that these sources can be manipulated by a Java application as if they were ordinary Java objects. An application may access objects from multiple JDO sources concurrently. In principle, JDO subsumes OR-mapping or, more accurately, an OR-mapping system would appear to a Java application as simply another JDO source.

The JDO does not attempt persistence independence. For example, the JDO defines a complex and separate "memory model" that an application programmer must understand. This model includes the concept of a "hollow" object, which is one that exists in the virtual machine but whose content has not yet been loaded from the external data source. Programmers must be prepared to deal with hollow objects in certain circumstances. As there isn't a straightforward transactional model for JDO we expect programmers will struggle with such responsibilities.

2.6 The Enterprise Java Beans (EJB) Framework

The Enterprise Java Beans (EJB) framework [63] aims to provide a complete solution to applications that manage distributed, heterogeneous data. EJB makes no pretence of persistence independence, programmers must follow strict rules about the structure and form of the classes that make up an EJB. In fact, each bean instance is represented by a total of three classes, the "EJB object", the "EJB home" and the actual bean instance. All access to the bean instance is routed through the EJB object and completely controlled by the EJB server. The benefit from following this protocol is that the EJB infrastructure promises to automate many aspects of persistence and transaction management. In addition, the EJB server can provide instance pooling and object-cache management.

Experience has shown that it is hard for programmers to adhere to strict rules. This difficulty is ameliorated by tools support, but it is hard to envisage tools support for EJB application synthesis that goes far beyond simple applications. Extensive interactions with large and complex graphs of objects are unlikely to be efficient if they depend on mediation.

2.7   Review of the Current Persistence Options for Java

All of the models described above have their strengths and weaknesses. JOS (↝2.1) is convenient and well matched for storing small and medium scale graphs of objects in a file system. This breaks down as soon as the graph is large, shared, multiply used, or contains instances that don't implement `Serializable`. JDBC and SQL/J (↝2.2) work well for legacy RDB interaction, but not for all *Java* data structures. Object-relational mappings (↝2.3) work if the data structures and traversal patterns required are not too complex. Object-database mappings (↝2.4) vary a lot between vendors, but there is at least one good example. The proposal for Java Data Objects (↝2.5) is very ambitious, but it is not yet realised. Enterprise Java Beans (↝2.6) require each application to fit within a rigid framework. Other models also exist, for example, mapping to XML. These may also exhibit similar problems, such as complex memory models or explicit mappings between disperate models.

This survey suggests that if it is possible to meet the ideals of orthogonal persistence the result may be a significantly improved environment for applications that need persistence — which is pretty much all of them. The 'if' and the 'may' are important words in that sentence.

3   Testing the Orthogonal Persistence Hypothesis

The PJama project was conceived as an opportunity to *properly* test the Orthogonal Persistence Hypothesis (OPH). We can state the hypothesis as:

> If application developers are provided with a well-implemented and well-supported orthogonally persistent programming platform, then a significant increase in developer productivity will ensue and operational performance will be satisfactory.

There were already a host of previously implemented orthogonally persistent languages [2,55]. The reviews [8,5] contain more complete lists. But, as we argue in [5], a conclusive test of the hypothesis had not been performed for a variety of reasons. Two important reasons were:

> Insufficient resources had been available to complete or evaluate the platform.
> The platform had not supported a language that was both popular and type safe.

We believed that the advent of Java gave us the opportunity to circumvent the latter problem, and that we could raise enough resource, in conjunction with Sun Microsystems Laboratories (SunLabs), to overcome the first problem. So PJava was proposed [6,3], as a platform to support this evaluation with the intention that the on-going tools project, Forest [43], would act as the user group, independently testing orthogonal persistence's impact on developer productivity and performance[4].

3.1   Requirements for PJama

In order that we could carry out evaluation at a reasonable scale, PJama had to deliver the reliability and functionality expected by application developers. We interpreted this "industrial strength" requirement as implying the following more detailed requirements had to be met simultaneously.

A *Orthogonality* — All instances of all classes must have the full rights to persistence.

B *Persistence Independence* — The language must be completely unchanged (syntax, semantics and core classes) so that imported programs and libraries of classes work correctly, whether they are imported in source form or as bytecodes.

C *Durability* — Application programmers must be able to trust the system not to lose their data.

D *Scalability* — Developers should not encounter limits which prevent their applications from running.

E *Schema Evolution* — Facilities to change any class definitions and to make consequent changes to instance populations must be well supported.

F *Platform Migration* — It must be possible to move existing applications and their data onto new technology (hardware, operating system, or Java virtual machine (JVM) [53]).

G *Endurance* — The platform must be able to sustain continuous operation.

H *Openness* — It must be possible to connect applications to other systems and to interwork with other technologies.

I *Transactional* — Transactional operation is required in order to combine durability and concurrency and to support appropriate combinations of isolation and communication.

J *Performance* — The performance must be acceptable.

Earlier systems have met some, but not all of these requirements simultaneously. This is unsurprising as many of them are difficult to reconcile with each other and some, e.g. transactions, require new technology, such as implicit lock management that is efficient for large numbers of objects [23].

---

[4] Prototypes based on the classic JDK have a subscript beginning with zero. The latest version, utilising JIT compilation, has subscript 1.

3.2   The Original Workplan

We planned to build a prototype in Glasgow based on the JDK, and to deliver this rapidly to SunLabs. The Forest group would use that for implementation, assessing its utility and providing feedback on the design. A version meeting all of the requirements would be developed in Glasgow, while the Forest group developed a set of tools intended to support distributed, co-operative development of Java applications [43,44]. *In some unspecified way* the experience of using PJama for this real application was to be distilled to yield evidence about the validity of the OP hypothesis. One benefit of this plan was that the developers were independent from the OP platform suppliers, which should reduce the chance that prejudice or common assumptions about applications or development would bias the outcome.

4   Progress with an Orthogonally Persistent Platform

Many projects are underway to explore orthogonal persistence for Java. They include [33,47,54,26]. We focus on our own experience, which is more fully described in [5].

4.1   Learning from a Prototype

Our prototype, built using JDK and RVM [61] (see Figure 1a), was operational in May 1996 (about seven months after we started) [7,3]. Of course, it was incomplete, but it was possible to use it to build applications.

At this point, we probably made our first significant mistake, by developing the prototype further [24]. That meant that we continued to wrestle with the complexity and unreliability of the JVM on which we were building. This was exacerbated by the rapid rate of change in the standard Java platform, with each release of the JDK. Two pernicious problems were that JVM's failure to maintain exact knowledge of all of the pointers and its extensive and unstructured use of C in the core classes, particularly the AWT[5]. Here again, with the benefit of hindsight, it might have been better to ignore AWT. But then we would have been far from orthogonal. We noticed that many of our users encountered substantial problems when AWT classes did not have full rights to persistence. They ended up writing mappings to capture information about their application's communication with its user in data structures that could persist, and reconstructing that state on restart; clearly a distraction from their application's logic.

Similarly, as we integrated communications and distribution with persistence we found it necessary to capture state at the start of a checkpoint and reconstruct it on restart. We recognised that it is a general requirement to handle intrinsically transient states, such as relationships with external systems. We therefore modified our API to support this through a listeners and events pattern [42,58]. This highlighted the equivalence between providing persistence and supporting

---

[5] A large collection of popular Java classes used to build GUIs.

long-term continuous execution. The paper [42] gives a good summary of our experiences with several versions of PJama based on the classic JDK.

Meanwhile, the circumstances of the team had changed. Laurent Daynès, moved from Glasgow to SunLabs to join the Forest group, which expanded and changed its emphasis from tools to persistence. Whilst both sites still shared the overall design, the division of implementation effort became:

PJ at SunLabs — modifying virtual machines, including JIT compilers, to deliver OP [51,52], handling the extension of orthogonality across the core classes, particularly Swing[6], developing the support for intrinsically transient states, pioneering technology for flexible transactions [25], and improved multi-application execution safety, based on application isolation [22].

Glasgow — object stores [57], recovery [36], evolution [4] and application trials [5].

4.2   Phase Two of PJama's Development

We decided, by late 1996, on the architecture of our new technology, shown in Figure 1.b. This continued with our fundamental decision to deliver persistence by modifying a JVM and moved completely away from using virtual-memory techniques. The persistent object store, Sphere, was designed and implemented from scratch, over a period of three years [57]. It is general purpose, but has novel mechanisms to support efficiently multiple data management regimes, bulk load, disk garbage collection, evolution [59,4] and independence from particular virtual machines.

A greater challenge, was to decide how best to achieve a new, modified virtual machine, including modified JIT. Several choices were available, when the decision was made in 1998.

EVM — Derived from the classic JVM, to support research into main-memory space management and garbage collection [67], this was emerging as a product to run on Enterprise servers under Solaris[7]. It precisely tracked pointers and most of the C code obeyed the JNI-discipline, that supported this. It had a JIT.

HotSpot — A new, and sophisticated JVM, that had two JIT technologies. This was primarily targeted at Microsoft NT platforms at that time.

External JVM — Any other JVM, such as those produced by other companies or the Open Software Foundation.

New Implementation — Starting again with the requirements of orthogonal persistence in mind.

We chose to build with the EVM, even though some people warned us that it would probably lose out politically in the long run to HotSpot. We selected this

---

[6] A set of classes supporting more sophisticated GUI interaction that depend on AWT classes and still use C.

[7] It is now called the SunLabs Research Virtual Machine.

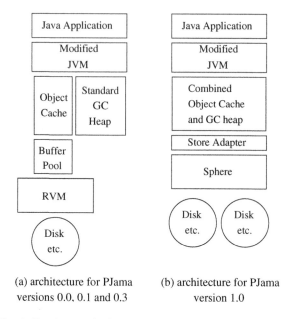

(a) architecture for PJama
versions 0.0, 0.1 and 0.3

(b) architecture for PJama
version 1.0

Fig. 1. Persistence Architectures used for Versions of PJama

path because it targetted support for large and long-running applications, which matched our expected primary use. We also had good working relationships with the EVM team. In contrast, *at that time* HotSpot appeared complex to modify, relatively unstable and oriented to running shorter-term executions. A major factor was probably that it was a much smaller step from the classic JDK, with which we were familiar, to use the EVM. An "External" JVM was scarcely considered for political, legal and practical reasons and a new JVM was infeasible, as producing a JVM of sufficient quality takes a much larger team than we could muster.

With the benefit of hindsight, choosing EVM, rather than HotSpot[8], was a mistake, as work was stopped on EVM much more rapidly than we had expected and work related to it was immediately considered inappropriate by Sun. This occurred during the summer of 1999, before PJama$_{1.0}$ became completely robust, and sapped the energy of the team modifying the EVM for our purposes. For research based on PJama to continue, it is necessary to once again choose and modify a JVM[9] — a task that takes two experienced engineers at least two years. A more detailed summary of the major decisions taken during the development of PJama can be found in Chapter 15 of [5].

---

[8] Which has advanced very rapidly for both platforms.

[9] EVM is not an option, as its source is not publically available.

4.3   Achievements of PJama$_{1.0}$

The achievements of PJama are summarised here relative to the requirements enunciated in ↝3.1.

A *Orthogonality* — An approximation to this has been achieved[10], which is good enough to allow many applications to be written without their developers being distracted by persistence requirements. The ability to stop and restart the Swing demonstration, restoring the whole interactive state is a powerful demonstration of how far we persevered with handling the AWT challenge. We have not had resources to process several important packages, such as JDBC and CORBA but do not expect them to expose new technical difficulties[11]. One class, intimately connected with the implementation of the JVM, Thread, has proved much more problematic. There are often references to threads, particularly in libraries, such as the core classes, that developers find useful. Not being able to make threads persist is therefore a serious handicap, as it once again forces developers to manage aspects of their own persistence. However, with the JVMs, operating systems and hardware we have used, it has not been possible to recover all of the necessary information at every checkpoint, to restore threads correctly. A general solution appears to be a research problem [5] Chapter 16.

B *Persistence Independence* — This has been completely achieved. Apart from the very few lines of code that explicitly call the PJama API to set up an application's persistent context, all code runs with unchanged behaviour in the persistent and non-persistent contexts.

C *Durability* — The ARIES-based recovery works well. As a back up for media failure and catastrophies, there are also logical and binary archiving mechanisms, but these conflict with endurance [G], since they require that the application programs be stopped.

D *Scalability* — We have tested stores up to 10 Gbytes and with more than 300 million objects. The largest single object used by any application so far was about 30 Mbytes. We do not anticipate major problems with increasing the scale.

E *Schema Evolution* — Our technology that supports evolution will permit virtually any change to the set and definitions of classes. It verifies that the set of changes are mutually consistent, that the final state conforms with the specification of Java and that it is consistent with known applications. It

---

[10] It is achieved completely for some specialised JVMs, such as the PalmTop version and the JVM written in Java — but these examples do not meet all of the other requirements.

[11] It is frustrating that many of the library classes use programming styles that assume the external context of an object only has to be constructed once as a class is loaded, when a resumable programming style would have been more robust, and straightforward — widespread use of resumable programming would make adaption to persistence, simply a matter of registering listeners for the checkpoint and restore events.

provides default and developer defined transformation of instances to transfer information between their old and new version. The system is made more convenient for developers by being integrated with a build and recompilation system [4,30]. But the present system conflicts with endurance [G] because, at present, it requires that the applications be stopped while evolution is performed.

F *Platform Migration* — Our current provision is a logical archive and restore. It was challenging to deliver, as classes that are intimately connected with the JVM's implementation need to be treated specially. The present algorithm is limited in the scale of data it can accommodate and we have little experience of its use. We believe that support for migration is essential and that the current approach will suffice. However, an incremental implementation is needed — the present implementation stops application processing, in conflict with endurance [G] and needs to get all data into main memory, conflicting with scalability [C].

G *Endurance* — Many applications, such as web servers, mail servers, news servers, business services, biological databases, etc., have to deliver a continuous service. These include just those applications for which improved persistence would (*we hypothesise*) be highly beneficial. Our performance here is mixed. Apart from the cases listed above, we also have to stop applications to perform disk garbage collection[12]. More critically, at present, bugs prevent heavily multithreaded applications from running for more than a few minutes, whereas we have run applications using only a few threads for more than 6 days without interruption[13].

H *Openness* — This depends on our generic facilities for explicitly preserving and reconstructing the state of external connections. We demonstrate the solution with `sockets`, `RMI` and the `Swing` subsystems. As mentioned in [A] above, more work is needed to cover the remaining core classes used for external connection.

I *Transactional* — The implicit transaction start, series of checkpoints and committing checkpoint, supported at present, provide a simple transactional facility, roughly equivalent to long-running transactions. Our more sophisticated plan for flexible transactions [6,3] is nearing fruition [23,25]. Its expressivity and semantics was explored using a Java-in-Java implementation, which, of course, did not offer acceptable performance [J]. For some applications, the present system is problematic, in that all threads have to reach a consistent state before a checkpoint is performed, as the checkpoint applies to the whole virtual machine.

J *Performance* — Execution of the modified JVM/JIT is slowed by 15% to 20% compared with the unmodified JVM/JIT for executions that are not

---

[12] A prototype concurrent disk garbage collector exists [57], but it is not yet in our released system.

[13] The unresolved bugs appear to be race conditions in the modified JVM. They mostly occur as interactions between code written by two different teams, the EVM team's main-memory management and the PJ team's object-cache management. Bugs of this kind are very time-consuming to locate with today's debugging tools!

accessing data on disk. A more relevant comparison, is to compare with applications using other forms of persistence ($\leadsto$2). We have observed cases where PJama gives speed up by a factor of more than 100, but the gain is highly application dependent. Therefore, useful comparisons depend on the development of appropriate benchmarks. There is much opportunity to improve over the present performance, e.g. by using known optimisations [13]. It is unlikely that performance deficiencies will be a significant impediment to evaluation and use.

In summary, the overall achievement is tantalisingly close to a platform ready to support a serious test of the orthogonal persistence hypothesis. There is probably enough functionality and performance. Lack of endurance and limits to the transactional facilities are the two major flaws. On the other hand, it is capable of running the benchmark that simulates an Enterprise middleware server load [29,52], with 24 warehouses, each running 5 threads of activity. It also runs the *large* 007 benchmark [15,52]. It is probable that PJama is as robust, scalable and comprehensive as many relational systems were when they were first used commercially. Today expectations are rightly higher.

This poses a fundamental question, "Why are we in this position?". That is, "Why has support from Sun for this experiment stopped?" and "Why didn't we complete it, or at least deliver a firm platform for experiments, in the time (nearly 5 years) and with the resources (probably about US$10 million)?" The rest of this paper is concerned with answering these questions, and trying to expose general lessons from the particular story.

Three general forms of explanation have to be considered:

We were either incompetent managers or poor engineers.
We tackled an ill-conceived project.
We were simply unlucky.

5   Analysis of the Impact of PJama

It is difficult to assess or estimate the impact or influence of PJama. It is evident that it is not going to be incorporated into a product immediately and there are only a few users; about 150 registered sites and about a dozen reported applications [48,50,49,32,10,5,52,68,69,20]. On the other hand, the future derivatives are unknown. Taking an optimistic view, we could imagine an impact analogous to that of self [18,38][14]. That work at SunLabs and Stanford was never used directly by Sun, but it had two major impacts.

It entered the culture and influenced further work. The most dramatic example being the formation of Anamorphic to build an efficient Smalltalk system based on the self experience. This was changed to target Java and forms the nucleus of the HotSpot system.

---

[14] Intriguingly, they now share the same resting place on Sunlab's web site, http://www.sun.com/research/previous.html.

It created a pool of exceptionally talented researchers and experienced language implementers, many of whom have contributed significantly to Java and other technologies.

It would be over ambitious to claim at this stage that the same will happen with PJama. But there are hints that it could happen.

We now look more carefully at progress towards the original goal of testing the OP hypothesis. If these tests supported the hypothesis this would be a result along the lines of Snyder's "proof of concept" [31], i.e. the concept of orthogonal persistence is "proven" to significantly improve developer productivity. To be on track with this, we need a number of real uses of PJama that involve typical development teams building and evolving applications and typical users imposing typical workloads. The benefits of such an observable workload and developer group would be twofold.

An opportunity to observe and measure a development team's problems, successes and productivity.

An opportunity to gather measurements of the workloads placed on the components of the system, which could be used to improve its engineering and which should inform other (orthogonal) persistence engineering projects.

At this stage, the best we could have hoped for, would be one or two year's worth of such observations. They are not happening because the platform quality has not yet been achieved. For a company or research organisation to commit an engineering team and a project that was actually going to be used by real users with their own data and critical goals, would require confidence in the platform and its maintenance. Many is the time we've heard the question, "Is it supported?". If the answer had been "Yes", there were, and still are, many developers who would like to participate in an evaluation project. They are, of course, behaving correctly, under the engineering procedures that were identified in the introduction. To work with an unsupported platform would be to take an undue risk. But for a company to commit to supporting that platform, a new technology whose benefits, costs and problems have not been determined, would also be an undue risk. So, we are presented with a classic chicken-and-egg problem.

At the outset, the investment expected from Sun (which was actually exceeded by a substantial factor), from the University of Glasgow and from our Research Council, looked as if it might be sufficient to get beyond this impasse.

5.1   Reaching Critical Mass

If an orthogonally persistent platform can reach sufficient quality via a protype, then there is a chance that it will attract sufficient interest to persuade the technology providers and the application developers to collaborate on resourcing and completing an evaluation. There are various ways in which this might have happened.

By targeting a very specific subset of Java, that was nevertheless convincing and deliverable.

By choosing to focus on a particular application, as in our original plan, and then to deliver functionality, scale and parts of Java, as they were needed.

By prioritising the requirements differently, conciously omitting some to achieve reliabilty over a more moderate subset.

By making better technical decisions, so that a viable system could be delivered.

By communicating more persuasively the potential benefits of orthogonal persistence and convincing people that these benefits were within reach ($\rightsquigarrow$5.3).

A targeted subset — Officially the licence to modify the JDK's source requires that the result should still comply with conformance tests. This is obviously a sensitive issue, when protecting the strength of Java that code can be compiled once and run anywhere. The core classes are an essential environment for this, as they abstract over the facilities provided by operating systems. At the start of our project we underestimated the cost of being complete, for two reasons. We did not anticipate how many classes would need special treatment, because of the way they were implemented. We never expected the rapid growth in the core classes, and in modifications to the language. Without a well identified target application, pressures from (potential) users tended to expand the set of classes on our "to do" list very rapidly.

A focus on one application — A partial solution is to focus on supporting a given application, or small group of applications. But, it is well known, that by doing so, one can develop high-level abstractions that support application development very well *within the common pattern*. Consequently, too narrow a goal would devalue the experiment. On the other hand, more sophisticated applications push up the requirements. The original goal of supporting the Forest project's distributed software production tools might have been a good focus, but it did require a very large proportion of Java's (early) facilities. Indeed, more or less the subset that we have actually implemented.

Prioritised Requirements — We sought to deliver a working response to all of the requirements set out in Section 3.1. We did order these, at least implicitly. Orthogonality [A] and persistence independence [B] were addressed first. Durability, scalability, evolution and openness [C, D, E, H], were then addressed. As we did this, our concern for performance [J], never far from our minds during design work, emerged as important — particularly when it brought an application's execution from 6.5 days to 3 hours. We considered transactions important from the start (concurring with Blackburn [12]) but found that fundamental machinery needed improving first [23,25,22]. Migration [F] has taken considerable investment, though it hasn't been fully addressed. Endurance [G] is clearly an issue for which we haven't yet delivered a solution. In short, project management required that we adopt priorities and these are evident from the state of PJama. Its current state also shows that we cannot omit any of our requirements and still have a foundation sufficient for testing the OP hypothesis.

Technical Decisions — as already indicated, some of our technical decisions might have been taken differently with hindsight. Perhaps the most fundamental are to use in-line tests for barriers, which implies modifying a JVM and JIT, and to manage objects rather than pages. Our intuition that these choices are essential for evolution and high performance with demanding application loads, is born out by observations of comparative performance with larger applications. Only one OODBMS appears to have comparable performance at large scale and that has taken a similar route. On the other hand, these choices have meant large amounts of difficult system-software development (though we're getting better at it [52]), which we seriously underestimated. Only when comparisons can be made for real workloads will we be able to determine under what circumstances these choices are appropriate. Other research, making different technical choices, shows promising results with small-scale, synthetic loads and with an incomplete delivery of our requirements, though it does promise good migration [54]. Research is needed, both to provide good information on which to base these choices, and to improve our engineering as we pursue them.

There are several reasons why taking different technical decisions alone, would not unravel our problem.

> When other combinations of technical choices are tried, and pursued to deliver *all* of the proposed requirements, they are likely to experience their own complexities.
>
> The technical problems posed by Java's rapid rate of change, extensive classes using non-Java implementations or non-resumable code, multiple external connection mechanisms, and semantic complexities of the language, would still have to be faced.
>
> The opportunity for eliminating barriers in compiled code [39] would still be worth exploring, as would many other aspects of the path we took.

Summary — Considering these three issues together, we could have made more progress by (1) using more focus, (e.g. not pursuing all of the changes in Java and attempting as many core classes), by (2) being driven by one application (e.g. distributed configuration and build management, as planned) and by (3) making better technical and political decisions (e.g. by building on a better JVM with a longer supported life). But I will argue that even with judgement that proves wise in hindsight, the original goal was unreachable with the feasibly available resources.

5.2   Experiments at an Appropriate Scale

We invested approximately US$10 million[15]. We started at a time when Java and its implementations were very volatile, which certainly decreased our efficiency

---

[15] UK costs were converted to US currency. All are based on the overheaded researcher salaries. These figures are simply indicative, as it is difficult to attribute work accurately and as cost is context dependent. The author is not privy to the actual US salaries and overheads.

[5]. Some of that investment went on other goals, developing the Forest tools [44], opening up new territory [23,22], with results in valuable technology, but which is not immediately applicable, and into education, which results in skilled engineers. Taking these effects into account, approximately US$6 million is a closer estimate of our investment into building an "industrial strength" platform. In contrast, it currently costs US$50 million to build a new DBMS ready for market [28]. A platform of the kind we sought probably needs at least half of that work. We were therefore attempting a task with quarter of the resource necessary.

But the ultimate goal was to test the OP hypothesis. To do that the platform would not only have to be built, it would need to be maintained for long enough for a complete experiment, say five years. Optimistically, that maintenance, for a limited group on a given hardware and operating system platform, would require five engineers (one to maintain the evolution system, two for the VM maintenance, two for the store maintenance, and sharing other work between them). This assumes a continued feed of language and core-class tracking updates from a VM source and only moderate expansion of the core-classes needing special treatment. That is at least another US$5 million expenditure[16].

This just provides and sustains the platform for the experiments. It does not include the cost of running those experiments, which would involve the application developers, the application users and a team of observers, measuring the properties of the software, the workload and the developers' productivity. But as the platform is expensive to build and maintain, it makes sense to use it to support a range of experiments, even though this probably doubles the maintenance and support costs. If the platform costs so much to set up, then it may also be sensible to use it for a much longer period than five years. In short, we have to recognise that the kind of research needed to tests hypotheses of the form:

X improves the productivity of application developers under realistic conditions of application scale, use and change.

requires a quantum leap in our resourcing and conduct of computing science experimentation (the topic of ⤳6). The attempt to use PJama to test the OP hypothesis was doomed to be inconclusive, not for the detailed reasons discussed above (though in retrospect we could have done better), but because it was an experiment conducted under procedures only appropriate for smaller scale and shorter term phenomena.

5.3   What about Industry?

Returning to our final postulated cause for failure, *being insufficiently persuasive*, it is appropriate to examine the industry's attitude to orthogonal persistence. We certainly didn't invest sufficiently in persuading industry, particularly in building partnerships to explore the potential of the technology. There were a number of contributory factors.

---

[16] Or £ 1 million (1.6 million Euros) if the work was carried out in the UK.

Commitment to Existing Practices — It is hard to persuade industry to consider changing practices: for good engineering reasons, described earlier, of not taking undue risks; because of the established training, habits and culture of application development engineers; because of massive existing investment and because the database and platform suppliers' marketing is committed to RDB and working well.

Displaced Problems — the groups who have greatest difficulty with the status quo are those building and maintaining large and complex enterprise systems. Whereas the platform builders and suppliers see little of this and are therefore disinclined to invest in addressing the developers' problem. Most application developers are unable to resource platform development — it needs to be amortised over many development projects.

Alternative Solutions — there is recognition that the demands for rapid development of many sophisticated enterprise applications is overwhelming development capacity and that they may well be becoming too complex to maintain. But other solutions are thought to be more likely to yield significant improvements quickly. The majority of these are the use of high-level notations and the automatic generation of code [17,11].

The Dominance of Glueware — our initial perception that many large applications were going to be built using Java has not been realised. A predominent use of Java for enterprise applications, is to write code that sits on a middle-tier computer and combines several pre-existing applications and data sources based on RDBs. Consequently, the components that are being combined provide persistence and the glueware combining them has little need for it.

Distribution Drives Application Structure — the need to scale up to support the rapid growth in e-business and the commensurate requirement for continuous services has made distribution virtually mandatory. Our failure to address distributed checkpoint because it depends on having transactions (↪4.3 item I) means that PJama is not deployable in this context. The weight of this requirement grew while we were developing against our original requirements.

Lack of Credibility — because much of the example research in orthogonal persistence has limitations (small scale, partial solutions, "obscure" languages, etc.) it lacks credibility among the decision makers of the software technology industry. They feel that the case is not proven (precisely what PJama set out to overcome) and that most of the research results we have could easily be reinvented and reconstructed in their context if this ever appeared relevant. Sometimes they go further, and say that has been tried already, and it didn't work. This is exacerbated by ignorance of current achievements. For example, they know schema edits are essential for persistence and suspect we can't perform them.

The Language Trap — There is a suspicion that orthogonal persistence implies adoption of a single language for all applications. A trap that is known to become serious over time, from which databases have rescued developers.

The situation is caricatured in Figure 2, where we see the forces of investment, existing practice and engineering caution piled up against the tiny mass of orthogonal persistence research, with its overall lack of cohesion and experimental evidence.

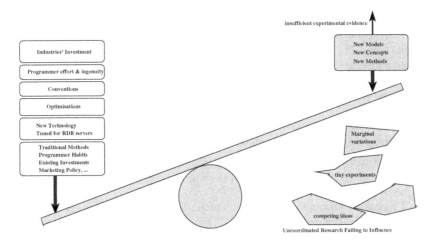

Fig. 2. Relationship between the Enterprise Platform Industries and Orthogonal Persistence Research

5.4 Why We Aren't Like Relations

It is informative to compare the advent of DBMS and particularly RDBMS with the current situation. In the 1960s and 1970s, the applications needed to run an organisation were being developed piece-meal and against separate structured files. Building and maintaining these was very difficult, as programmers had a great deal of responsibility for managing disk access, data format, concurrency, etc. The RDBs, by providing an abstraction that worked well for this class of application, promised the much needed reduction of the application complexity. The industry consequently invested, and the technology was adopted, despite many technical deficiencies still extant in that technology at its introduction. Most of those have been dealt with over the years by cohorts of researchers tackling particular problems arising in this context. A microcosm of that history is repeated in a recent review of triggers and constraints [17].

In contrast, orthogonal persistence doesn't offer such a simple message. For example, it doesn't offer to take away a substantial activity and automate it. On the contrary, when we say that indexes, etc. may be built above the platform, many people hear us say we are giving the application programmers extra work. We know that we'd normally expect those to be built by experts and delivered in libraries, but we haven't yet demonstrated that it is feasible. For example, we haven't measured the performance and shown it is acceptable, or demonstrated that we can deliver high concurrency because the algebra of index operations is well understood (that requires the non-isolated flexible transactions that was one of our goals ↝3.1 item I).

Similarly, though the application developers face difficult problems, their cause is not clear cut. Many complexities, from heterogeneity, distribution, multiple autonomous systems, mobility, intermittent connection, continuous service, all challenge the application developers. It is not clear that orthogonal persistence addresses these, and it is therefore not clear that it will contribute. The developers immediate hope is that the use of large, re-usable components, e.g. EJBs, and the generation of code from high-level descriptions, will alleviate their stress.

We believe that the principles of orthogonal persistence will benefit the real problems of application development and maintenance in three ways:

The principle of offering the same service, whatever the type (data structure) can be generalised and so developers will face fewer exceptions that have to be coded around.

The goal of encompassing all of a computation, including longevity, interaction with autonomous systems, and change in one consistent (programming) model, if met, will bring coherence and comprehensibility to the enterprise applications, their development and maintenance.

The two previous effects enhance code mobility through defining more of the computation completely. They also provide a context in which the generated code, and expertly prepared components may be more easily constructed, more easily combined and more easily used. We note that being able to combine such products is an essential requirement, not easily met in today's computational environments.

But these are *only* beliefs and they are all long-term effects. The apparent immediacy of alternative "rescue packages", such as code generation from high-level notations, is much more appealing, though it is equally an act of faith. For example, they may yield high productivity for narrow topics that they're able to handle, and generate much complexity combining or changing them in a total system. We also know that they are *not* rival approaches, but are potentially complimentary with orthogonal persistence.

We may conclude, as our act of faith, that future languages should be orthogonally persistent, and should automate mappings, disk management, transactions and recovery, just as those languages should have main-memory management and multi-threading. But we have to develop a much better way of communicating this.

6   Investigating Large-Scale Phenomena

The analysis of the previous section raises many questions, here we only consider one — the challenge of conducting large-scale and long-term investigations. It is no longer practical to try to convert the application development engineers to a new faith[17]. Instead, an engineering process of establishing the value of the new technology must be undertaken. It must be recognised that sometimes the hypothesis that a new technology has value will not be valid. In these cases, avoiding the cost of wider investment, justifies the cost of careful evaluation. In the successful cases, that evaluation may lead to more effective and faster take up of the new technology.

In computing science, we are faced with many putative advances. Some are relatively easily evaluated, because their effects are immediate and localised, e.g. a better index for a particular task, or a new network storage architecture. Others, because their effects are diverse and long term, are much harder to evaluate. In this paper, we have argued that orthogonal persistence is an example in this latter category. We now consider how research might proceed in such cases, using PJama to *illustrate* the possibilities. Although the envisaged process is set out as a sequence of steps below, actual practice will be iterative.

6.1   Is There a Case to Answer?

Before undertaking an expensive and long-term project, it has to be established to be worthwhile. A hypothesis must be well defined. For example, *"There is a significant class of applications for which, adding orthogonal persistence to the development platform would significantly improve developer productivity over application lifetimes"*. This obviously needs refinement. How big, how common and how important is this class of applications? What precisely does "adding orthogonal persistence" entail? How widespread and how substantial are the "productivity gains"? etc.

It is necessary to decide whether this is an important innovation. Does it have a large practical impact or a large conceptual value? Will it reveal new understanding of software engineering processes, that may well lead to further progress?

Does it have a chance of succeeding or of failing? If the result is a foregone conclusion *in either direction* there is little point in conducting the experiment. This step forces the research community to examine the practical details of the undertaking and to identify the likely risks. This discussion also has its own value. It will provoke refinement of terms such as "improvement", "performance" and "productivity" and will stimulate thought about potential detrimental effects as well as about the hypothesised benefits.

As we are considering an expensive undertaking, it will need to compete for resources. This requires that a community considers it a worthwhile investment. The debate and dialogue to achieve consensus that it is a worthwhile and viable issue to investigate has its own value. It forces the exposure and refinement of definitions, assumptions and criteria and will itself enhance our understanding of the processes involved in creating and sustaining enterprise applications. This

---

[17] Though Java appears to be a case where this happened — it certainly isn't a predictable process.

debate requires time and resources. We may expect subsidiary investigations to expose issues, for example, in the PJama case, analysis of existing suites of software and working practices to establish that there is potential for improvement. This requires a change in the research culture. It has to become appropriate to fund and publish such preparatory work, and that work has to be recognised in careers and PhDs.

6.2   Designing a Family of Experiments

As already explained ($\leadsto$16), the cost and complexity of the infrastructure for many software engineering experiments may make it sensible to conduct several experiments using the same context[18]. So it will normally be appropriate to consider a family of related experiments and design an infrastructure to support all of them. For simplicity, here we consider only one experiment within such a family.

If any theory is available, it should be considered as a means of refining the experiment. For example, it may show what factors are important, or even that in a particular case extrapolation from a smaller experiment is a reasonable first approximation. Considering the productivity of enterprise application developers the following kinds of theory may be relevant: models of program comprehension and construction, theories about how to quantify and manage change, theories about how engineers solve problems, etc. Ultimately, developing experimental protocols and developing theories that motivate and interpret their measurements must be concomitant activities.

It is necessary to identify what will be measured and what contextual parameters will be kept as stable as possible. In a software technology trial, such as that proposed for PJama, it would be necessary to measure developer productivity, predominantly as they maintain the system. Then it is necessary to establish how that can be measured. For example, several teams attempting tasks from a chosen set, with different technologies might be observed, directly to measure work hours and indirectly to measure actions. Similarly, the existing application and data context might be kept stable (i.e. reset for each trial). But how large should the tasks be? How should we deal with familiarity effects? How should we deal with communication or variation between teams? How should we set up the teams? How should we set up the application? etc. There are clearly many issues to be resolved at this stage of experimental design.

The great variability in the productivity of individual programmers is well known [14]. Though this tends to obscure the effects of the choice of technology it is clear that there are such effects and they may be large. Fortunately there is already practical experience in mounting experiments to expose these effects [46,45,66] and laboratories to study software engineering productivity are being established [62]. The existence of practitioners who are a hundred times more productive does not diminish the value of discriminating between technologies

---

[18] Just as the particle physicists do with a high-energy collider or the astronomers do with a high-resolution telescope.

that produce a large impact on each individual's productivity, particularly as there are never enough of the highly productive engineers.

An experimental protocol has to be prepared. For example, what warm up tasks will be used to (partially) eliminate familiarity effects? How are teams selected[19] and how are they allocated tasks[20]? How will the data from the experiments be processed? What differences in the measures will be disregarded "noise"? What differences in the measures will we judge significant?

Once designed, the experimental platform and context has to be constructed. This requires the technology to be built (the challenges here are well illustrated by the recent PJama saga) and the comparator technologies have to be acquired (the controls). It is necessary to build equivalent versions of the application, or convert an existing application to use the technologies in question. Mechanisms for acquiring the measurements which minimally perturb the development process have to be devised and built.

Such experimental planning and "apparatus" construction is an essential part of the research. The work will require innovation, creativity, high-quality engineering and scientific research skills. It is important to reach the intended scale, because software engineering and computing processes manifest new effects as the scale is increased. Again, the value of research into experimental methods for evaluating new software technologies must be recognised as a worthwhile contribution in its own right and an appropriate activity.

6.3   Conducting Experiments

Having designed an experiment, considerable effort is needed to conduct it accordingly. For example, the technology platforms for the experiments need to be kept in sufficiently good working order that software engineers participating as subjects believe that they are working with a viable and active systems. Similarly the applications have to be set up and maintained and users supported to obtain real user loads. The teams who will use the technology have to be chosen, briefed and managed. To obtain professionals with suitable experience, they may also need to be paid. The observations of the processes must be collected and monitored to ensure that they are being correctly and completely collected. This data must be carefully curated so that many subsequent analyses, that are unlikely to have been forseen, can be carried out by interested researchers.

6.4   Experimental Interpretation

Such technology trials will not admit simple, first-past-the-post analysis. There are likely to be many parameters that were impossible to maintain exactly constant, for example, the experience of the participating software engineers. There

---

[19] What experience and maturity mix is required from team members? How will they be paid and motivated? What will they be told? How will they be organised?

[20] Randomly for the total set? According to team background? To be done in any order? As a sequence of increasing scale? As a sequence of successive changes to related software and data?

are likely to be many measured parameters, all varying, and some that are hard to quantify. Experimental costs will limit the extent to which these problems can be overcome by repetition to increase sample size. Consequently, techniques derived from other testing regimes where similar difficulties of interpretation arise, such as clinical trials, may be needed. The statistical sophistication required may be considerably in excess of that used by many computer science experimenters at present. Then care must be taken as to how far the results derived from such experiments are extrapolated to other contexts.

6.5   Resources, Teams, and Communities

For the aspects of computing science research which require such large scale and sophisticated experimentation, we have to develop a mode of research which is capable of creating, managing, sustaining and resourcing such experiments. This can only happen with intellectual and practical support from peers (practitioners and researchers).

Intellectual support is needed in evaluating and discussing the incremental steps of the research outlined above. For example, grant application and paper reviewing, as well as PhD examination, has to assess fairly work that is only concerned with elucidating an aspect of the larger research programme. Since only a few of the large-scale experiments that are initially proposed will come to fruition, it is necessary to recognise as intellectually worthwhile investment in experimental planning, that may terminate.

A community of researchers interested in developing such experiments needs to form, in order to bring together the necessary range of skills and in order to provide the constructive criticism necessary to refine hypotheses, experimental designs, plans and procedures. It will need to collaborate closely on some experiments over substantial periods[21].

Computing differs from other experimental subjects in that software costs dominate the experimental budget, but are often hidden as the incidental work of researchers, PhD students, etc. The software for these larger experiments cannot be generated in this way. It has to be resourced over longer time scales and managed so that it achieves adequate quality. It may, with investment in coordination and management, be possible to do this through open source strategies, but in some cases, it will be an experimental cost that requires cash to pay software engineers' salaries.

6.6   Summary

In this section, the steps involved in large-scale technology evaluation experiments have been elucidated. Certain questions cannot be answered unless we take such an approach. Some of those questions may be important to the subject of computing science and to the users of its products in industry, commerce and government. The experimental procedures will require elapsed time and large

---

[21] Just as environmental scientists, astronomers, physicists, etc. do at present.

resources well beyond the currently accepted norms. For example, some of the effects on productivity that depend on the choice of technology may reverse as the scale changes.

This presents a challenge. How can we change the research culture so that this form of research is recognised as necessary and is properly supported? Currently such research is inhibited by negative attitudes towards those who try to measure properties of our technology that are difficult to quantify, even though they are important. Similarly, research into aspects of these larger problems is often disadvantaged relative to neatly packaged and complete research into smaller scale or easily measured phenomena even if those phenomena have much less significance. If computing science research is to be relevant to the massive networks of applications being built and deployed today then it must embrace larger-scale and longer-term experimental research. That will require fundamental changes in the ways in which we organise and assess research.

If the cost of all such research were to be so expensive for experiments, there would be a serious impediment to the development of computing science when it is applied to large and long-lived systems. Fortunately we can expect two benefits from the approach described above.

> The process of discussing and designing experiments will sharpen our experimental ingenuity so that smaller scale and lower cost procedures may sometimes be seen to offer sufficient evidence.
>
> The construction of the first large-scale experiments will teach us how to conduct them much more efficiently and will provide a legacy of understanding and evolving frameworks which will dramatically reduce the cost of future experimentation.

7   Conclusions

This paper has addressed three topics. The current options for providing persistence to Java programs were briefly reviewed ($\leadsto$2) and considered deficient, particularly when the cost of implementing changes to applications was considered. The next topic was a review of the PJama project, from its goal of testing the orthogonal persistence hypothesis ($\leadsto$3) to its more moderate but still significant outcome ($\leadsto$4). Analysis of that outcome ($\leadsto$5) leads to a recognition that some questions, such as the impact of orthogonal persistence on application developer productivity, can only be answered by large-scale and long-term experiments. The PJama project focused its efforts on constructing technology and failed to invest in an effective evaluation experiment. This was mainly because the need to plan, resource and conduct such an evaluation was seriously underestimated. This suggests that it is incumbent on projects developing new technologies that are intended to improve support for enterprise technologies to properly conduct such evaluations. That is not easy.

Whether or not the evaluation of PJama deserves the necessary investment, our experience exposes the question: How can we resource and conduct such evaluations? The third, and perhaps most important topic of the paper, an examination of that question ($\leadsto$6) generates the view that the modus operandi of computing science researchers needs to be radically changed to support large-scale and long-term experimentation whenever the goal is to better support large and long-lived applications.

Acknowledgements. The work was supported by grants from the British Engineering and Physical Sciences Research Council (GR/K87791) and from Sun Microsystems, Inc. The principal team members who developed PJama were Grzegorz Czajkowski, Laurent Daynès, Misha Dmitriev, Neal Gafter, Craig Hamilton, Brian Lewis, Bernd Mathiske, Tony Printezis, Susan Spence and Michael Van De Vanter. Many students at Glasgow and several summer interns at Sun, contributed in various ways.

Mick Jordan, the leader of the SunLabs Forest group, recognised the potential of orthogonal persistence for Java, initiated the work and organised a major proportion of the resources invested. He had a substantial influence on the design and development, and was a co-author of the report [5] on which parts of this paper are based. He also made valuable comments on an early version.

Ron Morrison read an early draft and provided both encouragement and helpful suggestions. Dag Sjøberg, Magne Jørgensen, Steve Blackburn and Ela Hunt suggested substantial improvements. Kathy Humphry, Gordon Cooke and Robert Japp suggested corrections.

References

1. A.E. Abbadi, M.J. Brodie, S. Chakravarthy, U. Dayal, N. Kamel, G. Schlageter, and K-Y. Whang, editors. *Proceedings of the Twentysixth International Conference on Very Large Databases.* Morgan Kaufmann, 2000.
2. M.P. Atkinson, P.J. Bailey, K.J. Chisholm, W.P. Cockshott, and R. Morrison. An approach to persistent programming. *The Computer Journal,* 26(4):360–365, November 1983.
3. M.P. Atkinson, L. Daynès, M.J. Jordan, T. Printezis, and S. Spence. An Orthogonally Persistent Java^{TM}. *ACM SIGMOD Record,* 25(4), December 1996.
4. M.P. Atkinson, M. Dmitriev, C. Hamilton, and T. Printezis. Scalable and Recoverable Implementation of Object Evolution for the PJama Platform. In Dearle et al. [27], pages 255–268 in the preprints, University of Oslo, Department of Informatics, Preprint 2000 No. 288.
5. M.P. Atkinson and M.J. Jordan. A Review of the Rationale and Architectures of PJama: a Durable, Flexible, Evolvable and Scalable Orthogonally Persistent Programming Platform. Technical Report TR-2000-90, Sun Microsystems Laboratories Inc and Department of Computing Science, University of Glasgow, 901 San Antonio Road, Palo Alto, CA 94303, USA and Glasgow G12 8QQ, Scotland, 2000.
6. M.P. Atkinson, M.J. Jordan, L. Daynès, and S. Spence. Design Issues for Persistent Java: A Type-safe, Object-oriented, Orthogonally Persistent System. In Connor and Nettles [21], pages 33–47.
7. M.P. Atkinson, M.J. Jordan, L. Daynès, and S. Spence. Design Issues for Persistent Java: A Type-safe, Object-oriented, Orthogonally Persistent System. In *The Proceedings of the Seventh International Workshop on Persistent Object Systems (POS 7),* pages 33–47, May 1996.

8. M.P. Atkinson and R. Morrison. Orthogonal Persistent Object Systems. *VLDB Journal*, 4(3):309–401, 1995.

9. M.P. Atkinson and R. Welland, editors. *Fully Integrated Data Environments*. Springer-Verlag, 1999.

10. S. Berman and E. Voges. A Spatiotemporal Model as the Basis for a Persistent GIS. In Dearle et al. [27].

11. P.A. Bernstein. Panel: Is Generic Metadata Management Feasible? In Abbadi et al. [1], pages 660–662.

12. S.M. Blackburn and J.N. Zigman. Concurrency — the Fly in the Ointment? In Morrison et al. [56], pages 250–258.

13. K. Brahnmath, N. Nystrom, A. Hosking, and Q.I. Cutts. Swizzle-barrier optimization for Orthogonal Persistence for Java. In Morrison et al. [56], pages 268–278.

14. Frederick P. Brooks, Jr. *The Mythical Man-Month — Essays on Software Engineering*. Addison-Wesley, Reading, MA, USA, anniversary edition, 1995.

15. M. Carey, D. DeWitt, and J. Naughton. The OO7 Benchmark. In *Proc. of the ACM SIGMOD Int. Conf. on Management of Data*, Washington D.C, May 1993.

16. R.G.G. Cattell, editor. *The Object Database Standard: ODMG-97 Third Edition*. Morgan Kaufmann, 1997.

17. S. Ceri, R.J. Cochrane, and J. Widom. Practical Applications of Triggers and Constraints: Successes and Lingering Issues. In Abbadi et al. [1], pages 254–262.

18. C. Chambers. *The Design and Implementation of the SELF Compiler, an Optimizing Compiler for Object-Oriented Programming Languages*. PhD thesis, Stanford University, March 1992. Available via anonymous ftp from self.stanford.edu.

19. G. Clossman, P. Shaw, M. Hapner, J. Klein, R. Pledereder, and B. Becker. Java and Relational Databases: SQLJ. *ACM SIGMOD Record*, 27(2):500, June 1998.

20. P. Collet and G. Vignola. Towards a Consistent Viewpoint on Consistency for Persistent Applications. In *ECOOP'2000 Symposium on Objects and Databases*, volume 1813 of *Lecture Notes in Computer Science*. Springer Verlag, June 2000. To appear.

21. R. Connor and S. Nettles, editors. *Persistent Object Systems: Principles and Practice — Proceedings of the Seventh International Workshop on Persistent Object Systems*. Morgan Kaufmann, 1996.

22. G. Czajkowski. Application Isolation in the Java^{TM} Virtual Machine. In *Proceedings of OOPSLA 2000*, 2000.

23. L. Daynès. Implementation of Automated Fine-Granularity Locking in a Persistent Programming Language. *Software — Practice and Experience*, 30:1–37, 2000.

24. L. Daynès and M.P. Atkinson. Main-Memory Management to support Orthogonal Persistence for Java. In Jordan and Atkinson [41], pages 37–60.

25. L. Daynès and G. Czajkowski. High-Performance, Space-Efficient Automated Object Locking, 2000. Submitted to ICDE'01.

26. A. Dearle, D. Hulse, and A. Farkas. Persistent Operating System Support for Java. In Jordan and Atkinson [40].

27. A. Dearle, G. Kirby, and D. Sjøberg, editors. *Proceedings of the Ninth International Workshop on Persistent Object Systems*. LNCS. Springer-Verlag, September 2000.

28. D. DeWitt. Comment on recent experiences starting a new company, Private Communication, August 2000.

29. R. Dimpsey, R. Arora, and K. Kuiper. Java Server Performance: A Case Study of Building Efficient, Scalable JVMs. *IBM Systems Journal*, 39(1), 2000.

30. M. Dmitriev. Class and Data Evolution Support in the PJama Persistent Platform. Technical Report TR-2000-57, Department of Computing Science, University of Glasgow, Glasgow G12 8QQ, Scotland, 2000.

31. Snyder L. *et al. Academic Careers for Experimental Computer Scientists and Engineers*. National Academic Press, Washington, USA, 1994.
32. A. Garratt, M. Jackson, P. Burden, and J. Wallis. A Comparison of Two Persistent Storage Tools for Implementing a Search Engine. In Dearle et al. [27].
33. A. Garthwaite and S. Nettles. TJava: a Transactional Java. In *IEEE International Conference on Computer Languages*. IEEE Press, 1998.
34. GemStone Systems, Inc. The GemStone/J 4.0 — The Adaptable J2EE Platform. http://www.gemstone.com/products/j/, 2000.
35. J. Gosling, B. Joy, and G. Steele. *The Java Language Specification*. Addison-Wesley, December 1996.
36. C.G. Hamilton. Recovery Management for Sphere: Recovering a Persistent Object Store. Technical Report TR-1999-51, Department of Computing Science, University of Glasgow, Glasgow G12 8QQ, Scotland, December 1999.
37. G. Hamilton, R. Cattell, and M. Fisher. *JDBC Database Access With Java: A Tutorial and Annotated Reference*. Addison-Wesley, 1997.
38. U. Hölzle. *Adaptive Optimization for Self: Reconciling High Performance with Exploratory Programming*. PhD thesis, Department of Computer Science, Stanford University, 1994.
39. A.L. Hosking, N. Nystrom, Q. Cutts, and K. Brahnmath. Optimizing the read and write barrier for orthogonal persistence. In Morrison et al. [56], pages 149–159.
40. M.J. Jordan and M.P. Atkinson, editors. *Proceedings of the First International Workshop on Persistence and Java*. Number TR-96-58 in Technical Report. Sun Microsystems Laboratories Inc, 901 San Antonio Road, Palo Alto, CA 94303, USA, November 1996.
41. M.J. Jordan and M.P. Atkinson, editors. *Proceedings of the Second International Workshop on Persistence and Java*. Number TR-97-63 in Technical Report. Sun Microsystems Laboratories Inc, 901 San Antonio Road, Palo Alto, CA 94303, USA, December 1997.
42. M.J. Jordan and M.P. Atkinson. Orthogonal Persistence for Java — A Mid-term Report. In Morrison et al. [56], pages 335–352.
43. M.J. Jordan and M.L. Van De Vanter. Software Configuration Management in an Object-Oriented Database. In *Proceedings of the Usenix Conference on Object-Oriented Technologies*, Monterey, CA, June 1995.
44. M.J. Jordan and M.L. Van De Vanter. Modular System Building with Java Packages. In *Proceedings of the Eighth International Conference on Software Engineering Environments*, Cottbus, Germany, May 1997.
45. M. Jørgensen and S. S. Bygdås. An empirical study of the correlation between development efficiency and software development tools. *Telektronikk*, 95(1):54–62, 1999.
46. M. Jørgensen, S. S. Bygdås, and T.Lunde. Efficiency Evaluation of CASE tools Method and Results. Technical Report 38/95, 1995.
47. A. Kaplan, J.V.E. Ridgeway, B.R. Schmerl, K. Sridar, and J.C. Wileden. Toward Pure Polylingual Persistence. In Dearle et al. [27], pages 54–68 in the preprints, University of Oslo, Department of Informatics, Preprint 2000 No. 288.
48. G.N.C. Kirby and R. Morrison. OCB: An Object/Class Browser for Java. In Jordan and Atkinson [41], pages 89–105.
49. G.N.C. Kirby and R. Morrison. Variadic Genericity Through Linguistic Reflection: A Performance Evaluation. In Morrison et al. [56], pages 136–148.
50. G.N.C. Kirby, R. Morrison, and D.W. Stemple. Linguistic Reflection in Java. *Software — Practice and Experience*, 28(10):1045–1077, 1998.

51. B. Lewis and B. Mathiske. Efficient Barriers for Persistent Object Caching in a High-Performance Java Virtual Machine. In *Proceedings of the OOPSLA'99 Workshop — Simplicity, Performance and Portability in Virtual Machine Design*, 1999.

52. B. Lewis, B. Mathiske, and N. Gafter. Architecture of the PEVM: A High-Performance Orthogonally Persistent Java Virtual Machine. In Dearle et al. [27].

53. T. Lindholm and F. Yellin. *The Java Virtual Machine Specification*. Addison-Wesley, 1996.

54. A. Marquez, S.M. Blackburn, G. Mercer, and J. Zigman. Implementing Orthogonally Persistent Java. In Dearle et al. [27], pages 218–232 in the preprints, University of Oslo, Department of Informatics, Preprint 2000 No. 288.

55. R. Morrison, R.C.H. Connor, Q.I. Cutts, G.N.C. Kirby, D.S. Munro, and M.P. Atkinson. The Napier88 Persistent Programming Language and Environment. In Atkinson and Welland [9], chapter 1.1.3, pages 98–154.

56. R. Morrison, M.J. Jordan, and M.P. Atkinson, editors. *Advances in Persistent Object Systems — Proceedings of the Eighth International Workshop on Persistent Object Systems (POS8) and the Third International Workshop on Persistence and Java (PJW3)*. Morgan Kaufmann, August 1998.

57. T. Printezis. *Management of Long-Running, High-Performance Persistent Object Stores*. PhD thesis, Department of Computing Science, University of Glasgow, Glasgow G12 8QQ, Scotland, May 2000.

58. T. Printezis, M. P. Atkinson, and M. J. Jordan. Defining and Handling Transient Data in PJama. In *Proceedings of the Seventh International Workshop on Database Programming Languages (DBPL'99)*, Kinlochrannoch, Scotland, September 1999.

59. T. Printezis and M.P. Atkinson. An Efficient Promotion Algorithm for Persistent Object Systems, 2000. To appear in *Software – Practice and Experience*.

60. C. Russell. JSR-12 Java Data Objects Specification (approved for development). http:/java.sun.com/aboutJava/communityprocess/jsr/jsr_012_dataobj.html, April 2000.

61. M. Satyanarayanan, H.H. Mashburn, P. Kumar, D.C. Steere, and J.J. Kistler. Lightweight Recoverable Virtual Memory. *ACM Transactions on Computers and Systems*, 12(1):33–57, February 1994.

62. D.I.K. Sjøberg and M. Jøgensen. A Proposal for a Laboratory for Software Engineering Experiments, 2000. in preparation.

63. Sun Microsystems, Inc. Enterprise Java Beans Specification 1.1, April 2000.

64. Sun Microsystems, Inc. Java Blend. http://www.sun.com/software/javablend/index.html, April 2000.

65. W.F. Tichy. Should computer scientists experiment more? *COMPUTER: IEEE Computer*, 31:32–40, 1998.

66. W.F. Tichy, P. Lukowicz, L. Prechelt, and E.A. Heinz. Experimental evaluation in computer science: A quantitative study. *The Journal of Systems and Software*, 28(1):9–18, January 1995.

67. D. White and A. Garthwaite. The GC interface in the EVM. Technical Report TR-98-67, Sun Microsystems Laboratories Inc, 901 San Antonio Road, Palo Alto, CA 94303, USA, 1998.

68. E. Zirintsis, V.S. Dunstan, G.N.C. Kirby, and R. Morrison. Hyper-Programming in Java. In Morrison et al. [56], pages 370–382.

69. E. Zirintsis, G.N.C. Kirby, and R. Morrison. Hyper-Code Revisited: Unifying Program Source, Executable and Data. In Dearle et al. [27], pages 202–217.

Parametric Polymorphism and Orthogonal Persistence *

Suad Alagić and Tuong Nguyen

Department of Computer Science,
Wichita State University,
Wichita, KS 67260-0083, USA
alagic@cs.twsu.edu

Abstract. Parametric classes come with non-trivial subtleties even in the paradigm of orthogonal persistence. Orthogonal persistence guarantees that objects of any type, including class objects, may persist. But a parametric class is not a Java type, and its class object does not exist. Further subtleties in the Java technology extended with orthogonal persistence are caused by the existence of both the persistent store and Java class files. Neither store was designed with parametric classes in mind. This paper presents a technique for implementing parametric classes in the Java technology extended with orthogonal persistence. The technique is based on a suitable representation of a parametric class as a Java class file, an extended class loader which handles instantiation of such a class, and an extension of the Java Core Reflection classes. Extending these final classes is a non-trivial experiment and requires complete recompilation of the Java system. The overall effect amounts to a new Java Virtual Machine that extends the standard one. However, this extension does not affect correct performance of Java programs.

1 Introduction

Collections and queries are the essential components of most database technologies. Parametric polymorphism is critical for such technologies because it allows static type checking of both collections and queries. This is why extending the Java technology with parametric polymorphism has particular importance for database technologies. This extension is in fact a major requirement for developing a full-fledged Java database technology.

Extending the Java technology with parametric polymorphism poses a non-trivial challenge. The problem is not in extending the language, but rather in extending the underlying software technology. In addition, most existing proposals for extending Java with parametric polymorphism do not consider the implications of persistence. In this paper we show that those implications are non-trivial. We also develop an implementation technique for parametric polymorphism in Java in an environment that supports orthogonal persistence.

---

* This material is based upon work supported by the NSF under grant number IIS-9811452.

K.R. Dittrich et al. (Eds.): Objects and Databases 2000, LNCS 1944, pp. 32–46, 2001.

The subtlety of the problem of parametric polymorphism in persistent environments comes from the fact that a parametric class is not a Java type. Only classes obtained from a parametric class are types. Orthogonal persistence guarantees that objects of any type may be persistent. But this does not apply to parametric classes, which are in fact patterns for constructing classes. Class objects of parametric classes never exist! Only class objects of instantiated parametric classes exist.

A parametric class is a type function. But functions are not first class objects in Java [14], and hence promoting a parametric class to persistence is formally not possible even in an environment that supports orthogonal persistence.

In this paper we address this controversy for the Java technology, which in fact includes additional subtleties. In section 2 we first explain briefly the implications of the lack of parametric polymorphism in Java for typing collections and queries. In section 3 we show how parametric polymorphism allows static type checking of collections and queries. We also discuss the form of parametric polymorphism which is required for database technologies (section 4).

The Java class file structure is described in section 5. The issues in adapting the Java class file structure to represent parametric classes are elaborated in section 6. Our specific technique for solving the problem of parametric polymorphism in Java is described in section 7.

The role of an extended class loader in this technique is discussed in section 8. A more sophisticated technique for extending Java with parametric polymorphism also requires extending Java Core Reflection classes [19]. A model of orthogonal persistence suggested in the paper requires an extension of the Java root class `Object`. As these are system classes (and the Java Core Reflection classes are also final), these extensions are non-trivial, and require a complete re-compilation of the Java platform. This experiment is explained in section 9.

Related research is summarized in section 10 and the conclusions are given in section 11.

2 Collections and Queries

Problems caused by the lack of parametric polymorphism in typing collections and queries are discussed in detail in our earlier papers ([6], [2], [3], [4]). These problems are explained briefly in this section and in the section 3 that follows.

Consider an abbreviated Java interface which specifies a generic collection type:

```
public interface Collection
{ public boolean add(Object obj);
  public boolean contains(Object obj);
  public boolean isEmpty();
  public Iterator iterator();
  public boolean remove(Object obj);
  public int size();
  ...
}
```

The only way to specify a generic collection type in the Java type system is to specify that the elements are of the type `Object`. This fact has far reaching implications. Static typing of collections and processing of collections with static type checking is impossible. Extensive dynamic type checking is unavoidable. Every time an object is retrieved from a collection, a type cast must be applied to it in order to perform specific actions on the object. Otherwise, only the methods from the class `Object` may be invoked on an object from a collection.

These limitations of the Java type system have non-trivial implications for type checking OQL queries [2]. In order to illustrate the problem, consider a Java collection `persons`:

```
Collection persons;
```

Note that it does not help to use inheritance to derive `PersonCollection` from `Collection`. The signatures of the methods inherited from `Collection` would have to remain the same. This is yet another limitation of the Java type system. It is actually needed in order to guarantee type safety when dynamic binding of messages to methods is in place. Because of all this, the following simple OQL query fails a type check:

```
select x.name
from   x in persons
where  x.age() >= 50
```

The reason for the above query to fail type checking is that the range variable `x` in the above query stands for an element of the collection `persons`. But the type of elements of the collection `persons` is `Object`. `Object` is not equipped with attributes or methods `name` and `age`.

The above observations show that Java and OQL do not have compatible type systems. Problems caused by the lack of support for parametric polymorphism are particularly serious in the ODMG Standard [12]. Indeed, the ODMG Object Model and the Java binding of the ODMG Standard do not support parametric polymorphism. Yet both are meant to work with OQL as components of a unified technology which is based on a unified type system!

3   Parametric Polymorphism

A strictly more sophisticated type system is obtained from the Java type system by introducing parametric polymorphism. This is illustrated by the parametric interface `Collection<T>` given below. The interface has one type parameter which ranges over the set of all types. This basic form of parametric polymorphism is called universal type quantification.

```
public interface Collection<T>
{ public boolean add(T obj);
  public boolean contains(T obj);
  public boolean isEmpty();
```

```
public Iterator<T> iterator();
public boolean remove(T obj);
public int size();
  ...
}
```

It is now possible to statically type collections. The same applies to programs that operate on collections, database transactions in particular. Instantiating parametric types is carried out at compile time, as in the example of the **persons** collection given below.

```
Collection<Person> persons;
```

It is now possible to process collections with no type casts. Static type checking of OQL queries also becomes possible. The query given above, which fails type checking in the Java type system, now type checks [2]. The reason is that it is now possible to infer at compile time the specific type of the range variable x. The inferred type of the range variable x is now **Person**, because the type of the collection **persons** is now **Collection<Person>**.

4   Bounded and F-Bounded Polymorphism

Universal type quantification is not sufficiently powerful for the object-oriented database technology. Typing ordered collections requires the form of parametric polymorphism called constrained genericity [17], or bounded type quantification. This is illustrated by the following example:

```
public interface Comparable {
  ...
 public boolean lessThan(Comparable obj);
}

public class OrderedCollection<T implements Comparable>
                 implements Collection<T> {
 ...
}
```

The parametric class **OrderedCollection<T implements Comparable>** has a constraint on the type parameter T. This is why this form of parametric polymorphism is called bounded type quantification. The corresponding actual type parameter to be substituted for T must implement the interface **Comparable**. This means that the actual parameter must have the ordering methods such as **lessThan**, etc.

This form of parametric polymorphism is required in typing keyed collections and indices. In fact, an even more sophisticated form of parametric polymorphism, called F-bounded polymorphism, is preferable ([6], [19]). In F-bounded polymorphism the bound itself is parametric, as illustrated below.

```
public interface Comparable<T> {
  ...
  public boolean lessThan(T obj);
}

public class OrderedCollection<T implements Comparable<T>>
                      implements Collection<T> {
  ...
}
```

It is particularly important to note that most published proposals for extending Java with parametric polymorphism include both bounded type quantification (constrained genericity) and F-bounded polymorphism. A detailed analysis is given in [19].

F-bounded polymorphism allows static type checking in some situations where static type checking with just bounded quantification is not possible [20]. However, F-bounded polymorphism amounts to structural subtyping which does not exist in Java. In Java, B is a subtype of A if either B extends A or B implements A. This is why the F-bounded condition T implements Comparable<T> is hard to reconcile with Java.

5   Java Class Files

Java classes are compiled into Java class files. The structure of the Java class files is described below in the Java programming notation.

```
public class ClassFile {
    int             magic;
    short           majorVersion;
    short           minorVersion;
    ConstantPoolInfo  constantPool[];
    short           accessFlags;
    ConstantPoolInfo  thisClass;
    ConstantPoolInfo  superClass;
    ConstantPoolInfo  interfaces[];
    FieldInfo       fields[];
    MethodInfo      methods[];
    AttributeInfo   attributes[];
    ...
}
```

A class file contains a magic number which indicates that the file is a class file. A class file also contains the minor and the major version number of the Java compiler that produced the file. A Java Virtual Machine must not attempt to run code with a different major version.

The information collected in the process of compilation of a Java class is stored in a table of the generated class file. This table is called the constant pool.

A class file also contains a field which encodes the access modifiers for the class (ACC_PUBLIC, ACC_INITIAL, ACC_SUPER, ACC_INTERFACE, ACC_ABSTRACT).

The fields **thisClass** and **superClass** of a class file refer to the constant pool information about the class itself and about its superclass. A class file also contains an array of references to the constant pool items that contain information about the interfaces implemented by this class.

The information about fields and methods of a class is collected into arrays **fields** and **methods** of the class file. The structure of the corresponding array elements for methods is given below in the Java notation. The structure for fields is actually the same.

```
public class MethodInfo {
    short          accessFlags;
    ConstantPoolInfo    name;
    ConstantPoolInfo    signature;
    AttributeInfo    attributes[];
    ...
}
```

Access flags of a method (ACC_PUBLIC, ACC_PRIVATE, ACC_PROTECTED, ACC_STATIC, ACC_FINAL, ACC_SYNCHRONIZED, ACC_NATIVE, ACC_ABSRACT) are encoded into a two byte field **accessFlags**.

The name of the method is given as a reference to a constant pool item which contains the actual string. The signature of a method consists of types of its parameters and the result type. This type descriptor is represented as a specially formatted string. The structure of type descriptors is determined by a grammar which is a part of the Java Virtual Machine Specification.

In the Java class file structure an array of attributes is associated with each class, each field, and each method. The structure of an attribute item is given below.

```
public class AttributeInfo {
    ConstantPoolInfo    name;
    byte          data[];
    ...
}
```

The predefined attributes are: SourceFile, ConstantValue, Code, Exceptions, InnerClasses, Synthetic, LineNumberTable and LocalVariableTable. Out of these, the attributes Code, ConstantValue and Exceptions must be correctly recognized in order for the Java Virtual Machine to function correctly. An important point is that in addition to the above mentioned attributes, optional attributes are also allowed. These optional attributes should have no effect on the correct functioning of the Java Virtual Machine.

6 Parametric Class Files

The class file structure is a significant component of the Java Virtual Machine Specification [16]. The current Java technology actually depends quite heavily on the predefined structure of class files as specified in [16]. We have explored several possibilities for representing a parametric class as a class file.

One option follows the generic Java idiom. In general, this generic Java idiom ([10],[18]) amounts to replacing the type parameters with their bound types. So `Collection<T>` would be represented by `Collection<Object>`. `OrderedCollection<T implements Comparable>` is represented by the class `OrderedCollection<Comparable>`. This technique has been used in [10] and [18]. However, we have shown [19] that the technique is in fact questionable with respect to correctness, particularly regarding the correct functioning of Java Core Reflection.

The main advantage of this representation is that the representation of a parametric class is a valid Java class file. The main disadvantage is the confusion between the type parameters and the bound types. In order to avoid this confusion we have carried out experiments in using the standard class file in such a way that the distinction between the type parameters and the bound types is properly encoded.

The generic Java idiom used in ([10],[18]) is problematic not only from the viewpoint of correct functioning of Java Core Reflection. It is actually particularly problematic in an environment that supports orthogonal persistence. The reason is that all instantiated classes of a particular parametric class are represented by the identical class object. This is the class object obtained by the above described substitution of the type parameters with their bound types. So for example, both `OrderedCollection<Employee>` and `OrderedCollection<Student>` would be represented by the class object for `OrderedCollection<Comparable>`.

The above situation does not create problems in executing methods because Java applies single dynamic dispatch. Hence, selection of a method is based only on the run-time type of the receiver object. However, when an object of an instantiated parametric class is promoted to persistence, so is its class object (reachability). This class object carries incorrect (or at least imprecise) type information. In the above example, persistent objects of classes `OrderedCollection<Student>` and `OrderedCollection<Employee>` would have the identical associated persistent class object which is in fact the class object for `OrderedCollection<Comparable>`. So the type information in the persistent store is incorrect!

The other option is that the Java class file structure is modified in such a way that it correctly represents a parametric class. The disadvantage is that the Java Virtual Machine would not know anything about this modified class file structure. The most important implication is that an extended class loader is required in order to handle loading of class objects of classes obtained by instantiation of a parametric class.

In either option the class file is marked appropriately as a generic class file. The new flags are illustrated in the Figure 1. These non-standard flags cause no problem in correct functioning of the Java Virtual Machine because these files are handled by an extended class loader which loads correct Java class objects produced from these files. The extension of the Java Core Reflection explained in section 9 must also recognize these non-standard tags. In fact, according to the Java Virtual Machine Specification [16] the unused bits of the access flag item in the Java class file structure are reserved for future use and should be ignored by implementations of the Java Virtual Machine. So this is one feature of the Java class file specification which allows some flexibility needed for correct representation of parametric classes.

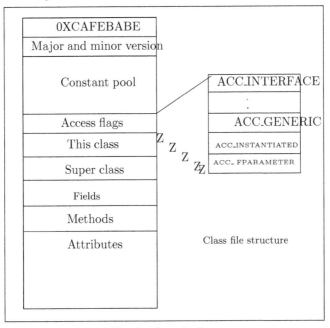

Fig. 1. Class file flags

The other source of flexibility in the Java class file structure is in the attributes associated with classes, fields, and methods. Optional attributes allow non-standard information to be associated with classes, fields and methods. These optional attributes may be used for representation of parametric classes. The extended class loader will, of course, know the full details of this additional encoding contained in Java class files.

The type information related to fields and methods is represented in class files by type descriptors which are in fact strings of a particular form. Type descriptors offer an interesting possibility for correct representation of parametric classes. Rather than confusing the type parameters with the bound types, the type parameters are encoded correctly in type descriptors. When an extended class loader is dealing with an instantiated parametric class, it should replace the formal type parameters with the actual type parameters. This produces a valid Java class file which my be loaded by the standard loader.

7   The Technique

The details of our technique are described below.

- *Compiling a parametric class* proceeds as follows:
  - A parametric class is compiled into a valid Java class file by replacing the type parameters with their bound types.
  - In addition, the number of type parameters and their bound types are recorded in the attributes of the class.
  - For each formal type parameter and for each method, the positions at which this parameter occurs in the type descriptors are recorded in the method's attributes.
  - The same is done for fields of the class.
- Two important points about the *class file generated this way* are:
  - The attributes set for the class, its fields, and its methods are optional attributes. They have no effect on the correct functioning of the Java Virtual Machine.
  - The generated class file is a valid Java class file which may be used as such.
  - If the class object is loaded from the class file generated in the above manner, usage of bound types in place of type parameters will have no negative implications on correct invocation of methods.
- *Loading an instantiated parametric class* proceeds as follows:
  - The class file representing the parametric class is located. Checking the number of the actual parameters and their conformance to the corresponding bound types could be done at this time. Of course, this should be preferably done at compile time.
  - For each type parameter its occurrences are replaced with the actual type parameter in the type descriptors for fields and methods. This step is based on the information recorded in the optional attributes for the class itself, its fields and its methods.
  - The class is loaded using the standard loading procedure.
- The *features of the above described technique* are:
  - The loaded class objects of instantiated parametric classes contain correct type information.
  - The run-time type information reported by the Java Core Reflection is correct.
  - The type information promoted to persistence is also correct.
  - The code for methods contains bound types in place of the actual type parameters, but this presents no problem for correct functioning of method invocations.
  - All the class files generated by this technique are valid Java class files.

8   Extended Class Loader

Unlike the technique based on the generic Java idiom, our techniques always require an extended class loader. The reason is that in our techniques the loaded class object of an instantiated parametric class carries correct run-time type information about the actual type parameter. This makes our techniques similar to the heterogeneous techniques [1] for extending Java with parametric polymorphism.

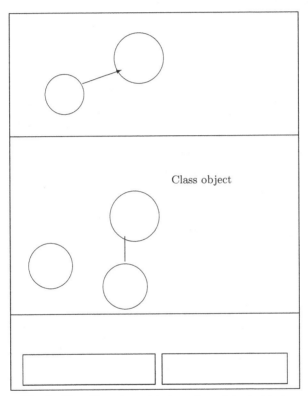

Class object

Fig. 2. Class files, class objects and persistent objects

Loading a class object for `OrderedCollection<Employee>` requires that the extended class loader locates the class file representing the parametric class `OrderedCollection<T implements Comparable>`. If the type constraint was not checked at compile time, the extended loader would also have to check the constraint `Employee implements Comparable`. The extended loader then performs instantiation generating a valid Java class object for `OrderedCollection<Employee>`. Whatever the chosen representation of a parametric class as a class file is, the extended class loader must know all about it.

For example, if a collection object `employees` of the type `OrderedCollection<Employee>` is promoted to persistence, so is the class object of `OrderedCollection<Employee>`. This is an implication of reachability. Unlike the technique based on the generic Java idiom, this technique guarantees two things: (i) The run-time type information is correct and (ii) The type information in the persistent store is correct.

However, note that the parametric class itself never resides in the persistent store. One could argue that this decision is an implication of orthogonality. A parametric class is not a Java type, its objects never exist, and hence the above decision. All of this is illustrated in the Figure 2.

As objects of a parametric class never exist, one could argue that there is no need for class objects of a parametric class to exist. But class objects of instantiated parametric classes must exist, because objects of such classes do exist. Objects of interfaces and abstract classes do not exist either per se. But objects of classes that implement them do exist. This is why class files and class objects of both interfaces and abstract classes must and do exist. All of this leads back to the fundamental problem: parametric classes are not Java types. Representing them by the existing Java types leads to non-trivial problems [19].

9   Extended Java Core Reflection

With the usage of an extended class loader and either a standard or a non-standard class file representation for a parametric class, we obtain correct run-time type information in the loaded class objects. Java Core Reflection reports this information correctly. However, it does not know anything about parametric classes. One could argue that this is exactly the way it should be.

A more ambitious approach presented in [19] extends the Java Core Reflection in such a way that it makes it aware of the existence of parametric classes. It also reports the type information associated with parametric classes, such as type parameters, bound types etc. Furthermore, if a class is in fact an instantiation of a parametric class, the extended Java Core Reflection reports that information. According to [19] Java Core Reflection also allows access from an instantiated class to its parametric class.

It is probably a debatable issue whether this level of generality is required. However, one could also argue that this level of generality is an implication of the fact that class loading is dynamic in Java. Loading of an instantiated parametric class requires knowledge about parametric classes themselves.

One novelty of this paper in comparison with [19] are the results on the actual experiment in extending the Java Core Reflection with additional functionalities for parametric classes. Some of the possible extensions are illustrated in the Figure 3.

All Java Core Reflection classes are final for good reasons. This feature protects the integrity of the Java type system at run-time. Since these classes cannot be extended, doing it actually produces a new version of the Java platform.

The diagram shows one more extension of the Java platform which is not required for parametric polymorphism. This extension actually associates persistence capabilities with the root class `Object`. This immediately guarantees orthogonality of persistence. We argued [3] that this is the most natural way for extending Java with parametric polymorphism. This model of persistence also requires persistent name spaces (environments). An environment is a dynamic name space which includes bindings for both classes and objects. A technique for implementing persistent environments in the Java technology is discussed in our related paper [5].

A rough equivalent of this model of persistence in the current Java technology would be obtained by making the root class `Object` implement the interface `Serializable`. This, of course, is currently not the case. This is precisely the reason why the Java model of persistence is not orthogonal. In addition, the Java model of persistence is low-level, because it requires a user to deal with files (`InputObjectStream` and `OutputObjectStream`), reading and writing objects, etc. Similar remarks apply to the model of persistence in Eiffel [17], which in fact is not part of the language. All the low-level details of the persistence implementation architecture should be transparent to the users, which is not the case in either language.

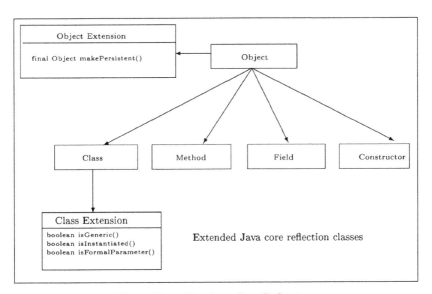

Fig. 3. Extending Java Core Reflection

We will explain briefly what is actually involved in extending Java system classes.

The process starts with the source of a standard system class. This source is extended by the new methods which are specified as native. Hence their implementation is in C. The newly added methods and the extended class are now compiled using GNU C compiler and JDK 1.1.7 toolkit. The effect of all of this is creation of a new Java compiler and a new Java platform. Now Java programs can make use of the extended class provided that the extended class is in the class path in place of the corresponding standard class. The actual re-compilation of the whole Java system takes around 3 hours on a Solaris 2.5 platform.

10   Related Research

The subtleties which parametric types bring to the notion of orthogonal persistence are not addressed in the classical papers on orthogonal persistence (such as [7]) nor in the papers on object-oriented databases (such as [9]). Furthermore, the only existing proposed standard for object-oriented databases (ODMG) does not support parametric polymorphism except in its C++ binding [12].

Two Java systems that support orthogonal persistence PJama [8] and GemstoneJ [11] do not address the issue of parametric classes. The reason is simple: both systems are based on Java as it is, and hence parametric polymorphism is not an issue.

Negative implications of the lack of parametric polymorphism in typing collections and queries are discussed in detail in our papers ([6], [2], [3], [4]). The impedance mismatch between Java and query languages is established in our paper [2].

Published proposals on extending Java with parametric polymorphism which are based on the generic Java idiom (Pizza [18], GJ [10], and NexGen [13]) are in fact not suitable for persistent systems. The reason is that this idiom represents all instantiated classes of a parametric class by an identical class object which carries incorrect (or at least imprecise) run-time type information.

There are two implications of this fact. One of them is that when a class object is promoted to persistence (by reachability!) it carries with it incorrect type information to the persistent store. The second implication is that Java Core Reflection reports incorrect information.

The idea that a correct solution for parametric polymorphism for Java requires considerations of the Java class file structure and an extension of the Java Core Reflection classes was suggested in our paper [19]. Although some implementation experiments were carried out around the time of the publication of [19], this paper is the first report which presents the experimental results.

11   Conclusions

Representing parametric classes in the Java technology extended with orthogonal persistence is subtle for two main reasons. The first one is that a parametric class is not a class at all. A class object of a parametric class never exists, and hence cannot be promoted to persistence even if orthogonality is guaranteed. The second problem is that Java class files have not been designed to represent parametric classes.

Our solution includes first of all a technique for representing a parametric class as a Java class file. The justification is the fact that the Java environment depends heavily on a specific and predefined class file structure [16]. We showed that such a representation is possible. However, a somewhat different design of the class file structure would make it more suitable for the representation of parametric classes.

A further conclusion is that even if the structure of the class files is changed, correct functioning of the Java environment may be guaranteed by an extended class loader. The extended class loader takes the name of the instantiated parametric class, locates the possibly modified parametric class file, and performs instantiation by loading the class object of the instantiated parametric class in main memory.

The solutions for parametric polymorphism in Java based on the generic Java idiom are not acceptable because of incorrect run-time type information and incorrect type information in the persistent store. The technique that we presented in this paper does not have this problem. The technique provides correct runtime type information which is reported correctly by Java Core Reflection. A major implication is that the type information promoted to persistence is correct. A further advantage of this technique is that it represents a parametric class as a valid Java class file.

Orthogonal persistence for Java requires a modified Java Virtual Machine. This is indeed what two systems that support orthogonal persistence for Java (PJama [8] and GemstoneJ [11]) have. We showed that two more extensions in fact may be preferable.

Java Core Reflection classes could be extended with suitable methods that deal with parametric classes, their parameters, and their instantiated classes [19]. Extending Java Core Reflection classes is not simple because these are final system classes. However, we have carried out a full and successful experiment showing what is involved in this extension. Of course, complete re-compilation of the whole Java system is required.

Although not required for parametric polymorphism, extending the Java class `Object` performed in this experiment is particularly relevant for orthogonal persistence. This extension associates persistence capabilities with the root class of the Java class hierarchy. Persistence capabilities in the root class immediately ensure orthogonality [3]. Since the extension consists of additional persistence related methods, this approach to orthogonal persistence is truly object-oriented. It is entirely based on message passing and inheritance.

References

1. O. Agesen, S. Freund, and J. C. Mitchell, Adding type parameterization to Java, Proceedings of the OOPSLA '97 Conference, pp. 49-65, ACM, 1997.
2. S. Alagić, Type checking OQL queries in the ODMG type systems, *ACM Transactions on Database Systems*, *24* (3), pp. 319-360, 1999.
3. S. Alagić, A family of the ODMG object models, invited paper, Proceedings of ADBIS '99, *Lecture Notes in Computer Science 1691*, pp. 14-30, 1999.

4. S. Alagić, O2 and the ODMG Standard: do they match?, *Theory and Practice of Object Systems*, *5* (4), pp. 239-247, 1999.

5. S. Alagić, J. Solorzano, and D. Gitchell, Orthogonal to the Java imperative, Proceedings of ECOOP '98, *Lecture Notes in Computer Science 1445*, pp. 212-233, Springer, 1998.

6. S. Alagić, The ODMG object model: does it make sense?, Proceedings of the OOPSLA '97 Conference, pp. 253-270, ACM, 1997.

7. M. Atkinson and R. Morrison, Orthogonally persistent object systems, *VLDB Journal 4*, pp. 319-401, 1995.

8. M. Atkinson, L. Daynes, M. J. Jordan, T. Printezis, and S. Spence, An orthogonally persistent Java^{TM}, ACM SIGMOD Record *25*, pp. 68-75, ACM, 1996.

9. M. Atkinson, F. Bancilhon, D. DeWitt, K. Dittrich, and S. Zdonik, The object-oriented database system manifesto, Proceedings of the First Object-Oriented and Deductive Database Conference (DOOD), pp. 40-75, Kyoto, 1989.

10. G. Bracha, M. Odersky, D. Stoutmire and P. Wadler, Making the future safe for the past: Adding genericity to the Java^{TM} programming language, Proceedings of OOPSLA '98, pp. 183-200, ACM, 1998.

11. B. Bretl, A. Otis, M. San Soucie, B. Schuchardt, and R. Venkatesh, Persistent Java objects in 3 tier architectures, in: R. Morrison, M. Jordan, and M. Atkinson: *Advances in Persistent Object Systems*, pp. 236-249, Morgan Kaufmann Publishers, 1999.

12. R. G. G. Cattell, D. K. Barry, M. Berler, J. Eastman, D. Jordan, C. Russel, O. Schadow, T. Stanieda, *The Object Data Standard: ODMG-3.0*, Morgan Kaufmann, 2000.

13. R. Cartwright and G. L. Steele Jr., Compatible genericity with run-time types for the Java^{TM} programming language, Proceedings of OOPSLA '98, pp. 201 -215, ACM, 1998.

14. J. Gosling, B. Joy, and G. Steele, *The Java^{TM} Language Specification*, Addison-Wesley, 1996.

15. M. Jordan and M. Atkinson, Orthogonal persistence for Java - A mid-term report, in: R. Morrison, M. Jordan, and M. Atkinson: *Advances in Persistent Object Systems*, pp. 335 - 352, Morgan Kaufmann Publishers, 1999.

16. T. Lindholm and F. Yellin, *The Java^{TM} Virtual Machine Specification*, Addison-Wesley, 1996.

17. B. Meyer, *Eiffel: The Language*, Prentice-Hall, 1992.

18. M. Odersky and P. Wadler, Pizza into Java: translating theory into practice, Proceedings of the POPL Conference, ACM, pp. 146-159, 1997.

19. J. Solorzano and S. Alagić, Parametric polymorphism for Java^{TM}: A reflective solution, Proceedings of OOPSLA '98, pp. 216-225, ACM, 1998.

20. K. K. Thorup and M. Torgesen, Unifying genericity, Proceedings of ECOOP '99, *Lecture Notes in Computer Science 1628*, pp. 186-204, Springer, 1999.

Towards a Consistent Viewpoint on Consistency for Persistent Applications

Philippe Collet and Greta Vignola

I3S Laboratory – CNRS – University of Nice - Sophia Antipolis
Les Algorithmes - Bât. Euclide B – 2000, route des Lucioles
BP 121, F-06903 Sophia Antipolis Cedex, France
{collet | vignola}@i3s.unice.fr

Abstract. Orthogonally persistent systems allow the use of a single object model to handle programs and data independently of their persistent condition. However, there is not yet any means to specify and control consistency in a single way, that is both program correctness and data integrity. This paper describes how the use of assertions can be extended to some important stages of the persistent application's life cycle: design, implementation, testing and evolution. We present our on-going implementation, the NightCap system, which aims at integrating assertions, with a mapping of the *Object Constraint Language* to Java, into a orthogonally persistent platform, namely PJama.

1   Introduction

One of the major problems of persistent systems is data integrity. As data persist through time, they must be kept consistent to remain usable. Object-oriented persistent languages provide a new kind of framework, where many points of view on consistency are present.

The software engineering viewpoint is mainly expressed in terms of reliability of the application. In this context, executable assertions are now recognised as an efficient technique for the specification of reliable object-oriented components. Associated with exceptions, they provide a pragmatic framework to ensure both correctness and robustness. On the other hand, the database viewpoint is concerned with ensuring data integrity and handling data inconsistencies. Two specific approaches have been developed to provide these features, using Event-Condition-Action rules or directly encoding constraints in the application. Persistent languages allow the use of a single object model for transient and persistent objects but there are still different approaches to ensure consistency in the transient and persistent programming fields.

As assertions are logical properties that are intended to be satisfied during software execution, we propose to make them *persist* so that they can be used to ensure the integrity of persistent data. While reconciling both the software engineering and database viewpoints, we thus describe a model extending the use of assertions to the life cycle of persistent applications, from design to testing and evolution. This model provides uniformity and reversibility of consistency specifications.

K.R. Dittrich et al. (Eds.): Objects and Databases 2000, LNCS 1944, pp. 47-60, 2001.

We also present its on-going implementation, the NightCap system, which aims at integrating assertions in the PJama platform to express and verify precise semantic properties and to control evolution on persistent stores. PJama provides support for persistence in the Java programming language, using an orthogonal approach. NightCap integrates assertions that come from the design stage using a mapping from the UML's Object Constraint Language to the Java language (OCL-J).

The remainder of this paper is organised as follows. Section 2 discusses our motivations to ensure consistency using assertions, leading to our proposed model. Section 3 describes the different parts of the NightCap system, presenting PJama and OCL-J. This section also describes the semantics of assertion evaluation and initial directions for optimisations. Section 4 discusses related work and section 5 concludes this paper by discussing future work.

2   Motivations

2.1   Ensuring Consistency in O-O Databases and Persistent Applications

Till now, two main approaches have been proposed to handle integrity constraints in object-oriented databases.

The first approach is based on rules [4,12], mainly ECA rules (Event-Condition-Action). Integrity constraints are attached to a specific event, a condition expresses the contradiction of the constraint and the associated action defines what to do in case of a violation. The definition and verification of ECA rules are detached from the application program and integrity checking on the whole database is managed by a large set of rules. A general problem of that kind of system is termination. The execution of ECA rules may not terminate, for example whenever the repair of a rule cyclically violates the constraints of other rules. The developer has to ensure that the execution of nested rules terminates. Moreover, ECA rule-based systems are hard to learn for the average developer as a constraint is often represented by many ECA rules with different events and actions. The global vision of the application semantics is partially lost or becomes fuzzy, and it is rather difficult to integrate such rules into programming languages.

The other main approach is usually qualified as *application-oriented* [5,6], as the programming or database language and its runtime system are modified to integrate consistency checking. Constraints are expressed using the programming language, which makes semantics less understandable, especially because the constraints must be specified for every transaction that might break them. Consequently, modifying constraints results in a difficult task. The developer is also completely responsible for the management of all aspects of constraints, as the means to arm and disarm constraints and to repair object inconsistencies are usually absent.

What persistent systems ensuring consistency need is a simpler model with a clear semantics, which also allows efficient checking. For a better integration in the software life cycle, this model must also maintain consistency using the same kind of formalism throughout the successive development stages.

2.2   Executable Assertions

Assertions are conditional annotations that describe object and method properties. Using all the functional features of an O-O language (constants, attributes, and functions), they specify conditions to be satisfied during software execution. Assertions annotate a class definition with preconditions, postconditions and invariants.

Preconditions define the conditions that must be satisfied before calling a method, constraining the state of the receiver object and the method parameters. Postconditions describe the state of the receiver after the method call for a procedure or the method result for a function. Within postconditions, one can refer to the old state of the receiver with a special keyword, so that postconditions can express properties over the old and new state. Invariants constrain the states of each instance of a class. They must hold for each instance between any public method call. Section 3.3 provides some examples of assertions through the OCL-J language.

Assertions define two kinds of contract [17]. The client contract expresses the obligations of the client through the method preconditions, whereas his benefits consist in the postconditions. On the contrary, the provider of the method regards the preconditions as acquired but must ensure that the postconditions are satisfied. The inheritance contract ensures the substitution rule for assertions along the inheritance hierarchy. That consists in the conjunction of postconditions and invariants, as well as the disjunction of preconditions. Contracts are checked at runtime during the implementation and testing stages. Evaluating assertions consists of verifying preconditions before its method call, while postconditions and invariants are checked after the method call. Any assertion violation is reported through an exception.

In a software engineering context, assertions allow programmers to formally specify properties of software components without using any new formalism, to verify programs that test themselves at runtime, while making it easier to locate programming errors inside components. Finally assertions document software components with an unambiguous specification, extracted from the code and in agreement with it.

2.3   Adapting Assertions to Persistent Applications

In a persistent context, assertions can be seen as a means to ensure both the correctness of the persistent program and the consistency of its persistent data. The correctness of the persistent application is enforced by the *common* use of assertions to specify semantic properties of classes. Using assertions as integrity constraints then enforces the consistency of the persistent data. In order to provide these features, the assertion mechanism must be enhanced in the following way:

- The assertion runtime (additional compiled classes that provide the necessary features for assertion checking at runtime) must be modified so that assertions might be checked on persistent instances.
- The assertion mechanism must handle object inconsistencies, by providing a way to declare and trigger repair actions.

We therefore integrate assertions inside classes, so that assertions will persist with the classes. In order to control assertion evaluation independently of an application, the assertion runtime is modified. This enables assertions such as invariants to be checked on a quiescent persistent store. The assertion runtime is then put in the store. Assertions are also described as objects [9] to precisely handle the evaluation of assertions on persistent data. We keep the *usual* semantics of assertion evaluation, which disarms checking inside assertions themselves, thereby avoiding non-termination problems.

From a software engineering viewpoint, the violation of an assertion is a correctness error and the exception raised by this violation should not be caught. But if we take the point of view of the engineering of persistent software, stored data must be preserved, and if at all possible eventually corrected whenever an error is detected. A DBMS usually provides a repair mechanism for inconsistent objects. We propose to apply this idea while preserving the original software engineering principles. Therefore, assertions will not include repair actions, but inconsistency handlers will be provided through a specialised API. These handlers will be associated with a specific scope (assertion, method, class, etc.) so that repair methods can be called after an assertion failure.

2.4   Assertions as a Common Basis for Consistency

To use assertions in both a programming and a persistent context, we use a persistent model in which the object model of the programming language becomes directly persistent, without any mapping to a different database model. Therefore, our work mainly focuses on the development of persistent applications, in particular using orthogonal persistence. Orthogonal persistence [3] is a language-independent model of persistence where objects of any type can persist, without any preliminary declaration in their class. This feature is often associated with persistence by reachability, that is all the information needed to correctly interpret persistent objects must also be made persistent. Reachability is determined from a set of *root* objects. We also add the property of persistence independence: it is almost indistinguishable whether the code is operating on long-lived or on transient data. These properties allow a seamless integration with the programming language, contrary to a model that separates programming and database management.

We thus consider an orthogonally persistent model, complemented with assertions. As assertions are now recognised as an efficient specification techniques for object-oriented components, their integration has been proposed since the design stage, like with the *Object Constraint Language* (OCL) [21], which is part of the UML standard [19]. We thus base our work on a quantified assertion language like OCL, which provides a reasonable expressiveness, while allowing the use of efficient implementation techniques during application testing [10,11].

Consequently we can apply assertions during some important stages of applications development:

- *Design*, in which assertions are expressed on classes through the OCL language.
- *Implementation and testing*, in which assertions are used for controlling the correctness of classes and persistent data. Assertions are then reversible

specifications, as changes on them can be propagated to the design assertions, as well as to the existing persistent instances.

- *Operational use*, in which some assertions may be checked to act as integrity constraints.
- *Evolution*, in which assertions may be used to verify the semantic consistency of the change on an evolved persistent store (see section 3.7).

3   The NightCap System

3.1   Overview of NightCap

NightCap is an assertion management system for orthogonally persistent applications. The system is based on PJama[1] [2] (see section 3.2), an orthogonally persistent platform for the Java language. NightCap uses a dedicated assertion language, OCL-J (see section 3.3), which is a mapping from the OCL language to Java. The *normal*

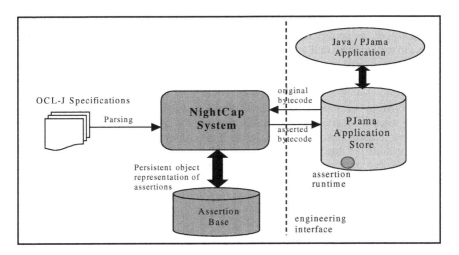

Fig. 1. Overview of the NightCap system.

Java platform is also supported for the use of assertions without orthogonal persistence.

Figure 1 gives an overview of NightCap. The system parses OCL-J specifications to store in the *assertion base* all knowledge regarding assertions. The assertion base is a persistent store containing *meta-information*, that is the internal object representation of assertions (complete syntax tree, related classes and methods,

---

[1] Substantially revised versions of PJama, including the ones we used in this work, PJama 1.6.4 and 1.6.5, are available from *http://www.dcs.gla.ac.uk/pjama/*.

specifications retrieved by inheritance, evaluation statistics, etc.). Using information on assertions, the system retrieves the Java bytecode of related classes from the application's persistent store to instrument it with assertions. The resulting bytecode then replaces the original one in the store. An assertion runtime is also put in the store, which contains the set of Java classes that handle assertion evaluation. The NightCap system organises assertion evaluation on applications and persistent data. It controls assertions on persistent data and associates repair actions with potential assertion violations (see section 3.5). An evolution guard will take advantages of the operational PJama evolution system to control proposed evolution steps according to assertion-based tests (see section 3.7).

3.2   Persistent Platform: PJama

PJama [2] is a platform developing orthogonal persistence for the Java language, which is developed in collaboration between Sun Microsystems Laboratories and the University of Glasgow. PJama is a prototype implementing the specification of *Orthogonal Persistence for the Java platform* (OPJ), which is based on type orthogonality, persistence by reachability and persistence independence. The efficiency and scalability of PJama have been demonstrated and the platform is now a reliable prototype. But to be used on a large scale, the platform needs a complete evolution tool, as application classes undergo changes and Java libraries are often subject to evolution as well.

The PJama persistent class evolution tool is under development. It currently supports the evolution of individual classes, class hierarchies and persistent objects [13]. A persistent class can be substituted by its new version and persistent objects can be converted to conform to the new definition of their classes. The evolution tool verifies whether classes are substitutable and, if the action has successfully completed, replaces the classes in the store. If the conversion cannot be automatic, the developer must provide a *conversion class*. The evolution tool ensures that changes brought to the store are valid, but this validity is only checked in terms of the compatibility of Java types. The NightCap system will complete this validity checking with assertion-based verifications.

3.3   Assertion Language: OCL-J

OCL [21] is a typed functional language, dedicated to design, which uses *basic* types and classes (`boolean`, `int`, `float`, `String`, etc.) and predefined generic collections. These collections support some high-order operations, such as `select` (to get a sub-collection of elements fulfilling a condition), `collect` (to filter elements according to a condition), `forAll` and `exists` as quantifiers, etc. Each of these operations rests on a general iteration method.

OCL-J establishes a mapping from OCL to the Java programming language by reusing basic types, enhancing Boolean operations and using the Java-2 collection hierarchy together with the OCL specialised operations. Some counterintuitive and criticised facilities [15] are not present in OCL-J, such as the automatic flattening of collections, or the arrow notation to access collection properties. This last feature is only a shortcut, so that OCL *arrowed* expression can be directly translated in an OCL-J compatible counterpart. Therefore OCL-J only supports access through the Java dot notation. A complete definition of the OCL-J language can be found in [8]. The following specification gives an example of its main features using a design example borrowed from [7]:

```
context Student inv UniqueCardNb:
  Student.allInstances().forAll(Student s1,s2 \ s1 != s2 ==>
                                         s1.cardNb != s2.cardNb)

context void Student.register(Section s, Course c)
  pre: c.hasSection().includes(s)
  pre: ! takes.includes(s)
  pre: c.openForRegistration()
    post: takes.includes(s)
    post: takes.size == takes.size@pre + 1
    post: classes.includes(c)
```

A `context` allows a programmer to describe the specified class or method. Invariants are specified by the keyword `inv` followed by an optional documentation label and the expression stating the invariant. This expression may contain any functional Java expression, as well as the special higher-order OCL-J expressions, such as the call of `forAll` on the set of all `Students` instances, with a predicate as parameter. This invariant checks that the attribute `cardNb` is unique among all students.

As for methods, their Java signature is described, followed by `pre` and `post` clauses, respectively for pre and postconditions. The above example is the specification of the method `register` in class `Student`. The preconditions state that section s must be part of the course c, that the student must not be registered yet in that section (`takes` is the collection of the sections in which the student is registered), and finally that the course c is still open for registration. The postconditions define the new state: the section s is in the collection `takes`, there is one element more in that collection and the course c is in the collection of registered classes. Inside postconditions, the `@pre` postfix keyword denotes the value of an expression before the method call, in order to express state change in postconditions.

3.4 Semantics of Assertions

Each OCL-J context clause allows us to produce the corresponding assertions in a Java class. The code corresponding to the assertion checking is added to the class' bytecodes to produce the following semantics.

When a method is called over an object, the preconditions of this method are checked in the order of their definition. If all the preconditions evaluate to true, the method body is executed. If a precondition evaluates to false or if the evaluation terminates with an exception, the assertion runtime looks for an associated repair action (see next section). If a repair action is found, its code is executed, otherwise an assertion exception is raised. Postconditions and invariants follow the same evaluation scheme, but they are checked at the end of the method body; postconditions are evaluated before invariants.

As an assertion violation without repair leads to a raised exception, the PJama system interprets this exception as a failure in the implicit transaction that occurs between stabilisations of the store, thereby aborting the transaction. Using this exception-based approach, the evaluation scheme of assertions will be able to be adapted when PJama provides more sophisticated transaction facilities.

The assertion runtime also builds special structures in order to provide access to type extents through the method `allInstances()` (cf. example page 53). Type extents are only accessible when they are needed for assertion checking. They are transient collections built using information from the store and are maintained during runtime.

Note that as invariants are conditions that must also hold on inactive objects, they can also be checked when a persistent store is quiescent.

3.5   Dealing with Inconsistencies

As assertions are used to check integrity constraints over persistent PJama stores, the NightCap system must provide a mechanism to handle object inconsistencies. This facility is provided through a specialised API that allows the programmer to define repair actions as Java code.

The abstract class `AssertionRuntime` gives access to an inconsistency manager in which one can add and remove inconsistency handlers. Different inconsistency handlers are provided according to their scope: the whole store, a package, a class, invariants of a class, a method, preconditions or postconditions of a method.

An inconsistency handler mainly consists of a method `repair` with the following signature:

```
repair(Object o, Exception e)
```

This method body contains the actions to repair the object `o` , `e` is the exception that has been raised.

When an assertion evaluation fails, the assertion runtime calls the most specialised inconsistency handler (if any), which calls the repair method. After this call, the assertion clause that was violated is checked again. If it fails again, the assertion runtime checks might either call a more general inconsistency handler or raise an appropriate exception to abort the transaction. To provide a flexible approach, each inconsistency handler defines a boolean that states whether the runtime can call a surrounding handler.

Finally, to avoid any composition problem at runtime, the system ensures that it activates only the most specialised inconsistency handler in any scope. However, a means to simply compose existing handlers is provided through constructors.

3.6   Dealing with Complexity: Initial Tactics

The OCL-J language provides the expressiveness of the first-order predicate calculus. By including function calls, the complexity of OCL-J expressions may easily result in inefficient evaluations.

We have previously developed efficient evaluation techniques for assertion checking during application testing [10,11]. These techniques are based on the reduction of assertions to be evaluated, as well as the number of objects to be checked. An assertion triggering system detects changes in the application and classifies classes according to their stability, which is given by their dependencies against the changes. The more unstable a class is, the more of its assertions that need to be checked. This selection of assertions is coupled with adaptive evaluation schemes. For example, when less control is demanded, universal quantifications are sampled, and assertions over type extents only use a shallow subset of the extent. These techniques can be reused when the persistent application is tested, but other optimisation techniques must be devised when assertions are used as integrity constraints.

We are currently studying the application of known optimisation techniques to our assertion language. The static analysis performed for the Thémis database programming language [5] seems to be partially applicable. In Thémis, integrity constraints contain methods, but they are restricted to the proposed database language, whereas OCL-J can use any Java function.

More generally, optimisation techniques that consist of reducing the checked constraints to the optimal subset by a static analysis can be adapted to our language [18], but the analysis of constraints will certainly be more difficult as it cannot be limited to a navigation path through the schema.

It should be noted that prior work on statically checkable constraints [6] is not directly applicable because such constraint languages cannot include function calls and they depend on updates on the database being done through a restricted language.

Using the information stored in the assertion base, we intend to experiment with the combination of different optimisation techniques. Some assertion checking may be disarmed on functions, as they should not change the state of persistent objects. Some assertion evaluation on transient objects may be deferred until they are promoted to the persistent store. Finally profiling may be used over methods to evaluate the cost of functions inside assertions.

3.7   Using Assertions to Control Evolution

The evolution guard of the NightCap system will aim at checking the validity of the evolved store according to assertions. During an evolution step, this system will verify that changes have not affected the semantics of stored instances of evolved classes, as well as their dependencies on objects that have not evolved.

We propose three stages of assertion checking during an evolution step (figure 2):

- *Stage A* checks the consistency of stored instances (V1) before their evolution. Invariants of the instances to be converted (V1) will be evaluated on each instance (V1) before the execution of its conversion method, by making them the preconditions of this method.

– *Stage B* aims at checking consistency of the evolved stored instances (V2). As assertions may express inter-object constraints, a completely evolved store is needed. Therefore invariants will be checked in one step after the evolution of the entire store.

– *Stage C* is a testing stage. It aims at verifying the correctness of the application V2 against the part that has not evolved and against persistent instances. Assertions V2 will be checked on instances and on the application V2, while executing it. In particular invariants will be checked on the store and on the application. Pre and postconditions will be armed in the application to verify the correctness of methods.

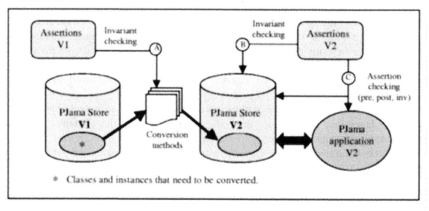

Fig.2. Assertion checking during an evolution step.

In order to evaluate assertions during the three checking stages, a straightforward solution would be to check the entire set of assertions. But the huge number of evaluations would lead to a considerable inefficiency, making the solution impracticable. Then, it becomes necessary to only verify a set of relevant assertions, in order to achieve a trade-off between the selected set of assertions and their evaluation cost.

In particular, in stage A only the invariants of classes to be converted will be checked during the evolution system's scan of the store. In stage B the set of assertions will be restricted to assertions of modified classes and those depending on them by inheritance or use relationships. In stage C it would be possible to provide levels of verification according to the amount and the kind of armed assertions during the application's execution. This would allow NightCap to determine an essential set of assertions to be checked, in order to provide acceptable performances in case of operational use.

Other relevant aspects must also be considered as, in practice, changes on classes may also include changes in the assertions. Therefore their evolution and checking must also be taken into account. As assertions describe semantic properties within a given framework (`pre`, `post`, `inv`), it is possible to detect assertion clauses that have been modified by a structural comparison between the new and old version of classes. This will allow us to map old assertion clauses to the new ones, so that assertions to be checked can be automatically selected.

In connection with assertion selection, it could also be useful to mark the weakest points in the store and in the new code, those that have evolved the most, so that assertion checking could go on during the application executions, for a certain time. A compromise between efficiency and a growing degree of confidence in the application should be found, related to the number of assertions already checked, thereby allowing a reduction of the number of checks. All assertion checks, successes and failures, would then be noted in the assertion base to provide the notion of confidence.

4   Related Work

In the field of object-oriented databases, the study of integrity constraints has been a subject of great interest, using either ECA rules or an application-oriented approach.

The ECA rules [4,12] approach faces problems regarding the non-termination of rule evaluation, the management of its large set of rules and its fuzzy and hard to learn semantics. Assertions have been integrated into active databases like SAMOS [14], but this approach also leads to non-termination problems as assertions are implemented through ECA rules.

In the application-oriented approach, constraints are encoded in application programs to provide efficient consistency checking [5]. Using this approach, the generated checking code may become too complex and further optimisations are then necessary. Moreover, the developer is completely responsible for the management of all aspects regarding constraints.

Even if it is not as powerful as a rule-based approach, our model provides an intuitive semantics, easy to understand by the average developer. Our approach allows easy enabling and disabling of assertions checking. Handling of object inconsistencies is also supported, as repair actions may be associated to the exceptions raised by assertion violations.

In [18], an approach for consistency management in object-oriented databases is proposed. This approach introduces a constraints catalogue, which is a meta-database of constraint specifications, which separates them from applications. Integrity constraints are also treated as first class citizens by considering them as objects. This approach also structures constraints to enable efficient checking. The assertion base of the NightCap system is similar to this constraints catalogue as it contains assertions as objects, which is a technique we used in our previous work on assertions [9,10]. This also provides the integrity independence feature to manage constraints without changing application programs.

Regarding assertions, there exist a lot of proposals for the integration of executable assertions into specific programming languages. But when they include quantifications[2], their implementation is basic and inefficient, such as in the iContract system for Java [16]. The OCL-J language has the advantage of the mapping with OCL from the UML standard. Lately an extension for assertions has been officially proposed for Java [20], but its expressiveness is limited.

A different approach [1] proposes assertions through a declarative constraint language on top of a Java Virtual Machine extended with orthogonal persistence. This declarative language is expressive, but it is a completely different formalism as it uses temporal Horn clauses. Our approach has the advantage of a single formalism from the design stage and, in our opinion, is easier to understand for the developer.

5   Conclusion

In this paper, we have proposed an approach that uses assertions to ensure consistency during the life cycle of persistent applications. This approach allows programmers to use a single formalism during the design and the implementation of persistent applications, to specify constraints that are used to check both the correctness of the application and the integrity of the persistent data.

Our approach uses a simpler model than ECA rules to provide integrity constraints for persistent data. However, our model has an intuitive semantics that is easy for the developer to understand and learn. Assertions are also completely integrated in the life cycle of persistent applications. They are used during the design stage to specify classes and during implementation to control the code against the specification. Finally, they are embedded in persistent stores to act as integrity constraints and they can also be used to validate evolution steps over those stores. Using the same formalism, our model provides traceability and reversibility of specifications between all development stages of a persistent application.

The NightCap system is currently undergoing implementation. The prototype can be used without access to the source code in order to handle code available only in bytecode form. We aim at using NightCap on real persistent applications to get feedback both on the performance side and on the use of assertions in persistent systems.

Future work will focus on the complete implementation of the NightCap system, as well as on the study and the experimentation of optimisation techniques for our assertion language.

Acknowledgements

This work is partly funded by the *Alliance* programme PN 00.214 (Franco-British joint research programme), between the Object and Software Components Group at

---

[2] It now becomes common for assertion languages to provide universal and existential quantifications over collections. Except for the Eiffel assertion system [17] and the Simple Assertion Facility [20] proposed for Java, all executable assertion systems we are aware of now include such quantifiers.

the I3S laboratory (University of Nice – Sophia Antipolis) and the PJama group at the University of Glasgow.

We greatly acknowledge the PJama group led by Malcolm Atkinson for giving us access to the PJama platform. We would also like to thank Malcolm Atkinson for valuable comments on this paper, as well as Pierre Crescenzo and the anonymous referees for their helpful suggestions.

References

1. Alagić, S., Solorzano, J., Gitchell, D., *Orthogonal to the Java Imperative* In Proc. of the 12th European Conf. on Object Oriented Programming (ECOOP'98).
2. Atkinson, M. P., Daynès, L., Jordan, M. J., Printezis T., Spence S., *An Orthogonally Persistent Java*, ACM SIGMOD Record (25)4, December 1996.
3. Atkinson, M. P., Morrison, P. *Orthogonally Persistent Object Systems,* VLDB Journal, 4(3), 1995.
4. Bauzer-Medeiros, C., Pfeffer, P, *Object Integrity Using Rules*, In Proc. of the 5th European Conference on Object Oriented Programming (ECOOP'91).
5. Benzaken, V., Doucet, A., *Thémis: A Database Programming Language Handling Integrity Constraints*, VLDB Journal, 4(3), 1995.
6. Benzaken, V., Schaefer, X., *Static Integrity Constraint Management in Object-Oriented Database Programming Languages via Predicate Transformer.* In Proc. of the 11th European Conf. on Object Oriented Programming (ECOOP'97).
7. Cattell, R.G.G. (ed.) *The Object Database Standard: ODMG 2.0*, Morgan Kaufmann Publishers, 1997.
8. Collet, P., *The OCL-J Specification*, Technical Report, I3S Laboratory. Feb. 2000.
9. Collet, P., Rousseau, R., *Assertions are Objects Too!* In Proc. of the 1st White Object-Oriented Nights (WOON'96), St-Petersburg, Martinus Nijhoff Intern., 1996.
10. Collet, P., Rousseau, R., *Towards Efficient Support for Executing the Object Constraint Language,* In Int. Conf. on Technology of Object-Oriented Languages and Systems (Tools 30, USA'99), Santa Barbara (Cal.), August 1-5, 1999, IEEE Computer Society Press.
11. Collet, P., Rousseau, R., *Efficient Implementation Techniques for Advanced Assertion Languages*, In L'Objet, 5(4), Hermès Sciences, 1999.
12. Diaz, O., *Deriving Active Rules for Constraint Maintenance in an Object-Oriented Database.* In Proc. of the 3rd Int. Conf. on Database and Expert System Applications (DEXA'92) , p. 332-337, Springer-Verlag, 1992.
13. Dmitriev, M., Atkinson, M.P., *Evolutionary Data Conversion in the PJama Persistent Language.* In Proc of the Workshop on Object and Databases, in the 13th European Conf. on Object Oriented Programming (ECOOP'99).
14. Geppert, A., Dittrich, K. R., *Specification and Implementation of Consistency Constraints in Object-Oriented Database Systems: Applying Programming-by-Contract*, In Proc. of GI-Conference DatenBanksysteme in Büro, Technik and Wissenschaft (BTW). March 1995.
15. Hamie, A., Civello, F., Howse J., Kent S., Mitchell R., *Reflections on the Object Constraint Language*, In UML'98 Int. Workshop, Mulhouse (France), 3-4 June 1998.
16. Kramer, R., *iContract - The Java Design by Contract Tool*, In International Conference on Technology of Object-Oriented Languages and Systems (Tools 26, USA'98) Santa Barbara (Cal.), August 3-7, 1998, IEEE Computer Society Press.
17. Meyer, B., *Applying Design by Contract*, IEEE Computer, 25(10), Oct.1992, p. 40-51.

18. Oakasha, H., Conrad, S., Saake, G., *Consistency Management in Object-Oriented Databases*. In Proc of the Workshop on Object and Databases, in the 13th European Conf. on Object Oriented Programming (ECOOP'99).
19. OMG Revision Task Force, *Unified Modeling Language Specification,* The Object Management Group Inc. Version 1.3, June 1999.
20. Sun Microsystems, Block, J., *Simple Assertion Facility*, Java Specification Request 041, `java.sun.com/aboutJava/communityProcess/jsr_041_asrt.html`, 1999.
21. Warmer, J., Kleppe, A., *The Object Constraint Language: Precise Modeling with UML,* Addison-Wesley Publishing Co. 1999.

Towards Scalable and Recoverable Object Evolution for the PJama Persistent Platform

Misha Dmitriev and Craig Hamilton

Department of Computing Science, University of Glasgow,
Glasgow G12 8RZ, Scotland, UK
{misha, craig}@dcs.gla.ac.uk

Abstract. Two developing technologies, namely Java Platform based on the Solaris Research VM and Sphere persistent store, have been recently combined to provide a new version of orthogonally persistent Java — PJama$_1$. Having these powerful technologies, the developers were given an excellent window of opportunity to provide evolution support as a standard, scalable and reliable mechanism. This paper describes the issues arising during the design of the store level foundation for the evolution technology, and our solutions. We have achieved our goals of making evolution scalable and recoverable, yet retaining the unchanged view of the "old object world" during object conversion, at a price of minor constraints to the semantics of custom evolution (conversion) code. A way to remove this constraint is proposed.

1 Introduction

1.1 Schema Evolution and Object Conversion for PPL and OODB

The requirement for schema evolution support is common for persistent programming languages (PPL) and object databases. The quality of the evolution subsystem is particularly important if a large amount of valuable data has been accumulated in a database (persistent store) and there is no easy *ad hoc* way of evolving it, apart from discarding the data, re-creating the database and re-reading the data into the database. To be useful, an evolution subsystem should support the facility to *convert* persistent objects of an evolved class if the formats of instances defined by the old and the new versions of this class are different. The effect of conversion is that every evolving object is transformed, but its identity remains the same, i.e. all links between objects, unless they are changed explicitly during the evolution, are preserved.

Object conversion can be supported in multiple ways. First of all, it may be eager or lazy. That is, all objects may be converted into the new format once and forever as soon as their class is evolved (eager or immediate conversion). Alternatively, this can happen for each object of an evolved class only when the object is requested by some application operating over the database (lazy conversion). The latter approach can be used when classes are changed immediately

K.R. Dittrich et al. (Eds.): Objects and Databases 2000, LNCS 1944, pp. 61–70, 2001.

and irrevertibly, but also if some kind of class or schema *versioning*, i.e., in broad terms, coexistence of old and new class versions which is unlimited in time, is used.

Object conversion can also be *default* or *custom*. In the first case, data transfer between the old and new copies of an evolving object is done automatically. It is typically limited to copying the values of fields with the same name and type and initialising new fields with default or user-defined constant values. Support for custom conversion means that the developer can provide high-level *conversion code* which performs arbitrary data copying and transformations.

1.2   PJama Evolution Model

PJama [7,1,9] is an experimental persistent programming system for the Java programming language. It has much in common with object database systems used together with Java. PJama is being developed as a collaborative project between the University of Glasgow and Sun Microsystems Inc.

The class evolution and object conversion model of PJama is described in detail in [5,4]. In brief, it looks as follows. Conversion is always performed eagerly. It can be default or custom. To perform custom conversion, the developer provides the Java code that transfers information from old objects to new and performs the necessary transformations. For example, old objects of class **Person** can contain a single field **name** for a person's name, whereas in the new class definition thre are two fields: **firstName** and **lastName**. Splitting a single string into two can't be done automatically. Instead, the programmer can write the following *conversion method*:

```
public static void convertInstance(Person$$_old_ver_ po,
                                   Person pn) {
  pn.firstName = getFirstName(po.name);   // Methods get...Name
  pn.lastName = getLastName(po.lastName); // not shown
}
```

A special *old class temporary renaming* mechanism is used to distinguish between old and new versions of an evolving class in the conversion code, as shown above. The system then scans the persistent store sequentially. For every object of an evolving class that it finds, it creates an empty new object. Its contents are first initialized using the default conversion mechanism which copies the values of the fields with the same names and compatible types from the old object to the new one. Then the conversion method is called. Old objects are atomically replaced with the new ones, which take their identity, only after all old objects are converted. Thus, a very important semantic property is supported: at any time during conversion, the "old world" of unevolved objects remains unchanged and completely visible to the conversion code.

Several other flavours of conversion methods are available, which can return new objects of any subclasses of an evolving class, or even arbitrary classes. The last option is unsafe and should be used with care, however it might be required if the data is re-structured deeply. Conversion methods are also available for the case when a class is deleted and its "orphan" instances should be *migrated* to other classes.

Another form of conversion, called *fully controlled* (as opposed to the above form called *bulk*), is also supported in PJama. Fully controlled conversion means that instead of individual methods, one for each evolving class, the programmer provides conversion code that should contain a single method called `conversionMain()`. If this method is present, it is treated as a single entrypoint and is called only once. The conversion code should then "manually" find and convert all necessary objects. Fully controlled conversion is useful if evolution is combined with major persistent data rearrangement, e.g. if an array of evolving objects is replaced with a linked list where the objects should be in some particular order.

1.3   Sphere Persistent Storage Layer

At present PJama is equipped with the persistent object store called Sphere [8, 10,11]. This system, among other merits, has a number of features that facilitate evolution. The most important of them is that the object PID in Sphere is logical. This means that instead of a physical offset of the object in the store, a PID contains a combination of the logical ID of the *store partition* where the object resides, and the index of the object's entry in the *indirectory* of this partition (Figure 1). Partitions, introduced to permit incremental store management algorithms, such as disk garbage collection and evolution, can be moved and resized within the store. Objects can be moved within partitions without changing their PIDs. A single partition can contain only certain *kinds* of objects. For example, instances and large scalar arrays are always kept in separate partitions. This can greatly speed up the lookup of evolving objects, since partitions containing unsuitable object kinds simply do not need to be inspected.

Each Sphere object that corresponds to a Java instance holds a reference to a *descriptor*. Descriptors are internally used objects that describe the layout (e.g. location of reference fields) of objects of the same type. A descriptor is lazily replicated in each partition that contains objects that need to be described by it. If an instance object exists within a partition, then a copy of its descriptor must be in that partition, and vice versa. There is a descriptor index in each partition. Using these properties of descriptors we can to rapidly discover whether any instances of a class exist within a partition, without the need to maintain exact class extents.

Sphere is also fully transactional. If a computation that runs on behalf of some transaction modifies the contents of the store and then crashes before committing the updates, the store layer will automatically perform *recovery* on restart, returning its contents to the initial state, as they were before the failed transaction started. Transactional behaviour is achieved by *logging* operations which change the contents of the store (see [6]).

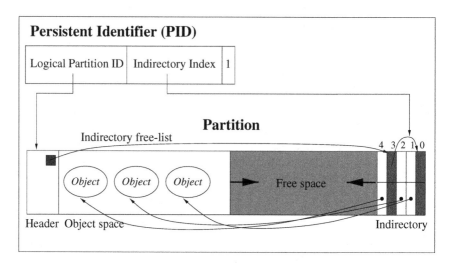

Fig. 1. PID format and partition organisation.

1.4 Our Goals

Our requirements to the evolution mechanism for PJama were formulated as follows:

1. Evolution should scale, i.e. work for any amount of objects that a Sphere store can accomodate, without substantial dependence of performance on the amount of objects to evolve.
2. Evolution should be performed atomically: it should either complete or abort. Failure at any stage of evolution, whether caused by an exception in the programmer-defined conversion code or an OS/hardware problem, should either allow the original state to be recovered or the evolution to complete on restart.
3. During evolution, the user must be provided with the consistent unchanged view of the old object world.

The development is facilitated by the fact that evolution in PJama is performed eagerly and "off-line". No persistent application and no additional background threads, e.g. a concurrent disk garbage collector, can run concurrently with the evolution transaction on the same store.

The reasons why the implementation of lazy conversion is currently not considered are related to both high-level and low-level aspects of this implementation. Quite serious high-level side concerns are described in [3]. The most important one is how to satisfy requirement 3 above if we don't want to keep old versions of objects in the store for unlimited time. The main concern about the Sphere-level part is that the implementation of primitive store operations that are necessary for lazy evolution (of them the most important one should look like "update a

store object, changing its type, and possibly size, without changing its PID"),
can hardly be done as a local update to the existing Sphere code. Instead, we
suspect that it will be necessary to change many parts of the code. This will
lead to higher code complexity and can possibly compromise its present high
level of robustness and performance. Since our present approach is to first deliver reliability and then additional features, and since we have not yet devised
an appropriate solution to high-level problems of lazy evolution, we decided to
defer the implementation of lazy object conversion.

2   Making Evolution Scalable

2.1   Context

During evolution, we load *old* objects (that is, old versions of evolving objects)
into the PJama VM main memory and convert them, creating the corresponding *new* objects. An unpredictable number of *newly-created* objects can also be
produced by conversion code, e.g. if we replace an integer field `date` in an evolving object with a new instance of class `Date`. Because of the requirement 3 in
the previous section, the evolution foundation is not allowed to replace any old
objects in the store with their new counterparts until the end of the evolution
transaction. However, we can't rely on holding the new objects in memory either,
since for most real-life applications, main memory would simply be insufficient
to accomodate all new objects. That's the main scalability issue with our approach to object conversion. We have to seek a better alternative for temporary
new object storage to make our technology scalable.

2.2   Temporary Storage of New Objects

Two places suitable for temporary storage of new objects can be envisaged: some
kind of custom virtual memory and the persistent store itself. The first variant
can be outruled almost immediately, the main reason being that Sphere stores,
and thus the space that evolving objects occupy, can grow to sizes much larger
than the limit of virtual memory on the most popular 32-bit hardware. Therefore,
taking the second approach, we can now consider the following general design.
Evolving objects are processed in portions small enough to fit into main memory.
As soon as all objects in the portion are processed, all new objects are saved
(promoted) into the store. Both the old and the new objects are then evicted
from main memory, either immediately or lazily, as further portions of objects are
processed. This process is repeated until there are no more unprocessed evolving
objects, and has the effect of producing two "worlds" - of old (unevolved) and
new objects. Then the old and new worlds are *collapsed*: the contents of each
old object are replaced with the contents of the corresponding new one, such
that the identity of the evolving object (which is essentially its PID) remains
the same.

2.3   Associating and Replacing Old and New Objects

The presented design addresses the most fundamental issue — scalability. However, it leaves a number of others. The first of them is the problem of how to store the association between old and new objects, i.e. all "old PID, new PID" pairs. This association should be preserved throughout the conversion process until collapsing starts, when this information is required. A straightforward solution — a main memory table that contains PID pairs (the global `pidTable` in memory) can, unfortunately, cause scalability problems again. For example, assume that we need to convert 2^{29} objects (Sphere allows us to store more, but let us consider a realistic case when just some proportion, not all objects in the store, are converted). An object PID is currently 32-bit, therefore a pair of PIDs will occupy 8 bytes. So we will need 2^{32} bytes to store the `pidTable` — the whole virtual memory available on a 32-bit machine. This is unacceptable, so we have to think of how to save parts of this table to disk during conversion, or how to preserve the association between objects in some other way.

Saving parts of the table to the store is possible if the table itself is made a persistent object. Further, the overhead can be relatively low if this table is constructed as a linked list of arrays (sub-tables). Every time a portion of objects is converted and promoted into the store, the next sub-table is also promoted. The disadvantage of this approach is that the table itself occupies space in the store, which may be comparable to the space occupied by the evolving objects, as we have just seen. Managing this persistent table also increases log traffic.

Another issue is how to replace old objects with the respective new ones in the store. The main problem is that a new object can be (and in practice almost always is) physically larger than the old object version. Therefore we can't store a new object over the old one, unless we move all objects in the partition that follow the old object. However, the size of the partition may be insufficient to accomodate the total difference in size between the new and old objects. Therefore the only reliable way to replace objects will be to create a new partition of sufficient size and copy all objects from the old partition into it, replacing old versions of evolving objects with new ones. Then the logical ID of the old partition should be transferred to the new one.

2.4   The Limbo Object Solution

The solution that we have adopted as a primary one, and have already implemented, addresses both of the above issues efficently. It is based on maintaining an implicit relation between objects and re-using the existing code of the disk garbage collector. Its key feature is preserving new objects in the store in the *limbo* form. A limbo object does not have its own PID and physically resides immediately after the live object it corresponds to. The implementation of object conversion now operates as follows. First all evolving objects of a partition are loaded into main memory and converted (Figure 2(a)). Then the new objects are promoted into a separate partition of the store (Figure 2(b)). After that the most important phase of low-level conversion begins: the contents of the evolving partition are copied into a completely new partition. Whenever the old copy of an evolving object is transferred, the corresponding new object is fetched and placed directly after it in the limbo form (Figure 2(c)). On completion of this partition sweep, the old partition copy is discarded immediately. At the same moment its logical ID is transferred to the partition where the new and the limbo objects are placed (Figure 2(d)). This is similar to two-space garbage collection, and in fact we have effectively reused the store garbage collection code in this case. New, or, rather, *temporary new* objects (objects 1' and 2' in partition #2, Figure 2(c)) are discarded, so that the partition can be re-used in future.

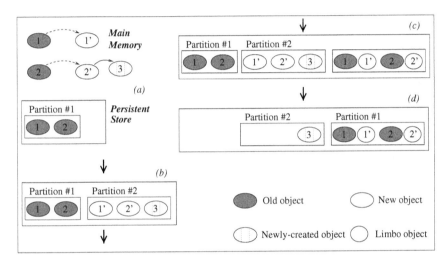

Fig. 2. PID Low-level conversion implementation using limbo objects

Thereafter, and until all objects in the store are converted, the relation between each new and old object is maintained implicitly. Finally, on transaction commit, the system just swaps objects in every "old object, limbo object" pair to make new objects live. This swap is done by updating the corresponding Sphere indirectory entries, avoiding physical moves of objects, therefore it is very fast.

2.5   Tradeoffs

The advantages of the above solution are its relative implementation convenience (the code of the disk garbage collector is largely reused), and lowest possible disk space and log traffic overhead. Having these properties, the implementation is also likely to perform well. However, its drawback is that during evolution, once a new object is turned into limbo state, it becomes inaccessible. That's because it does not have its own PID and is not recognised as a first-class store object. On the PJama VM level, once a new object is promoted into the store and made a limbo object, its PID (which is now meaningless) is discarded, and any updates to this object will not propagate to the store.

Our present experience shows that in most cases the conversion code does not need to revisit a new copy of an evolving object after the latter is created. However, if during conversion we want, for example, to create a forward chain of objects, we need to be able to revisit the new copies of evolved objects.

The limbo object solution also does not give any advantages in the case of fully controlled conversion where the order of faulting of evolving objects can be arbitrary. For this reason our present implementation of fully controlled conversion, though operational, does not scale. In this conversion mode, all evolving objects are loaded into memory on demand. Only after developer's conversion code terminates, evolved objects are sorted by partitions and the standard conversion operation described above is applied to each group, sequentially.

A solution which permits revisiting the new objects can be envisaged, that still exploits limbo objects. For it, Sphere operations to read and update a limbo object, given the PID of the corresponding live object, will be required. However, the main challenge will be to design and implement the management of limbo objects in the Java heap. Since in the PJama VM two objects can never have the same PID, limbo objects will have to be treated not as normal persistent objects. Probably a separate table that maps PIDs to memory objects, equivalent to the main PJama ROT (Resident Object Table), will be required for them. The PIDs of the corresponding live objects will be re-used for limbo objects. The garbage collection, eviction and update tracking/saving code of the PJama VM will have to be modified. But, provided that these changes are made in a comprehensible way and do not compromise the performance of ordinary PJama applications, this approach seems reasonable.

However, the problem of how to make fully controlled conversion scalable still remains. The only solution to it that we can currently see uses periodic saving of new objects to the store, plus a heavyweight persistent `pidTable`. When high-level conversion is finished, the same limbo object low-level conversion mechanism can be used to replace old objects with their new versions, ensuring conversion recoverability (see next section). The disadvantage of this approach is that it will lead to significant store growth during evolution, since at some point there will be three copies of an evolving object in the store: old live, new live and new limbo. It is also not clear yet how much additional code complexity it will introduce.

3   Making Evolution Recoverable

A big advantage of the limbo object solution, whether or not it is allowed to update limbo objects, is that the store can be recovered in a very simple way if a crash occurs during evolution. Indeed, the store essentially looks as unevolved (because old objects remain live and new objects are in limbo, not normally visible and accessible state) until the evolution operation is committed. At that moment the system starts swapping the live and limbo objects. If a crash occurs before the swapping has started, all we need to do to revert the store to its initial state is to discard the limbo objects. This actually happens in any case, whether or not evolution succeeded, and is done automatically by the disk garbage collector. The latter treats limbo objects as empty space, since they don't have their own PIDs and indirectory entries. If a crash occurs after commit begins, then on restart we roll forward and complete all swapping.

Other approaches based on this one, e.g. a scalable solution for fully controlled conversion presented in the previous section, will inherit its recoverability property.

4   Conclusion

We have recently made considerable progress with the design and implementation of the store level part of the evolution technology for PJama and Sphere. This technology, when it is used with standard (bulk) high-level conversion mode, is scalable and recoverable, which is confirmed by preliminary tests and measurements to be included elsewhere, e.g. [2]. It supports the fundamental requirement for the consistent view of all "old world" objects until the object conversion is complete. However, the presented technology currently imposes some (not very serious) limitations on the conversion code semantics. A sketch of the solution that will be free from these limitations is presented.

Our present low-level conversion implementation does not support scalability for fully controlled conversion. We have presented a preliminary solution still based on our current approach, that solves this problem, and now investigating it further.

References

1. M.P. Atkinson and M.J. Jordan. Issues Raised by Three Years of Developing PJama. In *Database Theory — ICDT'99*, C. Beeri and O.P. Buneman (Editors), pages 1-30. LNCS 1540, Springer Verlag, 1999.
2. M. P. Atkinson, M. Dmitriev, C. Hamilton and T. Printezis. Scalable and Recoverable Implementation of Object Evolution for the PJama Platform. Submitted to Ninth International Workshop on Persistent Object Systems (POS9), 2000, under review.
3. M. Dmitriev. The First Experience of Class Evolution Support in PJama. In *Proceedings of the 3rd Int. Workshop on Persistence and Java*, M.P. Atkinson, M.J. Jordan and R. Morrison (Editors), pages 279–296, Morgan Kaufmann, 1998.
4. M.Dmitriev. Class and Data Evolution Support in the PJama Persistent Platform. Technical Report TR-2000-57, University of Glasgow, Scotland, UK, June 2000. URL = http://www.dcs.gla.ac.uk/~misha/papers.
5. M. Dmitriev and M.P. Atkinson. Evolutionary Data conversion in the PJama Persistent Language. In *Proceedings of the 1st ECOOP Workshop on Object-Oriented Databases*, URL = http://www.disi.unige.it/conferences/oodbws99/, June 1999.

6. C.G. Hamilton. Recovery Management for Sphere: Recovering a Persistent Object Store. Technical Report TR-1999-51, University of Glasgow, Scotland, December 1999.

7. M.J. Jordan and M.P. Atkinson. Orthogonal Persistence for Java — a Mid-term Report. In *Proceedings of the 3rd Int. Workshop on Persistence and Java*, M.P. Atkinson, M.J. Jordan and R. Morrison (Editors), pages 335–352, Morgan Kaufmann, 1998.

8. T. Printezis, M.P. Atkinson and L. Daynès. The Implementation of Sphere: a Scalable, Flexible, and Extensible Persistent Object Store. Technical Report TR-1998-46, University of Glasgow, Scotland, May 1998.

9. PJama Team. PJama — API, Tools and Tutorials, web-based documentation. Sun Microsystems Laboratories, 901 San Antonio Road, MS MTV29-112, Palo Alto, CA 94303-4900, USA and Department of Computing Science, University of Glasgow, Glasgow G12 8QQ, Scotland. URL = `http://www.sun.com/research/forest`

10. T. Printezis. The Sphere User's Guide. Technical Report TR-1999-47, University of Glasgow, Scotland, July 1999.

11. T. Printezis. Management of Long-Running, High-Performance Persistent Object Stores. PhD Thesis, University of Glasgow, Scotland, 2000.

Dynamic Clustering in Object-Oriented Databases: An Advocacy for Simplicity

Jerome Darmont[1], Christophe Fromantin[2], Stephane Régnier[2+3],
Le Gruenwald[3], and Michel Schneider[2]

[1]E.R.I.C.
Université Lyon 2
69676 Bron Cedex, France
jdarmont@univ-lyon2.fr
[2]L.I.M.O.S.
Université Blaise Pascal
63177 Aubière Cedex, France
michel.schneider@isima.fr
[3]School of CS
University of Oklahoma
Norman, OK 73019, US
ggruenwald@ou.edu

Abstract. We present in this paper three dynamic clustering techniques for Object-Oriented Databases (OODBs). The first two, *Dynamic, Statistical & Tunable Clustering* (DSTC) and *StatClust*, exploit both comprehensive usage statistics and the inter-object reference graph. They are quite elaborate. However, they are also complex to implement and induce a high overhead. The third clustering technique, called *Detection & Reclustering of Objects* (DRO), is based on the same principles, but is much simpler to implement. These three clustering algorithm have been implemented in the Texas persistent object store and compared in terms of clustering efficiency (i.e., overall performance increase) and overhead using the *Object Clustering Benchmark* (OCB). The results obtained showed that DRO induced a lighter overhead while still achieving better overall performance.

Keywords: Object-Oriented Databases, Dynamic Object Clustering, Performance Comparison.

1. Introduction

Object-Oriented Database Management Systems (OODBMSs) always showed performance problems when compared to Relational Database Management Systems (RDBMSs). They really won an edge over RDBMSs only in niche markets, mainly engineering and multimedia applications. This performance problem is essentially caused by secondary storage Input/Output (I/O). Despite numerous advances in hard drive technology, I/Os still require much more time than main memory operations. Several techniques have been devised to minimize I/O transfers and improve the performances of OODBMSs, like query optimization, indexing, buffering, or clustering. Object clustering is a collaborative research topic at Blaise Pascal University (BPU) and the University of Oklahoma (OU) since the early 90's. The principle of clustering is to store related objects close to each other in order to

K.R. Dittrich et al. (Eds.): Objects and Databases 2000, LNCS 1944, pp. 71-85, 2001.

maximize the amount of relevant information returned when a disk page is loaded into the main memory.

Early clustering methods were static [1, 2, 12, 13, 14, 15], i.e., objects were clustered only once at creation time. With these methods, modifying the placement to suit changes in data usage necessitates reorganizing the whole database. This is a heavy task that can only be performed manually when the system is idle. To support databases that are intended to be accessible on a 7 days a week / 24 hours a day basis (e.g., web-accessed databases), dynamic clustering techniques that cluster and recluster objects automatically and incrementally have been designed both by researchers and OODBMS vendors. However, since publications by the latter are very few and research proposals are not always implemented or evaluated, it is hard to select the best technique in a given context.

The objectives of this paper are to propose an overview of the research dealing with dynamic object clustering techniques; to present two methods designed at BPU and OU called DSTC and StatClust, as well as a new one called *Detection & Reclustering of Objects* (DRO); and to compare these techniques in terms of efficiency and clustering overhead. These comparisons have been performed on the Texas system using the OCB benchmark [9], which has been specially designed to evaluate clustering algorithms.

The remainder of this paper is organized as follows. Section 2 establishes a state of the art regarding dynamic clustering techniques. Section 3 presents DSTC [3], StatClust [10], and eventually details DRO. Section 4 presents the performance evaluations we performed on Texas. We finally conclude the paper and discuss future research issues.

2. Related Work: Dynamic Object Clustering Methods

Most dynamic object clustering methods have been motivated by needs in engineering applications like CAD, CAM, or software engineering applications. A first class of clustering strategies is based on the analysis of database usage statistics. Chang and Katz [5] proposed a physical clustering method based on a particular inheritance link called *instance to instance* and the declaration of estimated access frequencies associated with three types of relationships (aggregation, equivalence, version). The idea is allowing inheritance of data along any type of attribute and particularly along inter-object links. For instance, it is interesting, when a new version of an object is created, to automatically make it inherit from its ancestor's aggregation links toward other objects. Inherited data are stored only once, which allows an important gain in terms of disk space, but forces a physical object to be placed as close to inherited data as possible. The access frequencies and the computation of inherited attributes costs help identifying the destination page of a newly created object. If the target page is full, the system can either split the page or elect the next best page as a target page. Dynamic clustering is also coupled with an appropriate buffering strategy that is a variation of *Least Recently Used* (LRU) allowing a better usage of existing clustering. It is based on prioritizing all pages in memory. Frequently used pages have their priority increased along with their structurally related pages, while unused pages have their priority decreased with time. This method has never been implemented, except within simulation models [5, 8, 10] that hint a potential increase in performance of 200% under certain conditions.

Another method based on statistics has been proposed by McIver and King [17], who advocate that object placement determination phases must be independent of the actual placement. The strategy leans on the exploitation of three modules running concurrently. The *statistics collection module* collects general database usage statistics and also selective database usage statistics concerning depth-first or breadth-first traversals, which are assimilated to navigational and associative accesses, respectively. The *cluster analysis module* uses a variation of the Cactis algorithm [12]. It first finds out the most referenced object in the database. Then, objects linked to it are grouped on the same disk page in depth-first, by decreasing order of co-usage frequency. An advised variation is to use depth-first traversals when navigational accesses are preponderant and breadth-first traversals when associative accesses are preponderant. The type of access to select is provided by usage statistics. Clustering analysis is triggered after collection of a significant amount of statistics. The *reorganization module* rearranges objects on disk so that the database physical organization corresponds to the page assignments suggested by clustering analysis. A reorganization phase is not always necessary after each clustering analysis phase. When a reorganization phase is triggered, it deals only with objects that have not been clustered. The performance of this method has been evaluated by simulation using the *Trouble Ticket Benchmark* [16]. This study shows that the collected statistics and the proposed clustering are pertinent, and that a high overhead is caused by the database reorganization phases, where the entire database is locked and the transactions are postponed.

Cheng and Hurson state that existing strategies are generally based on one single clustering criterion [7]. Their *multi-level clustering* allows clustering objects using several criteria at once. The method associates a criterion to each of three types of relationships identified by [5]: equivalence, aggregation, and version. A proximity degree between two objects can be elaborated using the values of these criteria. Clustering is recommended when this proximity degree is sufficiently small. The clustering algorithm actually orders objects on the basis of their proximity degree. Clustering is performed by the system, without any external intervention. Furthermore, this strategy is backed up by a cost model that evaluates the benefit of a possible dynamic reorganization. This proposal has never been implemented.

Finally, an innovative strategy has been proposed to handle object clustering in the EOS distributed system [11]. This method exploits the system's garbage collector and induces a very low overhead. Clustering specifications are provided by the database administrator, who weights arcs in the class aggregation graph according to estimated access probabilities. Objects are clustered with their stronger weighted parent when created. Placements are re-evaluated afterward by the disk garbage collection process and may be modified asynchronously. This proposal has not been implemented. The authors do provide elements regarding feasibility and low cost, but this technique is intimately related to the presence of a disk garbage collector continuously working, which is costly and thus not much used in existing OODBMSs.

3. Studied Dynamic Clustering Algorithms

3.1. DSTC

DSTC is actually both a dynamic object clustering policy and its associated buffering policy, which aims at clustering together objects that are used together at near instants in time [3]. It measures object usage statistics, while respecting the following constraints: minimize the amount of data managed, maximize the pertinence of collected statistics, reduce the cost of persistent storage for these data, and minimize perturbations on running transactions. This goal is achieved by scaling collected data at different levels and using gradual filters on main memory-stored statistics. Hence, it is possible to store on disk only presumably significant statistics.

Database usage statistics concern object access frequencies and inter-object reference usage frequencies. All types of links are considered as physical references, whether they are structural links built at the schema level or logical links depending on applications or induced by physical object fragmentation. All physical accesses from one object toward another are detected and counted. Physical object reorganization is started by a trigger mechanism. Object disk storage is organized through an ordering algorithm that builds linear sequences of objects that capture "attraction forces" between objects. This sequence is sequentially transcribed in a cluster, i.e., a contiguous disk segment of variable size. The underlying algorithm was inspired by [7]. Flexibility in this approach is achieved through various parameters allowing the adaptation of system reactivity to database behavior. These parameters are set up by the database administrator. The DSTC strategy is organized into five phases.

1. *Observation phase:* During a predefined *observation period*, object usage statistics are collected and stored in an *observation matrix* in main memory.
2. *Selection phase:* Data stored in the observation matrix are sorted and filtered. Only significant statistics are retained.
3. *Consolidation phase:* Results from the selection phase are used to update data collected in previous observation phases, which are stored in a persistent *consolidated matrix.*
4. *Dynamic cluster reorganization:* Statistics from the consolidated matrix are exploited to suggest a reorganization of the physical space. Existing *clustering units* can be modified and new *clustering units* can be created.
5. *Physical database reorganization:* Clustering units are eventually used to consider a new object placement on disk. This phase is triggered when the system is idle.

The principle of the buffering management associated with DSTC is the following. When an object belonging to a cluster is accessed, the whole cluster is loaded. This avoids useless I/Os since objects in the cluster have a good probability to be used by the current transaction. A page replacement algorithm named LRU-C is also proposed. Its principle is to date clusters in the buffer rather than pages.

The DSTC strategy has been implemented in Texas [18] on Sun workstations and PCs under Linux. Performance studies have been performed with a benchmark based on OO1 [4] and baptized DSTC-CluB. They showed the efficiency of DSTC compared to a no-clustering policy on simple cases.

3.2. StatClust (*Statistical Clustering*)

This method extends Chang and Katz' method (see Section 2) [5]. Its authors advocate replacing user-estimated access frequencies by more reliable usage statistics [10], for each of the considered types of links (aggregation, equivalence, version). Statistics regarding read or write accesses have also been added. Clustering is automatic at object creation or update time and when a bad clustering is detected. The user can influence the clustering process through a set of parameters. A bad clustering is detected when the ratio between the number of blocks (set of contiguous pages) read in the buffer and the number of blocks read on disk is smaller than a threshold computed by the system, and the amount of collected statistics is sufficient. The detection of a bad clustering ends the collection of statistics and starts up a reclustering phase that specifies which objects might be reclustered (i.e., which objects show satisfying usage statistics). The physical placement of objects uses an algorithm close to [5], but also supports object duplication. Objects may be duplicated to increase reference locality. An object that is more read than updated is a candidate for duplication.

StatClust has been compared by simulation to static clustering techniques (ORION and Cactis) [10], but not to dynamic clustering techniques, including Chang and Katz' method, on which it is based. The results are actually very similar to those reported in [8].

3.3. DRO

Overview. The design of DRO makes use of the experience accumulated with both the DSTC and StatClust clustering methods, especially at the implementation level. Since these methods were quite sophisticated, they were also very difficult to implement properly and lots of problems occurred in the development process. Furthermore, though they attempt to minimize the amount of usage statistics stored, they use various statistical data that are not easy to manage and whose size often increases drastically. DRO is much easier to implement. It exploits both basic usage statistics and the graph of inter-object references (derived from the schema) to dynamically cluster the database. Its principle is to store together the objects that are the most frequently accessed overall. DRO has been implemented in Texas.

Usage Statistics. DRO stores and exploits two principal types of indicators. They are updated dynamically when the database is in use.

- The *object access frequency* measures the number of times each object is accessed. During the clustering phase, only the objects with the highest access frequencies are taken into account.

▪ The *page usage rate* is the ratio between the size of the data effectively stored in the page and the page size, a page being the unit of transfer between disk and memory. This ratio helps determining which pages degrade the system performance. The mean usage rate for all pages and the number of pages loaded are also computed.

The data structure presented in Fig. 1 as a UML static structure diagram is used to store DRO's usage statistics. The *PageStat* class concerns page statistics. It has three attributes: a page identifier, the number of times this page has been loaded into memory, and its page usage rate. The *ObjectStat* class concerns object statistics. It also has three attributes: an object identifier, the object access frequency, and a boolean usage indicator. The *PageObjectStat* class allows large objects to be stored on several pages. It has only one attribute: the size occupied by a given object in a given page.

Fig. 1. DRO usage statistics

Whenever an object is accessed, its access frequency is incremented by 1 and its usage indicator is set to true. Page statistics are updated whenever a page moves from the main memory to disk. The statistics attached to all the objects on this page are used to compute the size occupied on the page by objects that have actually been used. The page usage rate is then computed and *Nb_Load* is increased by 1. If an object is deleted from the database, the corresponding usage statistics are also deleted. If the page that contains this object does not have any more objects in its associated *PageObjectStat* object, its statistics are also deleted. If an object is merely moved from one page to another, its usage indicator is reset to false and its link to the starting page is deleted. Its statistics will then be linked to the destination page's statistics when the object is used again.

Clustering. The clustering phase can be triggered manually or automatically. It is subdivided into four steps. Until physical object placement, a control procedure checks out after each step whether clustering must abort or resume.

Step 1: Determination of Objects to Cluster. This step helps defining the objects belonging to pages with usage rate lower than the minimum usage rate (*MinUR*) and that have been loaded in memory more times than the minimum loading threshold (*MinLT*). *MinUR* and *MinLT* are user-defined parameters. *MinUR* helps selecting pages containing a majority of unused objects or objects that are not used together. Objects stored into these pages and whose usage statistics (i.e., an *ObjectStat* object) are instantiated are selected for clustering. They are attached to instances of the *Clustering* class. Objects of class *Clustering* are linked together by two bi-directional relations called *Object_Sort* and *Object_Placement*, which store objects sorted by access frequency and a placement order of objects on disk, respectively. To proceed to step 2, two conditions must be met: a) the number of pages to cluster must be greater than one, and b) the ratio between the number of pages to cluster and the number of pages actually used is greater than the page clustering rate parameter (*PCRate*).

Step 2: Clustering Setup. This step helps defining a sequential placement order of objects on disk. The algorithm input is the list of objects to cluster sorted by decreasing access frequency. This step is subdivided into three phases.

- *Object clustering using inter-object references.* This first phase links objects regarding reference links. The algorithm shown in Figure 2 runs up to a user-defined maximum distance *MaxD*, i.e., the first iteration considers all the objects referenced by the starting object (distance 1), then the process reiterates for each object found, up to distance *MaxD*. When linking together objects O_i and O_j of access frequencies AF_i and AF_j, the dissimilarity rate $|AF_i - AF_j| / \max(AF_i, AF_j)$ must be lower than the maximum dissimilarity rate *MaxDR* not to link objects that are too weakly bound. Objects are sorted by descending order of access frequency to generate a list defining a placement order of objects so that they can be sequentially written on disk.
- *Linking of placement order lists.* This phase links together the list parts made up in the first phase to obtain a single list. The list parts are considered in their generation order and simply concatenated.
- *Resemblance rate computation.* The third phase establishes a resemblance rate between the current object placement and the new placement proposed by the clustering algorithm. This resemblance rate helps evaluating how different the new clustering proposal is from the current physical placement of the objects. If the new cluster is found similar (for instance, if the considered objects have already been clustered), no action is undertaken. The resemblance rate is the number of objects in the proposed cluster that are not moved regarding current object placement divided by the number of objects in the cluster.

Step 3: Physical Object Clustering. Physical clustering is performed if the resemblance rate computed at step 2 is lower than a user-defined maximum resemblance rate (*MaxRR*). This operation clusters objects identified in the previous steps, but must also reorganize the database in order to retrieve space made available by movement or deletion of objects.

Step 4: Statistics Update. This update depends on a user-defined statistics update indicator (*SUInd*). If *SUInd* is set to true, all statistics are deleted. Otherwise, only statistics regarding pages containing objects that have been moved are deleted.

DRO Parameters. The parameters defining the behavior of the DRO strategy are set-up by the database administrator. They are recapitulated in Table 1. We obtained the default values through many experiments on Texas.

```
D = 0
End = false
While D < MaxD and not End do
    D = D + 1
    // Browse objects to cluster
    Starting_object = Clustering.Sort_first
    While Starting_object ≠ NIL and
    Starting_object.Placement_previous ≠ NIL do
        Starting_object = Starting_object.Sort_next
    End While
    While Starting_object ≠ NIL do
        Object_to_link = Starting_object
        While Object_to_link ≠ NIL and
        Object_to_link.Placement_previous ≠ NIL do
            Object_to_link = Object_to_link.Placement_next
        End while
        Found = TRUE
        While Found do
            // Find an object to cluster different from
            // Starting_object, referenced on a distance lower
            // than MaxD, with a dissimilarity rate lower than
            // MaxDR, and attribute Clustering.Placement_previous
            // set to NIL
            Found_object = Research_procedure_result()
            If Found_object ≠ NIL then
                Object_to_link.Placement_next = Found_object
                Object_found.Placement_previous = Object_to_link
                Object_to_link = Object_found
            Else
                Found = FALSE
            End if
        End while
    While Starting_object ≠ NIL and
    Starting_object.Placement_previous ≠ NIL do
        Starting_object = Starting_object.Sort_next
    End while
End while
```

Fig. 2. Object clustering

Table 1. DRO parameters

Parameter	Name	Type	Default value
Minimum usage rate	MinUR	Real	0.8
Minimum loading threshold	MinLT	Real	1
Page clustering rate	PCRate	Real	0.05
Maximum distance	MaxD	Integer	1
Maximum dissimilarity rate	MaxDR	Real	0.05
Maximum resemblance rate	MaxRR	Real	0.9
Statistics update indicator	SUInd	Boolean	True

Example of Clustering with DRO. Let us consider the graph of inter-object references from Fig. 3 and the associated access frequencies from Table 2. With the

MaxDR parameter set up to 0.1, Fig. 4 shows how the clustering algorithm builds an ordered sequence of objects that will be sequentially written on disk.

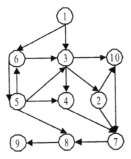

OID	Access Frequency
6	60
5	60
4	60
7	40
1	20
2	20
3	20
10	18
8	17

Fig. 3. Sample inter-object reference graph

Table 2. Sample access frequencies

Let *MaxD* be 1. Objects are considered by the order of access frequency. The dissimilarity rates between object couples (6, 5) and (5, 4) are both 0. The dissimilarity rates of the (6, 3), (5, 3), (5, 8), and (4, 7) couples are all greater than *MaxDR*, so the first sub-list we obtain is (6, 5, 4). The dissimilarity rate for the (7, 8) couple is 0.575 and hence greater than *MaxDR*, so (7) remains a singleton. The dissimilarity rates for the (1, 3), (3, 2), and (3, 10) couples are 0, 0, and 0.1, respectively (links to already treated objects are not considered), so the third sub-list is (1, 3, 2, 10). (8) forms the last sub-list since object #9 has never been accessed and thus must not be clustered. Now if *MaxD* is 2, we have to consider dissimilarity rates up to a "distance" (in number of objects) of 2 from the starting object. For instance, we must consider the (6, 10) couple. Its dissimilarity rate is 0.7, greater than *MaxDR*. The only change regarding the sub-lists obtained with *MaxD* set to 1 is the integration of object #8 in the (1, 3, 2, 10) sequence, because the dissimilarity rate of the (10, 8) couple is 0.05, lower than *MaxDR*. Eventually, the sub-lists are merged in one list by the order of creation.

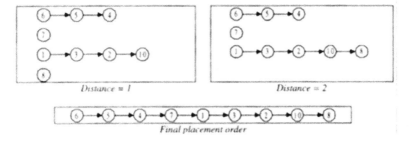

Fig. 4. Sample execution of the DRO clustering algorithm

4. Performance Comparison

4.1. Experiment Scope

Our initial goal was to compare the performances of StatClust, DSTC, and DRO. However, StatClust proved exceedingly difficult to implement in Texas. Since Texas exploits the operating system's virtual memory, it considers the memory buffer to be of infinite size. Thus, it is impossible to implement StatClust's module for detecting a bad clustering, because it needs to count the number of pages accessed from the disk and the buffer. Furthermore, substantial additions to Texas would be necessary to support the object replication process advocated by StatClust. Eventually, the object clustering algorithm initially builds a list of candidate pages containing objects related to the current object. To build this list, the database schema must be known. Techniques can be devised to automatically infer the schema, but none of them is easy to implement. In addition, when implementing StatClust, we found that Texas could not handle numerous transactions and the associated statistics on reasonably large databases and invariably crashed. Thus, we were not able to properly compare StatClust to the other algorithms. Hence, we only compare DSTC and DRO here.

To compare the performances of DSTC and DRO, we used a mid-sized OCB database composed of 50 classes and 100,000 objects, for a size of about 62 MB. The other OCB parameters defining the database were set to default. Two series of standard OCB transactions (1000 transactions and 10,000 transactions) were executed on this database, before and after object clustering. System performance was measured in terms of I/Os, response time, and relative performance improvement due to clustering. Only the results concerning I/Os are presented in this paper because response time plots present exactly the same tendencies and do not bring additional insight. Eventually, these experiments have been performed in several memory configurations. Since Texas makes an intensive use of virtual memory, it was interesting to see how the system behaved when the ratio *main memory size / database size* varied. The whole process was reiterated 100 times so that mean tendencies could be achieved. In each iteration, the same random seed was selected for the DSTC and DRO experiments so that they were rigorously identical.

4.2. Experiment Hardware and Software

The version of Texas we used is a prototype (version 0.5) running on a PC Pentium 166 with 64 MB of RAM, and version 2.0.30 of Linux. The swap partition size was 64 MB. StatClust, DSTC and DRO are integrated in Texas as a collection of new modules, and a modification of several Texas modules. Texas and the additional StatClust, DSTC and DRO modules were written in GNU C++ version 2.7.2.1.

4.3. Experiment Results

DSTC. Fig. 5 and 6 show that clustering with DSTC indeed allows a significant gain in performance, especially when the amount of main memory available is small. Clustering is definitely more useful when the database does not fit wholly within the main memory, since its effects are felt as soon as the system swaps and not only at page load time. This assumption is neatly confirmed by the clustering gain factor graph in Fig. 6. Clustering gain factor is equal to the number of I/Os necessary to execute the transactions after clustering divided by the number of I/Os necessary to execute the transactions before clustering. A discrepancy appears between Fig. 5 and 6 due to the fact that 1000 transactions are not enough: objects are used, clustered, but rarely reused following the same patterns, thus provoking an useless clustering) on small memory configurations. On the other hand, the 10,000 transaction workload appears more representative of actual database usage, allowing an average gain factor of about 2.5.

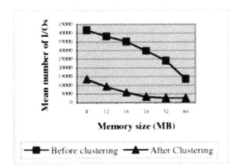
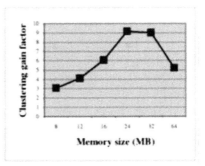

Fig. 5. DSTC results – 1000 transactions

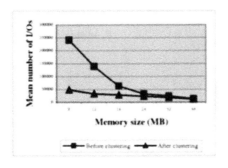
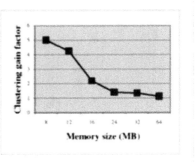

Fig. 6. DSTC results – 10,000 transactions

DRO. Fig. 7 and 8 show that DRO bears the same overall behavior as DSTC. However, the gain factor achieved with DRO on the 10,000 transaction workload looks much better. It is indeed about 15. The comparison is unfair, though, because we selected the optimal set of parameters for DRO clustering, while we could not do it for DSTC. Due to technical problems with big databases, we had to parameterize DSTC so that clustering was not the best possible. There was a threshold effect on a set of DSTC parameters. Below this "threshold", everything worked out fine but clustering was average. Beyond the "threshold", clustering units were too big for Texas to manage and the system invariably crashed.

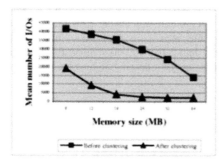 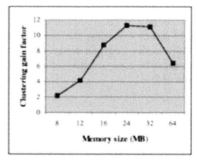

Fig. 7. DRO results – 1000 transactions

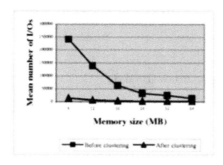 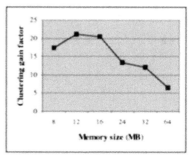

Fig. 8. DRO results – 10,000 transactions

Comparison of DSTC and DRO. To eventually compare DSTC and DRO on a fair ground, we used a smaller database so that DSTC could properly work. We used OCB's default database (50 classes, 20,000 instances, about 20 MB) and ran two series of typical transactions that were likely to benefit from clustering: depth-3 hierarchy traversals (that always follow the same type of reference) and depth-2 simple traversals (depth-first traversals). The depth of traversals was reduced regarding OCB's default parameters so that the generated clusters were not too big and the effects of clustering were clear. The traversals have been performed from 100 predefined root objects and each of them was executed 10 times.

Table 3 displays the mean number of I/Os concerning database usage before and after clustering. It shows that DSTC and DRO both achieve a substantial increase in performance (factor 6-7). DRO looks even better, though more tuning with DSTC should bring this method on the same level. Unfortunately, such tuning still provoked execution errors in Texas. The big difference between DSTC and DRO lies in clustering overhead (the number of I/Os necessary for an algorithm to cluster the database). DSTC induces a high overhead, which renders it difficult to implement truly dynamically. Its authors actually advocate its triggering when the database is idle. On the contrary, DRO, which is much simpler, present a lower overhead (about 4 times lower) and is certainly better suited to a dynamic execution.

Table 3. Clustering efficiency comparison between DSTC and DRO (I/Os)

	Hierarchy traversals		Simple traversals	
	DSTC	*DRO*	*DSTC*	*DRO*
Pre-clustering usage	1682.6	1686	1682	1683
Post-clustering usage	270.8	226	281.75	236.75
Clustering gain factor	*6.21*	*7.46*	*5.97*	*7.11*
Clustering overhead	12219.4	3286.8	12174	2804.5

5. Conclusion

We have presented in this paper a representative panel of dynamic object clustering techniques, including our first effort in this field: the DSTC and StatClust techniques, which both make an intensive use of statistical counters and include clustering mechanisms with elaborated features. We have also presented a new clustering method, DRO, whose principles are based on those of DSTC and StatClust, but that is much simpler and deals with fewer statistical counters. The idea behind DRO is to provide a clustering method equivalent to or better than DSTC and StatClust while achieving simplicity of implementation.

We validated the idea that a simple dynamic clustering technique could provide better results than an elaborated one by comparing DSTC and DRO. Our results showed that DRO indeed performed better than DSTC, which could not be set up in an optimal fashion due to its inherent complexity. Furthermore, the clustering overhead induced by DRO was much lower than that induced by DSTC, definitely proving that a simple approach is more viable in dynamic context than a complex one.

To summarize, we showed that DRO was a better choice than DSTC in all circumstances. We also underlined the fact that a dynamic clustering technique is perfectly viable in an OODBMS and could achieve significant gains in performances. Since DRO is based on usage statistics, it fits well with the concept of autoadmin databases that is currently researched in major companies to automate the database tuning process [6].

The perspectives opened by this study are divided into two axes. First, the evaluation of DRO should be carried on on other systems besides Texas, which is a persistent object store rather than a full OODBMS. Such evaluations could be conducted on real OODBMSs like O_2, or achieved by simulation. Second, DRO itself could be improved so that clustering overhead is minimized. Some optimizations can be achieved in its code itself (at the list manipulation level, for instance), while others relate more to tuning DRO's parameters, which could also be achieved by simulation.

References

1. T. Andrews, C. Harris, K. Sinkel: ONTOS: A Persistent Database for C++. In: Object-Oriented Databases with Applications to CASE, Networks and VLSI CAD (1991) 387–406
2. V. Benzaken, C. Delobel: Enhancing Performance in a Persistent Object Store: Clustering Strategies n O_2. 4th International Workshop on Persistent Object Systems (1990) 403–412
3. F. Bullat, M. Schneider: Dynamic Clustering in Object Database Exploiting Effective Use of Relationships Between Objects. ECOOP '96, Linz, Austria. LNCS Vol. 1098 (1996) 344–365
4. R.G.G. Cattell: An Engineering Database Benchmark. In: The Benchmark Handbook for Database Transaction Processing Systems. Morgan Kaufmann (1991) 247–281
5. E.E. Chang, R.H. Katz: Exploiting Inheritance and Structure Semantics for Effective Clustering and Buffering in an Object-Oriented DBMS. ACM SIGMOD Inter-national Conference on Management of Data (1989) 348–357
6. S. Chaudhuri, V. Narasayya: AutoAdmin "What-if" Index Analysis Utility. ACM SIGMOD International Conference on Management of Data, Seattle, Washington (1998) 367–378
7. J.R. Cheng, A.R. Hurson: Effective clustering of complex objects in object oriented databases. ACM SIGMOD International Conference on Management of Data (1991) 22–31
8. J. Darmont, L. Gruenwald: A Comparison Study of Clustering Techniques for Object-Oriented Databases. Information Sciences, Vol. 94, No. 1-4 (1996) 55–86
9. J. Darmont, B. Petit, M. Schneider: OCB: A Generic Benchmark to Evaluate the Performances of Object-Oriented Database Systems. 6th International Conference on Extending Database Technology (EDBT '98), Valencia, Spain. LNCS Vol. 1377 (1998) 326–340

10. J.-Y. Gay, L. Gruenwald: A Clustering Technique for Object Oriented Databases. 8th International Conference on Database and Expert Systems Applications (DEXA '97), Toulouse, France. LNCS Vol. 1308 (1997) 81–90
11. O. Gruber, L. Amsaleg: Object Grouping in EOS. IWDOM '92 Workshop on Distributed Object Management, University of Alberta, Canada (1992) 117–131
12. S.E. Hudson, R. King: Cactis: A Self-Adaptive Concurrent Implementation of an Object-Oriented Database Management System. ACM Transactions on Database Systems, Vol. 14, No. 3 (1989) 291–321
13. W. Kim, J. Banerjee, H.-T. Chou, J.F. Garza, D. Woelk: Composite Object Support in an Object-Oriented Database System. International Conference on OOPSLA (1987) 118–125
14. C. Lamb, G. Landis, J. Orenstein, D. Weinreb: The ObjectStore Database System. Communications of the ACM, Vol. 34, No. 10 (1991) 50–63
15. D. Maier, J. Stein, A. Otis, A. Purdy: Development of an Object-Oriented DBMS. ACM OOPSLA '86 (1986) 472–482
16. C. McGlenaghan: OODBMS Benchmark Specification. Technical Report No. At-12/99-001523-00.01, US West Advanced Technologies (1991)
17. W.J. Mc Iver Jr., R. King: Self-Adaptive, On-Line Reclustering of Complex Object Data. ACM SIGMOD Conference (1994) 407–418
18. V. Singhal, S.V. Kakkad, P.R. Wilson: Texas: An Efficient, Portable Persistent Store. 5th International Workshop on Persistent Object Systems (1992)

Opportunistic Prioritised Clustering Framework (OPCF)

Zhen He[1], Alonso Márquez[1], and Stephen Blackburn[2]

[1] Department of Computer Science, The Australian National University
Canberra, ACT 0200, Australia
`zhen@cs.anu.edu.au`, `alonso@upside.anu.edu.au`
[2] Department of Computer Science, University of Massachusetts
Amherst, MA 1003, USA
`steveb@cs.umass.edu`

Abstract. Ever since the 'early days' of database management systems, clustering has proven to be one of the most effective performance enhancement techniques for object oriented database management systems. The bulk of the work in the area has been on static clustering algorithms which re-cluster the object base when the database is static. However, this type of re-clustering cannot be used when 24-hour database access is required. In such situations *dynamic clustering* is required, which allows the object base to be reclustered while the database is in operation. We believe that most existing dynamic clustering algorithms lack three important properties. These include: the *use of opportunism* to imposes the smallest I/O footprint for re-organisation; the *re-use of prior research* on static clustering algorithms; and the *prioritisation of re-clustering* so that the worst clustered pages are re-clustered first. In this paper, we present OPCF, a framework in which any existing static clustering algorithm can be made dynamic and given the desired properties of I/O opportunism and clustering prioritisation. In addition, this paper presents a performance evaluation of the ideas suggested above.The main contribution of this paper is the observation that existing static clustering algorithms, when transformed via a simple transformation framework such as OPCF, can produce dynamic clustering algorithms that out-perform complex existing dynamic algorithms, in a variety of situations. This makes the solution presented in this paper particularly attractive to real OODBMS system implementers who often prefer to opt for simpler solutions.

1   Introduction

The current rate of performance improvement for CPUs is much higher than that for memory or disk I/O.

CPU performance doubles every 18 months while disk I/O improves at only 5-8 % per year. On the other hand, cheap disks mean object bases will become bigger as database designers realise that more data can be stored [12]. A consequence of these facts is that disk I/O is likely to be a bottleneck in an increasing

K.R. Dittrich et al. (Eds.): Objects and Databases 2000, LNCS 1944, pp. 86–100, 2001.
© Springer-Verlag Berlin Heidelberg 2001

number of database applications. It should also be noted, memory is also becoming a more prevalent source of bottleneck on modern DBMS [1]. However their study was conducted on relational DBMS. We believe for object-oriented DBMS where navigation is common, I/O may be a more common source of bottleneck.

Ever since the 'early days' of database management systems, clustering has proven to be one of the most effective performance enhancement techniques [7]. The reason for this is that the majority of object accesses in an object oriented database are navigational. Consequently, related objects are often accessed consecutively. Clustering objects in an object oriented database reduces disk I/O by grouping related objects into the same disk page. In addition to reduced I/O, clustering also uses cache space more efficiently by reducing the number of unused objects that occupy the cache.[1] Periodical re-clustering allows the physical organisation of objects on disk to closer reflect the prevailing pattern of object access.

The majority of existing clustering algorithms are static [15,2,8,6]. Static clustering algorithms require that re-clustering take place when the database is not in operation, thus prohibiting 24 hour database access. In contrast, dynamic clustering algorithms re-cluster the database while database applications are in operation. Applications that require 24 hour database access and involve frequent changes to data access patterns may benefit from the use of dynamic clustering.

In our view, there are a number of properties that are missing from most existing dynamic clustering algorithms. These properties include:

- The use of opportunism to impose the smallest I/O footprint for re-organisation;
- The re-use of existing work on static clustering algorithms; and
- A prioritisation of re-clustering so the worst clustered pages are re-clustered first.

The goal of dynamic clustering is to generate the minimum number of I/Os for a given set of database application access patterns. The clustering process itself may generate I/O, loading data pages for the sole purpose of object base re-organisation. However, most researchers have chosen to ignore these sources of I/O generation and instead concentrated on developing the dynamic clustering algorithm that minimises the number of data pages[2] loaded during normal database operation[3].

Despite the great body of work that exists on static clustering[15,2,8,6], there has been little transfer of ideas into the dynamic clustering literature. In this paper we address this omission by incorporating two existing and yet vastly contrasting types of static clustering algorithms into our dynamic clustering framework. These are the 'graph partitioning' and the 'probability ranking principle'

---

[1] Throughout this paper we use the term 'cache' to refer to the in-memory portion of an object base.

[2] Pages where the objects reside.

[3] Normal database operation as opposed to re-clustering operation.

(PRP) algorithms. We show that by using our framework these two existing static clustering algorithms outperform an existing and highly competitive dynamic clustering algorithm (DSTC [3]) in a variety of situations.

The disruptive nature of re-clustering dictates that dynamic clustering algorithms must be incremental. This means that only a small portion of the object base can be re-clustered in each iteration. When faced with a variety of different portions to target for re-organisation, the clustering algorithm must select the portion to re-cluster first. We term this the selection problem. To our knowledge, this problem has not been previously identified in the literature. To solve this problem we propose that it should be the worst clustered memory-resident page that should be selected first for re-clustering. To this end, our dynamic clustering framework, incorporates prioritisation.

In summary the main contributions of our paper include: a new framework (OPCF) by which any existing static clustering algorithm can be made into a dynamic clustering algorithm and given the desirable properties of I/O opportunism and clustering prioritisation; an example of how two existing static clustering algorithms, can be made dynamic using OPCF; a comparative performance evaluation between the two new dynamic clustering algorithm produced by OCPF, with an existing and highly competitive dynamic clustering algorithm, DSTC.

2   Related Work

The re-organisation phase of dynamic clustering can incur significant overhead. Two of the key overheads are increased write lock contention[4], and I/O.

To reduce write lock contention, most dynamic clustering algorithms are designed to be incremental and thus only consider a portion of the object base for clustering during each re-organisation. However, we are aware of only one algorithm [16] that takes care to not to introduce extra I/O during the re-organisation phase. Knafla [16] accomplish this by calculating a new placement when the object graph is modified, either by a link (reference) modification or object insertion. The algorithm then reclusters the objects that are effected by the modification or insertion. Once the new placement is determined, only the objects in memory are re-organised and the remaining objects are only rearranged as they are loaded into memory. However, the objects considered for re-organisation can include any object in the store. The drawback of this approach is that information about any object in the store may be needed. OPCF produces algorithms that differ from these algorithms by only needing information on objects that are currently in memory and only re-organising those objects. This makes dynamic clustering algorithms produced by OPCF more opportunistic[5] than existing algorithms.

---

[4] Note that in an optimistic system this would translate to transaction aborts.
[5] By opportunistic we refer to our opportunistic use of in-memory data in order to minimise both read and write I/O.

The incremental nature of dynamic clustering requires that only a small portion of the entire database to be re-clustered at each iteration. However, the choice as to which portion to re-cluster is where many existing algorithms differ. Chang and Katz [14] suggest targeting the portion that was accessed after the previous re-organisation. However, this may involve a very large portion of the database if the re-clustering is not triggered frequently. Wietrzyk and Orgun [16] re-cluster effected objects as soon as an object graph modification occurs. They use a threshold mechanism[6] to determine when re-clustering is worthwhile. However, this approach may still be too disruptive. An example of when its disruptiveness is likely to be felt is when the system is in peak usage and frequent object graph modifications are occurring. In such a scenario the object graph would be continuously re-clustered during peak database usage. The algorithm thus lacks a means of controlling when the re-clustering takes place. In contrast, the dynamic algorithms developed with OPCF can be easily made adaptive to changing system loads. This is due to the fact re-clustering can be triggered by an asynchronous dynamic load-balancing thread rather than a object graph modification.

A large body of work exists on static clustering algorithms [15,2,8,6]. However only relatively few static algorithms have been transformed into dynamic algorithms. Change and Katz [14] combined the existing static clustering algorithms, Cactis [10] and DAG [2] to create a new dynamic clustering algorithm. However Cactis and DAG are only sequence-based clustering algorithms which have been found to be inferior when compared to graph partitioning algorithms[15]. Wietrzyk and Orgun [16] developed a new dynamic graph partitioning clustering algorithm. However their graph partitioning algorithm was not compared with any existing static graph partitioning clustering algorithm. In this paper two existing static clustering algorithms were transformed into dynamic clustering algorithms using OPCF and compared to an existing dynamic clustering algorithm, DSTC [3].

The fact that dynamic clustering algorithms re-organise objects on-line mean that objects are required to be moved when application transactions are running. Care must be taken to make the movement as non-intrusive as possible. Lakhamraju, Rastogi, Seshadri and Sudarshan [13] presents a re-organisation algorithm that can be used in a complementary manner with OPCF, to produce less disruptive dynamic clustering algorithms.

3   The Opportunistic Prioritised Clustering Framework (OPCF)

The opportunistic prioritised clustering framework offers a generic way in which existing static clustering algorithms can be made dynamic. OPCF possesses two key properties : read and write I/O opportunism; prioritisation of re-clustering,

---

[6] Based on the heuristic that says that a more frequently accessed object that is clustered badly is more worth while re-clustering.

so the worst clustered page is re-clustered first. The framework ensures the resulting clustering algorithm can be made both read and write opportunistic[7] but does not limit the algorithms to opportunism.

OPCF works at the *page* grain, instead of *cluster* grain. This means that when re-clustering occurs, all objects in an integer number of *pages* are re-clustered. This contrasts with dynamic *cluster* grain algorithms like DSTC [3] where individual *objects* that are determined to need re-clustering are removed from existing pages and placed into *new* pages.

In order to apply OPCF, a series of steps must be applied. These steps are outlined below.

— *Define Incremental Reorganisation Algorithm*: In this step, a strategy is developed by which the existing static clustering algorithm is adapted to work in an incremental way. That is, at each iteration of re-organisation the algorithm must be able to operate with a limited scope.
— *Define Clustering Badness Metric*: OPCF prioritises re-clustering by re-clustering the worst clustered pages first. This means there must be a way of defining the quality of clustering at a page grain. We term this the clustering badness metric. The way in which clustering badness is to be defined for a particular static clustering algorithm depends on the goal of the clustering algorithm. For instance, the PRP clustering algorithm has the goal of grouping hot[8] objects together and therefore it may have a clustering badness metric that includes a measure of the concentration of cold objects in pages that contain hot objects.
  At each clustering analysis iteration[9] a user defined number of pages (NPA) have their clustering badness calculated. Once the page's clustering badness is calculated, the clustering badness is compared against a user-defined clustering badness threshold (CBT). If the page has a higher clustering badness value than the threshold then the page is placed in a priority queue sorted on clustering badness. At each re-organisation iteration a page is removed from the top of the priority queue and used to determine the scope of re-organisation for that re-organisation iteration. A user-defined number (NRI) of re-organisation iterations are performed at the end of each clustering analysis iteration.
— *Define Scope of Re-organisation*: To limit the work done in each re-organisation iteration of the dynamic clustering algorithm, a limited number of pages must be chosen to form the scope of re-organisation. The scope of re-organisation should be chosen in such a way that re-organisation of those pages will produce the maximum amount of improvement in clustering quality while preserving the property of incrementality.

---

[7] The distinction between read and write opportunism is that, read opportunism prevents read I/O to be generated during the clustering process and write opportunism prevents the clustering process from updating any cache page that is clean and thus reduces write I/O.

[8] By hot objects we mean objects accessed more frequently.

[9] Cluster analysis simply refers to calculating clustering badness of pages of the store.

The way the scope of re-organisation is chosen dictates whether the clustering algorithm is opportunistic or non-opportunistic. To achieve read opportunism, only *in-memory* pages are included in the scope of re-organisation. To achieve write opportunism, only *in-memory* and *updated* pages are included in the scope of re-organisation.

– *Define Cluster Placement Policy*: Because OPCF works at a page rather than cluster grain, the initial stages of each re-organisation iteration target an integer number of pages and so will, in general, identify multiple clusters, some of which may be small.[10] The existence of clusters which are smaller than a page size raises the important issue of how best to pack clusters into pages.

A simple way in which cluster analysis can be triggered in OPCF is by triggering cluster analysis when a user specified number of objects (N) has been accessed this is similar to the technique used in DSTC [3]. However any other triggering method may be used, including triggering via asynchronous thread for load balancing reasons.

4   Graph Partitioning

Partition-based clustering algorithms consider the object placement problem as a graph partitioning problem in which the min-cut criteria is to be satisfied for page boundaries. The vertices and edges of the graph are labeled with weights. Vertex weights represent object size and depending on the clustering algorithm, edge weights represent either the frequency with which a reference between the pair of objects is traversed, or the frequency with which the pair of objects were accessed in close temporal proximity.

There are two types of partition based static clustering algorithms: *iterative improvement* and *constructive partitioning*. Iterative improvement algorithms such as the Kernighan-Lin Heuristic (KL) [11], iteratively improve partitions by swapping objects between partitions in an attempt to satisfy the min-cut criteria. Constructive algorithms such as greedy graph partitioning (GGP) [8] attempt to satisfy the min-cut criteria by first assigning only one object to a partition and then combining partitions in a greedy manner.

The study carried out by Tsangaris and Naughton [15] indicates that graph partitioning algorithms perform best for both the working set size metric[11] and long term expansion factor metric[12]. However, they are generally more expensive in terms of CPU usage and statistic collection than sequence based algorithms [2,6]

---

[10] In contrast, when re-organisation occurs at a cluster grain, each re-organisation can be more strongly targeted towards a particular cluster or clusters, and so is more likely to identify larger clusters.

[11] Working set size [15] is a measure of the performance of the clustering algorithm starting with a cold cache.

[12] Long term expansion factor[15] is an indicator of the steady state performance of an object clustering algorithm when the cache size is large.

4.1   Online Graph Partitioning

This section outlines how we applied the opportunistic prioritised clustering framework onto static graph partitioning algorithms.

- *Incremental Reorganisation Algorithm*: At each re-organisation iteration the graph partitioning algorithm is applied to the pages in the scope of re-organisation as if these pages represent the entire database.
- *Clustering Badness Metric*: The static graph partitioning algorithms attempt to satisfy the min-cut criteria. This means that they minimise the sum of edge weights that cross page boundaries. In order to include this criteria into our clustering badness metric we have included external tension in the metric. External tension is the sum of weights of edges of the clustering graph which cross page boundaries. A page with higher external tension is worse clustered. In addition, heat is included in the metric to give priority for reorganising hotter pages. Below is a definition of clustering badness for page p:

$$CB(p) = \sum_{i \in p} heat_i \times \sum_{i \in p} external\ tension_i \qquad (1)$$

The calculation of external tension differs between the opportunistic version of the dynamic graph partitioning algorithm and the non-opportunistic version. In the read opportunistic version, the external tension is calculated from only weights of edges that cross the boundary of the page under consideration to other in-memory[13] pages. By contrast, the non-opportunistic algorithm also counts edge weights that crosses page boundaries onto disk pages.
- *Scope of Reorganisation*: The scope of re-organisation is the worst clustered page and its related pages. Two pages are considered to be related if at least one object link crosses the boundary between the two pages. If the dynamic clustering algorithm is to be run read opportunistically then only *in-memory related* pages are in the scope of re-organisation. See figure 2 for an example. When write opportunism is required the scope of re-organisation is further restricted, to only *updated* and *in-memory* pages.
- *Cluster Placement Policy*: For this application of OPCF, we have chosen to place clusters into pages in order of heat. The reason for this choice is that cold clusters will be placed away from hot clusters and thus pages containing hot clusters which are more likely to be in memory will have less wasted space occupied by cold clusters. This is similar to the goal of PRP (see section 5).

The particular graph partitioning algorithm implemented for the results section of this paper is the greedy graph partitioning[14] (GGP) algorithm [8]. However, the above methodology can be applied to any static graph partitioning

---

[13] In-memory and updated pages in the case of write opportunism.

[14] In our particular implementation we assigned edge weights to the clustering graph using the temporal proximity of object accesses, this was the same approach used in DSTC.

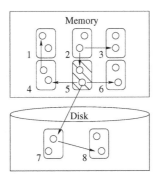

Fig. 1. In this example the worst clustered page is 5 and the scope of re-organisation for read opportunistic dynamic graph partitioning are pages 2, 4, 5 and 6. The scope of re-organisation for non-opportunistic dynamic PRP are pages 2, 4, 5, 6 and 7.

clustering algorithm. GGP first places all objects in a separate partition and then iterates through a list of edges in descending edge weight. If the two objects on the ends of the currently selected edge are in different partitions and the sum size of the two partitions are smaller than a page then the partitions are joined.

5   Probability Ranking Principle Clustering Algorithm (PRP)

The simplest static clustering algorithm is the probability ranking principle (PRP) algorithm[17]. PRP just involves placing the objects in the object graph in decreasing heat (where 'heat' is simply a measure of access frequency). This surprisingly simple algorithm yields near optimal long term expansion factor[15].

The reason that PRP achieves near optimal expansion factor is that it groups together those objects that constitute the active portion of the database. Therefore when the size of the active portion of the database is small relative to the available cache size and the steady state performance of the database is of interest, then this algorithm yields a near optimal solution. However, when a small traversal is conducted on a cold cache, PRP tends to perform poorly for working set size, since it does not take object relationships into consideration. [15]

The simplicity of the PRP algorithm combined with its minimal requirements with respect to statistics makes it particularly suitable for dynamic clustering[15]. However, to our knowledge, an dynamic version of PRP has not been suggested before in the literature.

Due to space constraints the way in which PRP is transformed into a dynamic algorithm is not included in this paper, however it can be found in [9].

---

[15] Where CPU and I/O resources are precious

6 Dynamic Statistical and Tunable Clustering Technique (DSTC)

DTSC is an existing dynamic clustering algorithm [3] which has the feature of achieving dynamicity without adding high overhead and excessive volume of statistics.

The algorithms is divided into five phases:

- *Observation Phase*: In order to minimise disruptiveness of statistics collection, DSTC only collects statistics at predefined observation periods and the information is stored in a transient observation matrix.
- *Selection Phase*: In order to reduce the volume of statistics stored, at the selection phase the transient observation matrix is scanned and only significant statistics are saved.
- *Consolidation Phase*: The results of the selection phase are combined with statistics gathered in previous observation phases and saved in the persistent consolidated matrix.
- *Dynamic Cluster Reorganisation*: Using the information in the updated consolidated matrix, new clusters are discovered or existing ones are updated. In order to achieve incrementality the re-organisation work is broken up into small fragments called clustering units.
- *Physical Clustering Organisation*: The clustering units are finally applied to the database in an incremental way (that is one clustering unit at a time). This phase is triggered when the system is idle.

DSTC is not an opportunistic clustering algorithm since its scope of reorganisation can be objects that are currently residing on disk. In order to make DSTC opportunistic we have chosen to restrict the scope of objects that can be chosen from when forming clustering units to those objects that are currently in *memory* for read opportunism and *updated* and in *memory* for write opportunism. In the results section, results of both opportunistic and non opportunistic DSTC are presented.

7 Results

In this section we present results of experiments we conducted with the object clustering benchmark OCB [4] using the virtual object oriented database simulator, VOODB [5]. VOODB is based on a generic discrete-event simulation framework. Its purpose is to allow performance evaluations of OODBs in general, and optimisation methods like clustering in particular.

OCB is a generic object-oriented benchmark that was designed to benchmark OODBM systems and clustering polices in particular. The OCB database has a variety of parameters which make it very user-tunable. A database is generated by setting parameters such as total number of objects, maximum number of references per class, base instance size, number of classes, etc. Once these parameters are set, a database conforming to these parameters is randomly generated. The database consists of objects of varying sizes. In the experiments conducted in this paper the objects varied in size from 50 to 1200 bytes and the average object size was 268 bytes. The parameters of OCB and VOODB used to conduct the experiments in this paper are specified in table 1.

Table 1. Parameters used for OCB and VOODB. VOODB parameters involving time have been omitted from this table, since the results reported are in terms of I/O performance.

Parameter Description	Value
number of classes in the database	50
maximum number of references, per class	10
instances base size, per class	50
total number of objects	20000
number of reference types	4
reference types random distribution	uniform
class reference random distribution	uniform
objects in classes random distribution	uniform
objects references random distribution	uniform

(a) OCB parameters

Parameter Description	Value
system class	centralised
disk page size	4096 bytes
buffer size	varies
buffer replacement policy	LRU-2
pre-fetch policy	none
multiprogramming level	1
number of users	1
object initial placement	optimised sequential

(b) VOODB parameters

Throughout the remainder of this section, we will use the following abbreviations:

NC   no clustering
DSTC dynamic statistical and tunable clustering technique [3]
GP   dynamic greedy graph partitioning [8]
PRP dynamic probability ranking principle clustering algorithm [17]

The algorithm names are given the suffix 'N' if the algorithm run was non-opportunistic and 'O' if the algorithm was read opportunistic. We conducted experiments with write opportunistic variants of all the above clustering algorithms. However the results showed that write opportunistic clustering performed in all situations nearly the same as no clustering and therefore the results of write opportunistic algorithms are not included in this paper[16].

---

[16] It appears the limitations placed on the clustering algorithms by only allowing updated pages to be involved in the clustering process was too restrictive.

The read workload used in the experiments consisted of simple traversals, hierarchical traversals and stochastic traversals[4]. The update transactions used consisted of object attribute updates, object insertions, object deletion, object link insertions and object link deletions.

The parameters used for the clustering algorithms investigated in this paper are presented in table 2. For a description of DSTC parameters, see [3].

Table 2. Parameters used for the clustering algorithms DSTC, PRP and GP.

Parameter	Value
n	200
n_p	200
p	1000
T_{fa}	0.0
T_{fe}	0.0
T_{fc}	0.0
w	0.0
s	10

(a)   DSTC parameters

Parameter	PRP Value	GP Value
N	200	200
CBT	0.1	0.1
NPA	50	50
NRI	25	25

(b) OPCF parameters

7.1   Varying Buffer Size Experiment

This experiment was designed to investigate the effects of changing buffer size in two different conditions, read only transactions and 10% update transactions. We divided the 20MB (20000 object) database into hot and cold regions. The hot region was made to be 1.5% of the total size of the database and 99% of transactions were directed at the hot region. (Skewing the access distribution has the effect of highlighting the importance of clustering. An algorithm that does not cluster well will perform very poorly under such a workload.)

The results are shown on figure 2. When updates are introduced into the workload, GP-O appears to outperform DTSC-O and DSTC-N algorithms by a large margin. A possible explanation for this behavior is that DSTC works at the cluster grain and thus places each newly constructed cluster of objects into a *new* page. This generates a lot of empty space in pages where the cluster size is small. The end result is that objects are more spread out and when random updates occur, a larger number of pages are updated, resulting in a larger number of write I/Os. This contrasts to the graph partitioning algorithm where multiple clusters may reside in the same page and thus random updates are confined to a smaller number of pages.

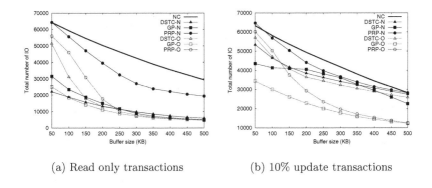

(a) Read only transactions   (b) 10% update transactions

Fig. 2. Effects of varying buffer size

Secondly, when the buffer size is small the PRP algorithms do not perform as well as GP. This result is consistent with the static behavior of the algorithms[15]. The reason for this is that PRP does not take inter-object relationships into consideration when clustering.

7.2   Varying Percentage of Updates Transactions

In this experiment we investigated what effect varying the percentage of update transactions has on the performance of the dynamic clustering algorithms. For this experiment we set the buffer size to 600 KB and the other system settings were the same as in section 7.1. The results of this experiment can be seen in figure 3.

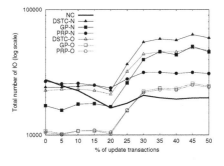

Fig. 3. Effects of varying update percentage

As observed in section 7.1, GP-O and PRP-O are the best performers when the buffer size is large. What is interesting here is the point at which clustering becomes worse than no clustering for the different algorithms. PRP-O and GP-O do not perform worse than no clustering until the percentage of update transactions is greater than 27% however DTSC-O becomes worse than no clustering at 8%.[17] This seems to indicate that the read opportunistic algorithms proposed by this paper are more robust to update transactions when compared to DSTC. The reason for this can again be explained by the fact GP and PRP have less empty spaces among pages. Therefore random updates become less dispersed when compared to DSTC which places every cluster on a separate page.

7.3   Varying Hot Region Size

In this experiment we investigated the effect that varying the size of the hot region has on the performance of the dynamic clustering algorithms. The buffer size was again set to 600 KB. The remaining settings with the exception of hot region size (which we will vary) were the same as for section 7.1.

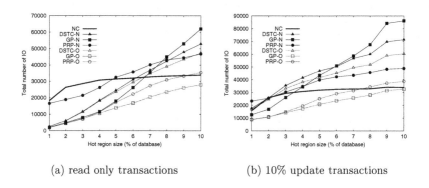

(a) read only transactions   (b) 10% update transactions

Fig. 4. Effects of varying hot region size

Figure 4 shows the results of running the experiment with both read only transactions and 10% update transactions. The most important observation that can be made from these graphs is that as the hot region's size increases, GP-O outperforms DSTC-O by an increasing margin. A possible reason for this observation is that when the size of the hot region is small, the hot objects are initially dispersed very thinly across the pages of the database and therefore a clustering algorithm such as GP which works at the page grain can only find a few

---

[17] This is not inconsistent with the results of section 7.1 since the buffer size used in this experiment is slightly larger than the maximum buffer size used in section 7.1

clusters per re-clustering iteration. However DSTC-O, which picks out objects that belong to the same cluster from anywhere in memory, and DTSC-N, which picks from anywhere in the database, can quickly form large clusters even if the objects are dispersed among many pages. However this advantage begins to diminish as the hot region size increases and every page begins to have a larger portion of hot objects. That is to say, as more hot objects appear in every page, each re-organisation iteration of GP (page grain re-clustering) becomes more productive. The bad performance of GP-N may be attributed to its tendency to generate excessive read I/O as the hot region size increases. As the hot region size increases, GP-N's scope of re-organisation increases dramatically because its scope of re-organisation is all the worst clustered page's related pages (anywhere in the database). Therefore any productive work that the algorithm performs gets quickly overshadowed by the excessive I/O generated by the clustering processes.

8   Conclusions

In this paper we have presented OPCF, a generic framework which when applied to static clustering algorithms, can produce dynamic clustering algorithms that possesses the two desirable properties of *opportunism* and *prioritisation of clustering*. In addition, application of the framework is straightforward and yet it produces clustering algorithms that outperform an existing highly competitive dynamic clustering algorithm, DSTC [3], in a variety of situations.

For further work, we plan to add more existing dynamic clustering algorithms to our simulation study. We would also like to experiment with transforming other static clustering algorithms using OPCF and see how they perform in relation to the algorithms presented in this paper.

Acknowledgements. The authors wish to acknowledge that this work was carried out within the Cooperative Research Center for Advanced Computational Systems established under the Australian Government's Cooperative Research Centers Program.

We would like to thank Jerome Darmont for creating VOODB and making the sources publicly available. We would also like to thank Jerome for creating OCB, the benchmark used to conduct the experiments presented in this paper. Finally we would like to thank Luke Kirby and Eliot Moss for their helpful comments and suggestions.

References

1. AILAMAKI, A., DEWITT, D. J., HILL, M. D., AND WOOD, D. A. Dbmss on a modern processor: Where does time go? In *The 25th VLDB conference, Edinburgh, Scotland* (September 1999), pp. 266–277.
2. BANERJEE, J., KIM, W., KIM, S. J., AND GARZA, J. F. Clustering a dag for cad databases. In *IEEE Transactions on Software Engineering* (November 1988), vol. 14, pp. 1684–1699.

3. BULLAT, F. *Regroupement dynamique dojets dans les bases de donnees*. PhD thesis, Blaise Pascal University, Clermont-Ferrand II, France, January 1996.

4. DARMONT, J., PETIT, B., AND SCHNEIDER, M. Ocb: A generic benchmark to evaluate the performances of object-oriented database systems. In *International Conference on Extending Database Technology (EDBT)* (Valencia Spain, March 1998), LNCS Vol. 1377 (Springer), pp. 326–340.

5. DARMONT, J., AND SCHNEIDER, M. Voodb: A generic discrete-event random simulation model to evaluate the performances of oodbs. In *The 25th VLDB conference, Edinburgh, Scotland* (September 1999), pp. 254–265.

6. DREW, P., KING, R., AND HUDSON, S. E. The performance and utility of the cactis implementation algorithms. In *16th International Conference on Very Large Data Bases* (Brisbane, Queensland, Australia, 13–16 Aug. 1990), D. McLeod, R. Sacks-Davis, and H.-J. Schek, Eds., Morgan Kaufmann, pp. 135–147.

7. GERLHOF, A., KEMPER, A., AND MOERKOTTE, G. On the cost of monitoring and reorganization of object bases for clustering. In *ACM SIGMOD Record* (1996), vol. 25, pp. 28–33.

8. GERLHOF, C., KEMPER, A., KILGER, C., AND MOERKOTTE, G. Partition-based clustering in object bases: From theory to practice. *In Proceedings of the International Conference on Foundations of Data Organisation and Algorithms (FODO)* (1993).

9. HE, Z., MARQUEZ, A., AND BLACKBURN, S. Opportunistic prioritised clustering framework. Tech. rep., The Australian National University, 2000.

10. HUDSON, E., AND KING, R. Cactis: A self-adaptive, concurrent implementation of an object-oriented database management system. In *ACM Transactions on Database Systems* (September 1989), pp. 291–321.

11. KERNIGHAN, B., AND LIN, S. An efficient heuristic procedure for partitioning graphs. *Bell System Technical Journal* (1970), 291–307.

12. KNAFLA, N. *Prefetching Techniques for Client/Server, Object-Oriented Database Systems*. PhD thesis, University of Edinburgh, 1999.

13. LAKHAMRAJU, M., RASTOGI, R., SESHADRI, S., AND SUDARSHAN, S. On-line reorganisation in object databases. In *Proceedings of the ACM SIGMOD conference on Management of Data* (May 2000).

14. MCIVER, W. J. J., AND KING, R. Self-adaptive, on-line reclustering of complex object data. In *Proceedings of the 1994 ACM SIGMOD International Conference on Management of Data, Minneapolis, Minnesota, May 24-27, 1994* (1994), R. T. Snodgrass and M. Winslett, Eds., ACM Press, pp. 407–418.

15. TSANGARIS, E.-M. M. *Principles of Static Clustering For Object Oriented Databases*. PhD thesis, University of Wisconsin-Madison, 1992.

16. WIETRZYK, V. S., AND ORGUN, M. A. Dynamic reorganisation of object databases. In *Proceedings of the International Database Engineering and Applications Symposium* (August 1999), IEEE Computer Society.

17. YUE, P. C., AND WONG, C. K. On the optimality of the probability ranking scheme in storage applications. *JACM 20*, 4 (October 1973), 624–633.

A Flexible Approach for Instance Adaptation During Class Versioning

Awais Rashid[1], Peter Sawyer[1], and Elke Pulvermueller[2]

[1]Computing Department, Lancaster University, Lancaster LA1 4YR, UK
{marash|sawyer}@comp.lancs.ac.uk
[2]Institut fuer Programmstrukturen und Datenorganisation, University of Karlsruhe, 76128 Karlsruhe, Germany
pulvermueller@acm.org

Abstract. One of the consequences of evolution can be the inability to access objects created using the older schema definition under the new definition and vice versa. Instance adaptation is the conversion of objects to a compatible definition or making objects exhibit a compatible interface. Existing evolution approaches are committed to a particular instance adaptation strategy. This is because changes to the instance adaptation strategy or an attempt to adopt an entirely different strategy would be very costly. This paper proposes a flexible instance adaptation approach for systems employing class versioning to manage evolution. Flexibility is achieved by encapsulating the instance adaptation code in *aspects* - abstractions introduced by aspect-oriented programming to localise cross-cutting concerns. This makes it possible to make cost-effective changes to the instance adaptation strategy. The flexibility of the approach is demonstrated by using two instance adaptation strategies: error handlers and update/backdate methods.

1 Introduction

The conceptual structure of an object-oriented database may not remain constant and may vary to a large extent [46]. The need for these variations (evolution) arises due to a variety of reasons e.g. to correct mistakes in the database design, to add new features during incremental design or to reflect changes in the structure of the real world artefacts modelled in the database. Two types of anomalous behaviour can arise as a consequence of evolution:

- Objects created under the older schema definition might not be accessible under the new definition and vice versa.
- Application programs ccessing the database prior to evolution might contain invalid references and method calls.

The former has been termed a *structural consistency* issue and the latter a *behavioural consistency* issue [49].

K.R. Dittrich et al. (Eds.): Objects and Databases 2000, LNCS 1944, pp. 101-113, 2001.

One of the various evolution strategies[1] employed to address the above issues is class versioning [11, 12, 33, 47, 50]. In this approach a new version of a class is created upon modification. Applications are bound to specific versions of classes or a common interface while objects are bound to the class version used to instantiate them. When an object is accessed using another type version (or a common type interface) it is either converted or made to exhibit a compatible interface. This is termed instance adaptation. This paper proposes a flexible instance adaptation approach for class versioning systems. From this point onwards instance adaptation (and hence structural consistency) will be the focus of the discussion. Behavioural consistency problems will not be discussed. An analysis of such problems in the context of both untyped and strongly typed programming languages can be found in [8].

Existing class versioning approaches are committed to a particular instance adaptation strategy[2]. For example, ENCORE [47] and AVANCE [11] employ error handlers to simulate compatible interfaces while CLOSQL [33] uses update/backdate methods to dynamically convert instances between class versions. Although it is possible to make changes to the instance adaptation strategy or adopt an entirely different strategy, such an attempt would be very costly. All the versions of existing classes might need to be modified to reflect the change. In other words, the evolution problem will appear at a different level. Therefore, existing systems are, to a great extent, bound to the particular instance adaptation strategy being used. Our case studies at an organisation where day-to-day activities revolve around the database have brought to front the need for application or scenario specific instance adaptation. One such case involved the need to simulate a *move attribute* evolution primitive. This could either be achieved by adding an additional primitive to the evolution taxonomy or customising the instance adaptation approach to simulate the primitive. Over the lifetime of the database there might also be a need to move to a better, more efficient instance adaptation strategy. Due to the lack of flexibility in existing instance adaptation approaches such customisation or exchange will be very expensive.

In this paper we propose a flexible approach which localises the effect of any changes to the instance adaptation strategy, hence making such changes possible and cost-effective. This is achieved by encapsulating the instance adaptation code into *aspects*. Aspects are abstractions introduced by aspect-oriented programming (AOP) [21, 22] to localise cross-cutting concerns. A detailed description of the applicability of aspects in OODBs has been provided in [44]. From the above discussion it is clear that the instance adaptation strategy cross-cuts class versions created over the lifetime of the database and, hence, can be separated using aspects. It can be automatically woven into the class versions when required and can also be automatically rewoven if the aspects are modified.

The next section provides an overview of aspect-oriented programming. This is followed by a description of the flexible instance adaptation approach. Section 4 uses

---

[1] Other evolution strategies include *schema evolution* [5, 14, 15, 26, 36, 48], where the database has one logical schema to which class definition and class hierarchy modifications are applied and *schema versioning* [3, 6, 23, 25, 34, 35, 38], which allows several versions of one logical schema to be created and manipulated independently of each other.

[2] This is also true of schema evolution and schema versioning approaches.

error handlers and update/backdate methods as examples to demonstrate the flexibility of the approach. Section 5 discusses related work while section 6 concludes the discussion and identifies directions for future work.

2 Aspect-Oriented Programming

Aspect-oriented programming [21, 22] aims at easing software development by providing further support for modularisation. *Aspects* are abstractions which serve to localise any cross-cutting concerns e.g. code which cannot be encapsulated within one class but is tangled over many classes. A few examples of aspects are memory management, failure handling, communication, real-time constraints, resource sharing, performance optimisation, debugging and synchronisation. Although patterns [17] can help to deal with such cross-cutting code by providing guidelines for a good structure, they are not available or suitable for all cases and mostly provide only partial solutions to the code tangling problem. With AOP, such cross-cutting code is encapsulated into separate constructs: the aspects. As shown in fig. 1 classes are designed and coded separately from code that cross-cuts them (in this case debugging and synchronisation code). The links between classes and aspects are expressed by explicit or implicit *join points*. These links can be categorised[3] as [20]:

- *open:* both classes and aspects know about each other
- *class-directional:* the aspect knows about the class but not vice versa
- *aspect-directional:* the class knows about the aspect but not vice versa
- *closed:* neither the aspect nor the class knows about the other

An *aspect weaver* is responsible for merging the classes and the aspects with respect to the join points. This can be done statically as a phase at compile-time or dynamically at run-time [19, 22].

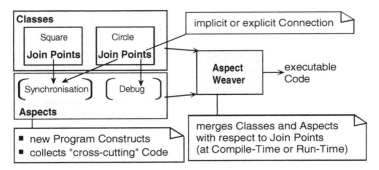

Fig. 1. Aspect-Oriented Programming

Different AOP techniques and research directions can be identified. They all share the common goal of providing an improved separation of concerns. AspectJ [4] is an aspect-oriented extension to Java. The environment offers an aspect language to

---

[3] The categorisation determines the reusability of classes and aspects.

formulate the aspect code separately from Java class code, a weaver and additional development support. AOP extensions to other languages have also been developed. [10] describes an aspect language and a weaver for Smalltalk. An aspect language for the domain of robust programming can be found in [16].

Other AOP approaches aiming at achieving a similar separation of concerns include subject-oriented programming [18], composition filters [1] and adaptive programming [29, 32]. In subject-oriented programming different subjective perspectives on a single object model are captured. Applications are composed of "subjects" (i.e. partial object models) by means of declarative composition rules. The composition filters approach extends an object with input and output filters. These filters are used to localise non-functional code. Adaptive programming is a special case of AOP where one of the building blocks is expressible in terms of graphs. The other building blocks refer to the graphs using traversal strategies. A traversal strategy can be viewed as a partial specification of a class diagram. This traversal strategy cross-cuts the class graphs. Instead of hard-wiring structural knowledge paths within the classes, this knowledge is separated.

Experience reports and assessment of AOP can be found in [20, 37].

3 The Flexible Instance Adaptation Approach

Our approach is based on the observation that the instance adaptation code cross-cuts the class version definitions. This is because existing systems introduce the adaptation code directly into the class versions upon evolution. Often, the same adaptation routines are introduced into a number of class versions. Consequently, if the behaviour of a routine needs to be changed maintenance has to be performed on all the class versions in which it was introduced. There is a high probability that a number of adaptation routines in a class version will never be invoked as only newer applications will attempt to access properties and methods unavailable for objects associated with the particular class version. The adaptation strategy is fixed and adoption of a new strategy might trigger the need for changes to all or a large number of versions of existing classes.

Since instance adaptation is a cross-cutting concern we propose separating it from the class versions using aspects (cf. fig. 2(a)). It should be noted that although fig. 2(a) shows one instance adaptation aspect per class version, one such aspect can serve a number of class versions. Similarly, a particular class version can have more than one instance adaptation aspect. Fig. 2(b) depicts the case when an application attempts to access an object associated with version 1 of *class A* using the interface offered by version 2 of the same class. The aspect containing the instance adaptation code is dynamically woven into the particular class version (version 1 in this case). This code is then invoked to return the results to the application.

It should be noted that the instance adaptation code in fig. 2 has two parts:
- Adaptation routines
- Instance adaptation strategy

An adaptation routine is the code specific to a class version or a set of class versions. This code handles the interface mismatch between a class version and the accessed object. The instance adaptation strategy is the code which detects the interface mismatch and invokes the appropriate adaptation routine e.g. an error handler [47], an update method [33] or a transformation function [14].

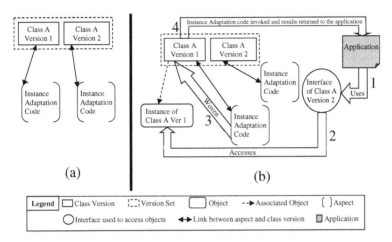

Fig. 2. Instance Adaptation using Aspects

Based on the above observation two possible aspect structures are shown in fig. 3. The structure in fig. 3(a) encapsulates the instance adaptation strategy and the adaptation routines for a class version (or a set of class versions) in one aspect. This has the advantage of having the instance adaptation code for a class version (or a set of class versions) in one place but unnecessary weaving of the instance adaptation strategy (which could previously be woven) needs to be carried out. This can be taken care of by *selective weaving* i.e. only weaving the modified parts of an aspect if it has previously been woven into the particular class version. Such a structure also has the advantage of allowing multiple instance adaptation strategies to coexist. One set of class versions could use one strategy while another could use a different one. This choice can also be application dependent. A disadvantage of this structure is the need to modify a large number of aspects if the instance adaptation strategy is changed. This is addressed by the structure in fig. 3(b) which encapsulates the instance adaptation strategy in an aspect separate from the ones containing the specific adaptation routines. In this case only one instance adaptation aspect exists in the system providing better localisation of changes as compared to the structure in fig. 3(a). Any such change will require aspects containing the adaptation routines to be rewoven. Issues relating to this and a solution based on assertions have been discussed in [24]. If more than one instance adaptation aspects are allowed to exist multiple instance adaptation strategies can coexist (similar to the structure in fig. 3(a)). If only one instance adaptation strategy is being used and the system is single-rooted (this implies that the system has a root class which has only one class version) the instance adaptation aspect can be woven into the root class version and rewoven only if the instance adaptation strategy is modified. Versions of subclasses will need a small amount of code to be woven into them in order to access the functionality woven in the root class. This code can be separated in an aspect if a generic calling mechanism is being used. Otherwise, it can reside in aspects containing the adaptation routines.

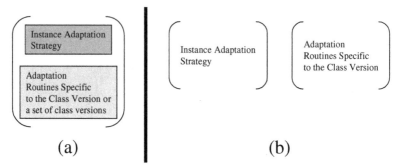

Fig. 3. Two Possible Aspect Structures

The above discussion shows that aspects help in separating the instance adaptation strategy from the class versions. Behaviour of the adaptation routines can be modified within the aspects instead of modifying them within each class version. If a different instance adaptation strategy needs to be employed only the aspects need to be modified without having the problem of updating the various class versions. These are automatically updated to use the new strategy (and the new adaptation routines) when the aspects are rewoven. The need to reweave can easily be identified by a simple run-time check based on timestamps.

The approach has been implemented as part of the SADES evolution system [39, 40, 41, 43, 45] which has been built as a layer on top of the commercially available Jasmine[4] object database management system. Applications can be bound to particular class versions or a common interface for the class. An example of switching between two different instance adaptation strategies in the SADES system is discussed in the following section.

4 Example Instance Adaptation Strategies

In this section we discuss the use of two different instance adaptation strategies in SADES: error handlers from ENCORE [47] and update/backdate methods from CLOSQL [33]. The example aims to demonstrate the flexibility of the approach. We first discuss how to implement the error handlers strategy using our approach. We then present the implementation of the update/backdate methods strategy. This is followed by a description of seamless transformation from one instance adaptation strategy to another.

---

[4] http://www.cai.com/

We have employed the aspect structure in fig. 3(b) in SADES as the class hierarchy is single-rooted with strictly one version for the root class. Versions of all classes directly or indirectly inherit from this root class version. Although not shown in the following example, it should be assumed that appropriate code has been woven into the class versions to access the adaptation strategy woven into the root class version.

4.1 Error Handlers

We first consider the instance adaptation strategy of ENCORE [47]. As shown in figure 4, applications access instances of a class through a *version set interface* which is the union of the properties and methods defined by all versions of the class. Error handlers are employed to trap incompatibilities between the version set interface and the interface of a particular class version. These handlers also ensure that objects associated with the class version exhibit the version set interface. As shown in fig. 4(b) if a new class version modifies the version set interface (e.g. if it introduces new properties and methods) handlers for the new properties and methods are introduced into all the former versions of the type. On the other hand, if creation of a new class version does not modify the version set interface (e.g. if the version is introduced because properties and methods have been removed), handlers for the removed properties and methods are added to the newly created version (cf. fig. 4(c)).

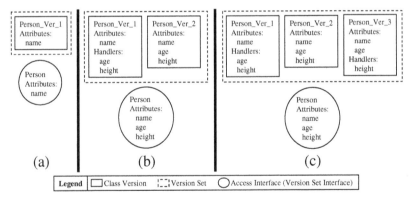

Fig. 4. Error Handlers in ENCORE

The introduction of error handlers in former class versions is a significant overhead especially when, over the lifetime of the database, a substantial number of class versions exist prior to the creation of a new one. If the behaviour of some handlers needs to be changed maintenance has to be performed on all the class versions in which the handlers were introduced. To demonstrate our approach we have chosen the scenario in fig. 4(b). Similar solutions can be employed for other cases. As shown in fig. 5(a), instead of introducing the handlers into the former class versions they are encapsulated in an aspect. In this case one aspect serves all the class versions existing prior to the creation of the new one. Links between aspects and class versions are *open* [20] as an aspect needs to know about the various class versions it can be applied to while a class version needs to be aware of the aspect that needs to be woven to exhibit a specific interface. Fig. 5(b) depicts the case when an application attempts to access the *age* and *height* attributes in an object associated with version 1 of *class Person*. The aspect containing the handlers is woven into the particular class version. The handlers then simulate (to the application) the presence of the missing attributes in the associated object.

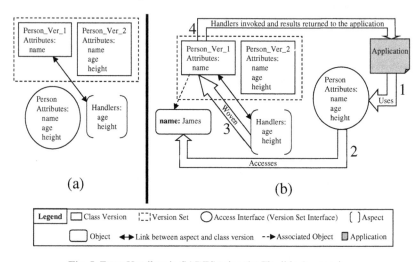

Fig. 5. Error Handlers in SADES using the Flexible Approach

4.2 Update/Backdate Methods

We now discuss implementation of the instance adaptation strategy of CLOSQL [33] using our approach. In CLOSQL, unlike ENCORE, instances are converted between class versions instead of emulating the conversion. The conversion is reversible, hence allowing instances to be freely converted between various versions of their particular class. When a new class version is created the maintainer specifies update functions for all the attributes in the class version. An update function specifies what is to happen to the particular attribute when it is converted to a newer class version. Backdate functions provide similar functionality for the conversion to older class versions. All the update and backdate functions for the class version are grouped into an *update method* and a *backdate method* respectively. Applications are bound to the class versions. Therefore, the access interface is that of the particular class version being used to access an object. When an instance is converted some of the attribute values can be lost (if the class version used for conversion does not define some of the attributes whose values exist in the instance prior to conversion). This is addressed by storing removed attribute values separately.

Figure 6 shows the implementation of the update/backdate methods strategy using our approach. As shown in fig. 6(a) an aspect containing an update method is associated with version 1 of *class Person* in order to convert instances associated with version 1 to version 2. An aspect containing a backdate method to convert instances associated with version 2 to version 1 is also introduced. Although not shown in fig. 6(a) when an instance is converted from *class Person* version 2 to version 1 a storage aspect will be associated with the converted instance in order to store removed information. Fig. 6(b) depicts the case when an application attempts to access an object associated with version 1 of *class Person* using the class definition in version 2. The aspect containing the update method is woven into version 1. The method then converts the accessed object to the definition in version 2. The converted object is now associated with the new class version definition (i.e. version 2) and returns information to the application.

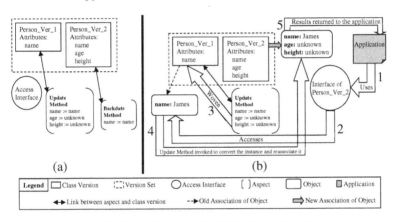

(a)   (b)

Fig. 6. Update/Backdate Methods in SADES using the Flexible Approach

4.3 Changing the Instance Adaptation Strategy

This section describes how the flexible approach allows seamless transformation from one instance adaptation strategy to another. As discussed earlier such a need can arise due to application/scenario specific adaptation requirements or the availability of a more efficient strategy. We assume that the system initially employs the error handlers strategy (as shown in fig. 5) and discuss how this strategy can be replaced by the update/backdate methods strategy (as shown in fig. 6). In order to adopt this new strategy in SADES the aspect containing the instance adaptation strategy in fig. 3(b) (in this case error handlers) is replaced by an aspect encapsulating the new strategy (in this case update/backdate methods). The instance adaptation strategy aspect is rewoven into the root class version. There is no need to reweave access from subclass versions as the code for this is independent of the instance adaptation strategy in SADES. The aspects containing the handlers are replaced by those containing update/backdate methods. Let us assume that the scenario in fig. 6 corresponds to the one in fig. 5 after the instance adaptation strategy has been changed. As shown in fig. 6(a) the aspect containing error handlers for version 1 of *class Person* will be replaced with an aspect containing an update method to convert instances associated with version 1 to version 2. An aspect containing a backdate method to convert instances associated with version 2 to version 1 will also be introduced. Since the approach is based on dynamic weaving the new aspects will be woven into the particular class version when required. It should be noted that it is also possible to automatically generate the aspects encapsulating update/backdate methods from those containing error handlers and vice versa. This eases the programmer's task who can edit the generated aspects if needed.

5 Related Work

A number of approaches have been employed to ensure structural consistency. [7, 9] provide theoretical foundations for the purpose. [13] proposes the use of a special consistency checking tool. [14] employs transformation functions and object migration. [5] suggests *screening* deleted or modified information from application programs instead of deleting or modifying it physically. Only conversion functions have access to the screened information. The screening information and transformation functions can be encapsulated in aspects. [25] exploits the difference between old and new definitions through a program generator used to produce transformation programs and tables. A similar approach can be employed to generate required aspects upon creation of a new class version.

Separation of concerns in object-oriented databases has been explicitly considered in [44] which identifies some of the cross-cutting concerns in object databases and proposes an aspect-oriented extension to capture these explicitly. Some existing work has also addressed separation of concerns implicitly. The concept of object version derivation graphs [31] separates version management from the objects. A similar approach is proposed by [39, 40, 41, 43, 45] where version derivation graphs manage both object and class versioning. Additional semantics for object and class versioning are provided separately from the general version management technique. [30] employs propagation patterns [27, 28] to exploit polymorphic reuse mechanisms in order to minimise the effort required to manually reprogram methods and queries due to schema modifications. Propagation patterns are behavioural abstractions of application programs and define patterns of operation propagation by reasoning about the behavioural dependencies among co-operating objects. [42] implements inheritance links between classes using semantic relationships which are first class-objects. The inheritance hierarchy can be changed by modifying the relationships instead of having to alter actual class definitions. In the *hologram approach* proposed by [2] an object is implemented by multiple instances representing its many faceted nature. These instances are linked together through aggregation links in a specialisation hierarchy. This makes objects dynamic since they can migrate between the classes of a hierarchy hence making schema changes more pertinent.

6 Conclusions

We have proposed a flexible approach for instance adaptation during class versioning. The approach has been implemented as part of the SADES system. Changes to the instance adaptation strategies in existing systems are expensive due to the cross-cutting nature of the instance adaptation code. The adaptation routines are spread across various class versions making maintenance difficult. We have employed aspects to separate the instance adaptation code from the class versions. This localises the effect of any changes to the instance adaptation code. As a result the behaviour of adaptation routines can be modified in a cost-effective manner. It is also possible to seamlessly move to an entirely different instance adaptation strategy. This has been demonstrated by using error handlers and update/backdate methods as examples. Our approach also allows multiple instance adaptation strategies to coexist in the system. This makes it possible to use different strategies for different parts of the system or to use one strategy when data is accessed using one application and a different one when using another application.

One of the essential requirements for the approach to be effective is the need for a highly efficient weaver. Reflecting on experiences with our initial prototype we are building a sophisticated weaver for the purpose. Our future work will explore the applicability of the approach in systems employing schema evolution and schema versioning as evolution strategies. We are also interested in developing an aspect-oriented evolution framework for object-oriented databases.

References

1. Aksit, M., Tekinerdogan, B., "Aspect-Oriented Programming using Composition Filters", *Proceedings of the AOP Workshop at ECOOP '98, 1998*
2. Al-Jadir, L., Leonard, M., "If We Refuse the Inheritance …", *Proceedings of DEXA 1999, LNCS 1677, pp. 560-572*
3. Andany, J., Leonard, M., Palisser, C., "Management of Schema Evolution in Databases", *Proceedings of the 17th International Conference on Very Large Databases, Morgan Kaufmann 1991, pp. 161-170*
4. AspectJ Home Page, http://aspectj.org/, *Xerox PARC, USA*
5. Banerjee, J., Kim, W., Kim, H., Korth, H. F., "Semantics and Implementation of Schema Evolution in Object-Oriented Databases", *Proceedings of ACM SIGMOD Conference, SIGMOD Record, Vol. 16, No. 3, Dec. 1987, pp. 311-322*
6. Benatallah, B., Tari, Z., "Dealing with Version Pertinence to Design an Efficient Schema Evolution Framework", *Proceedings of the International Database Engineering and Applications Symposium, Cardiff, Wales, U.K., IEEE Computer Society 1998, pp. 24-33*
7. Bergstein, P. L., "Object-Preserving Class Transformations", *Proceedings of OOPSLA 1991, ACM SIGPLAN Notices, Vol. 26, No. 11, pp. 299-313*
8. Bergstein, P. L., Huersch, W. L., "Maintaining Behavioral Consistency during Schema Evolution", *Proceedings of the International Symposium on Object Technologies for Advanced Software, Springer-Verlag 1993, pp. 176-193*
9. Bergstein, P. L., "Maintenance of Object-Oriented Systems during Structural Evolution", *TAPOS - Theory and Practice of Object Systems, Vol. 3, No. 3, pp. 185-212*
10. Boellert, K., "On Weaving Aspects", Proc. of the AOP Workshop at ECOOP '99

11. Bjornerstedt, A., Hulten, C., "Version Control in an Object-Oriented Architecture", *In Object-Oriented Concepts, Databases, and Applications (eds: Kim, W., Lochovsky, F. H.), pp. 451-485*

12. Clamen, S. M., "Type Evolution and Instance Adaptation", *School of Computer Science, Carnegie Mellon University, Technical Report CMU-CS-92-133R, June 1992*

13. Delcourt, C., Zicari, R., "The Design of an Integrity Consistency Checker (ICC) for an Object Oriented Database System", *Proceedings of ECOOP 1991, Lecture Notes in Computer Science 512, pp. 97-117*

14. Ferrandina, F., Meyer, T., Zicari, R., Ferran, G., "Schema and Database Evolution in the O2 Object Database System", *Proceedings of the 21st Conference on Very Large Databases, Morgan Kaufmann 1995, pp. 170-181*

15. Fishman, D. H. *et al.*, "Iris: An Object Oriented Database Management System", *ACM Transactions on Office Information Systems, Vol. 5, No. 1, 1987, pp. 48-69*

16. Fradet, P., Suedholt, M., "An Aspect Language for Robust Programming", *Proceedings of the AOP Workshop at ECOOP '99, 1999*

17. Gamma, E. *et al.*, "Design Patterns - Elements of Reusable Object-Oriented Software", *Addison Wesley, c1995*

18. Harrison, W., Ossher, H., "Subject-Oriented Programming (A Critique of Pure Objects)", *Proceedings of OOPSLA 1993, ACM SIGPLAN Notices, Vol. 28, No. 10, Oct. 1993, pp. 411-428*

19. Kenens, P., *et al.*, "An AOP Case with Static and Dynamic Aspects", *Proceedings of the AOP Workshop at ECOOP '98, 1998*

20. Kersten, M. A., Murphy, G. C., "Atlas: A Case Study in Building a Web-based Learning Environment using Aspect-oriented Programming", *Proceedings of OOPSLA 1999, ACM SIGPLAN Notices, Vol. 34, No. 10, Oct. 1999, pp. 340-352*

21. Kiczales, G., Irwin, J., Lamping, J., Loingtier, J., Lopes, C., Maeda, C., Mendhekar, A., "Aspect-Oriented Programming", *ACM Computing Surveys, Vol. 28, No. 4, Dec. 1996*

22. Kiczales, G., Lamping, J., Mendhekar, A., Maeda, C., Lopes, C., Loingtier, J., Irwin, J., "Aspect-Oriented Programming", *Proceedings of ECOOP '97, LNCS 1241, pp. 220-242*

23. Kim, W., Chou, H.-T., "Versions of Schema for Object-Oriented Databases", *Proceedings of 14th International Conference on Very Large Databases, Morgan Kaufmann 1988, pp. 148-159*

24. Klaeren, H., Pulvermueller, E., Rashid, A., Speck, A., "Supporting Composition using Assertions", *Cooperative Systems Engineering Group, Computing Department, Lancaster University, Technical Report No: CSEG/4/00*

25. Lerner, B. S., Habermann, A. N., "Beyond Schema Evolution to Database Reorganisation", *Proceedings of ECOOP/OOPSLA 1990, ACM SIGPLAN Notices, Vol. 25, No. 10, Oct. 1990, pp. 67-76*

26. Li, Q., McLeod, D., "Conceptual Database Evolution through Learning in Object Databases", *IEEE Transactions on Knowledge and Data Engineering, Vol. 6, No. 2, April 1994, pp. 205-224*

27. Lieberherr, K. J., Huersch, W., Silva-Lepe, I., Xiao, C., "Experience with a Graph-Based Propagation Pattern Programming Tool", *Proceedings of the International CASE Workshop, IEEE Computer Society 1992, pp. 114-119*

28. Lieberherr, K. J., Silva-Lepe, I., Xiao, C., "Adaptive Object-Oriented Programming using Graph-Based Customization", *CACM, Vol. 37, No. 5, May 1994, pp. 94-101*

29. Lieberherr, K. J., "Demeter", http://www.ccs.neu.edu/research/demeter/index.html

30. Liu, L., Zicari, R., Huersch, W., Lieberherr, K. J., "The Role of Polymorphic Reuse Mechanisms in Schema Evolution in an Object-Oriented Database", *IEEE Transactions of Knowledge and Data Engineering, Vol. 9, No. 1, Jan.-Feb. 1997, pp. 50-67*

31. Loomis, M. E. S., "Object Versioning", *JOOP, Jan. 1992, pp. 40-43*

32. Mezini, M., Lieberherr, K. J., "Adaptive Plug-and-Play Components for Evolutionary Software Development", *Proceedings of OOPSLA 1998, ACM SIGPLAN Notices, Vol. 33, No. 10, Oct. 1998, pp.97-116*

33. Monk, S., Sommerville, I., "Schema Evolution in OODBs Using Class Versioning", *SIGMOD Record, Vol. 22, No. 3, Sept. 1993, pp. 16-22*

34. Odberg, E., "A Framework for Managing Schema Versioning in Object Oriented Databases", Proceedings of the International Conference on Database and Expert Systems Applications (DEXA) 1992, pp. 115-120

35. Odberg, E., "A Global Perspective of Schema Modification Management for Object-Oriented Databases", *Proceedings of the 6th International Workshop on Persistent Object Systems (POS) 1994, pp. 479-502*

36. Peters, R. J., Ozsu, M. T., "An Axiomatic Model of Dynamic Schema Evolution in Objectbase Systems", *ACM Transactions on Database Systems, Vol. 22, No. 1, March 1997, pp. 75-114*

37. Pulvermueller, E., Klaeren, H., Speck, A., "Aspects in Distributed Environments", *Proceedings of GCSE 1999, Erfurt, Germany (to be published by Springer-Verlag)*

38. Ra., Y.-G., Rundensteiner, E. A., "A Transparent Schema-Evolution System Based on Object-Oriented View Technology", *IEEE Transactions on Knowledge and Data Engineering, Vol. 9, No. 4, July/Aug. 1997, pp. 600-624*

39. Rashid, A., Sawyer, P., "Facilitating Virtual Representation of CAD Data through a Learning Based Approach to Conceptual Database Evolution Employing Direct Instance Sharing", *Proceedings of DEXA '98, LNCS 1460, pp. 384-393*

40. Rashid, A., "SADES - a Semi-Autonomous Database Evolution System", *Proceedings of PhDOOS '98, ECOOP '98 Workshop Reader, LNCS 1543*

41. Rashid, A., Sawyer, P., "Toward 'Database Evolution': a Taxonomy for Object Oriented Databases", *In review at IEEE Transactions on Knowledge and Data Engineering*

42. Rashid, A., Sawyer, P., "Dynamic Relationships in Object Oriented Databases: A Uniform Approach", *Proceedings DEXA '99, LNCS 1677, pp. 26-35*

43. Rashid, A., Sawyer, P., "Transparent Dynamic Database Evolution from Java", *Proceedings of OOPSLA 1999 Workshop on Java and Databases: Persistence Options*

44. Rashid, A., Pulvermueller, E., "From Object-Oriented to Aspect-Oriented Databases", *In review at DEXA 2000*

45. "SADES Java API Documentation",

46. *http://www.comp.lancs.ac.uk/computing/users/marash/research/sades/index.html*

47. Sjoberg, D., "Quantifying Schema Evolution", *Information and Software Technology, Vol. 35, No. 1, pp. 35-44, Jan. 1993*

48. Skarra, A. H., Zdonik, S. B., "The Management of Changing Types in an Object-Oriented Database", *Proceedings of the 1st OOPSLA Conference, Sept. 1986, pp. 483-495*

49. Tamzalit, D., Oussalah, C., "Instances Evolution vs Classes Evolution", *Proceedings of DEXA 1999, LNCS 1677, pp. 16-25*

50. Zicari, R., "A Framework for Schema Updates in an Object-Oriented Database System", *Proceedings of the International Conference on Data Engineering 1991, IEEE Computer Society Press, pp. 2-13*

51. Zdonik, B., "Maintaining Consistency in a Database with Changing Types", *ACM SIGPLAN Notices, Vol. 21, No. 10, Oct. 1986*

Optimizing Performance of Schema Evolution Sequences *

Kajal T. Claypool, Chandrakant Natarajan, and Elke A. Rundensteiner

Worcester Polytechnic Institute, 100 Intitute Road,
Worcester, MA, USA
{kajal, chandu, rundenst}@cs.wpi.edu
http://davis.wpi.edu/dsrg

Abstract. More than ever before schema transformation is a prevalent problem that needs to be addressed to accomplish for example the migration of legacy systems to the newer OODB systems, the generation of structured web pages from data in database systems, or the integration of systems with different native data models. Such schema transformations are typically composed of a sequence of schema evolution operations. The execution of such sequences can be very time-intensive, possibly requiring many hours or even days and thus effectively making the database unavailable for unacceptable time spans. While researchers have looked at the deferred execution approach for schema evolution in an effort to improve availability of the system, to the best of our knowledge ours is the first effort to provide a direct optimization strategy for a sequence of changes. In this paper, we propose heuristics for the iterative elimination and cancellation of schema evolution primitives as well as for the merging of database modifications of primitives such that they can be performed in *one* efficient transformation pass over the database. In addition we show the correctness of our optimization approach, thus guaranteeing that the initial input and the optimized output schema evolution sequence produce the same final schema and data state. We provide proof of the algorithm's optimality by establishing the confluence property of our problem search space, i.e., we show that the iterative application of our heuristics always terminates and converges to a unique minimal sequence. Moreover, we have conducted experimental studies that demonstrate the performance gains achieved by our proposed optimization technique over previous solutions.

Keywords: Schema Evolution, Object-Oriented Databases, Optimization.

* This work was supported in part by the NSF NYI grant #IRI 94-57609. We would also like to thank our industrial sponsors, in particular, IBM for the IBM partnership award and Informix for software contribution. Kajal T. Claypool would like to thank GE for the GE Corporate Fellowship. Special thanks also goes to the PSE Team specifically, Gordon Landis, Sam Haradhvala, Pat O'Brien and Breman Thuraising at Object Design Inc. for not only software contributions but also for providing us with a customized patch of the PSE Pro2.0 system that exposed schema-related APIs needed to develop our tool.

K.R. Dittrich et al. (Eds.): Objects and Databases 2000, LNCS 1944, pp. 114–127, 2001.
© Springer-Verlag Berlin Heidelberg 2001

1   Introduction

Not only is it difficult to pre-determine the database schema for many complex applications during the first pass, but worst yet application requirements typically change over time. For example [17] documents the extent of schema evolution during the development and the initial use of a health management system at several hospitals. There was an increase of 139% in the number of relations and an increase of 274% in the number of attributes, and every relation in the schema was changed at least once during the nineteen-month period of the study. In another study [13], significant changes (about 59% of attributes on the average) were reported for seven applications which ranged from project tracking, real estate inventory and accounting to government administration of the skill trades and apprenticeship programs. These studies reveal that schema changes are an inevitable task not only during the development of a project but also once a project has become operational. For this reason, most object-oriented database systems (OODB) today support some form of schema evolution [18,3, 14,10].

The state of the art in OODB evolution is to offer seamless change management by providing transparency between the database schema and the application source files representing the schema. Systems such as ObjectStore [14] allow users to directly edit the application source leaving the OODB system to handle the propagation of this sequence of changes to the database schema. Other systems such as Itasca [10] provide a graphical user interface (GUI) that allows the users to specify a set of their schema changes graphically while the system again is responsible for propagating the schema changes to the database. Other systems such as O_2 [18,2], TESS [12] and SERF [5] all deal with more advanced schema changes, such as merging of two classes, which are often composed of a sequence of schema evolution primitives. All of these systems deal with applying not a *single schema change* but a *sequence of schema changes* to the underlying database.

Unfortunately, schema evolution remains a very expensive process both in terms of system resource consumption as well as database unavailability [9]. Even a single simple schema evolution primitive (such as add-attribute to a class) applied to a small database of 20,000 objects (approx. 4MB of data) has been reported to already take about 7.4 minutes [7]. With the current database technology for the specification of schema changes as a sequence of changes the performance of the system is further compromised, with evolution costs for large databases possibly escalating to hours, perhaps even days for entire sequences.

In previous work, researchers have looked at improving system availability during schema evolution by proposing execution strategies such as deferred execution [18,9]. No work, however, has been undertaken to actually optimize or reduce the sequence of operations that are being applied to a given schema. Kahler et al. [11] have looked at pre-execution optimization for reducing the number of update messages that are sent to maintain replicated sites in the context of distributed databases. In their approach, the messages are simple data updates on tuples. He sorts the number of messages by their tuple-identifier, and then condenses (with merge or remove) the change history of the tuple into one update operation.

We now present a similar approach (merge, cancel, eliminate) for optimizing a sequence of schema evolution operations. Our optimization strategy, called CHOP, exploits two principles of schema evolution execution within one integrated solution:

- Minimize the number of schema evolution operations in a sequence by for example canceling or eliminating schema evolution operations. For example, adding an attribute and then deleting the same attribute is an obvious case of cancellation where neither operation needs to be executed.
- Merge the execution of all schema evolution changes that operate on one extent to amortize the cost of schema evolution over several schema changes. For example, consider a sequence that adds two or more attributes to the same class. Object updates for these done simultaneously can potentially half the cost of executing these sequentially.

To the best of our knowledge ours is the first effort to provide an optimization strategy for a sequence of changes prior to execution a la Kahler [11]. Our approach is orthogonal to the existing execution strategies for schema evolution, i.e., it can in fact be applied to both immediate and the deferred execution strategies [9].

To summarize, in this paper, we present a general strategy for the reduction of a given sequence of schema evolution operations **prior** to its actual execution. Our work is based on a taxonomy of schema evolution operations we developed for the ODMG object model but it can easily be applied to any other object model. We present here an analysis of the schema evolution operations and of the schema to characterize the conditions under which operations in a sequence can be optimized. Based on this analysis we present the *merge*, *cancel* and *eliminate* optimization functions and the conditions under which they can be applied. We have also been able to show both formally and experimentally that the order in which these functions are applied is not relevant for the final optimized sequence, i.e., they will all produce the same *unique* final sequence. As a conclusion to our work we also present a summary of our experimental results.

Outlook. The rest of the paper is organized as follows. Section 3 presents the taxonomy of schema evolution primitives on which we base our analysis. Section 4 gives a formalization of the schema evolution operation properties. Section 5 presents the actual optimization functions while Section 6 describes how these are combined to form the overall CHOP strategy. Section 7 presents our experimental evaluation. We conclude in Section 8.

2   Related Work

Current commercial OODBs such as Itasca [10], GemStone [3], ObjectStore [14], and O_2 [18] all provide some schema evolution - be it a set of schema evolution primitives or some mechanism for global changes. Some work in schema evolution has focused on the areas of optimization and database availability, in particular on deciding when and how to modify the database to address concerns such as efficiency and availability. In [9,8], a deferred execution strategy is proposed for the O_2 database system that maintains a history of schema evolution operations for a class and migrates objects only when actually accessed by the user. This allows not only for high database availability but also amortizes the cost of the object transformations with that of a query lookup. However, no optimizations are applied to this sequence of schema evolution operation(s) and the performance of this deferred mechanism deteriorates as the set of queried objects grows larger. Our approach, while primarily optimizing the immediate update mode, also complements the deferred mechanism by offering time savings as the queried set of objects and the number of schema evolution operations to be applied on it grows larger.

Similar work has also been done in database log recovery mechanisms. In [11], Kahler et. al use hashing to compute the net effect of changes in a log by eliminating and/or collapsing redundant log enteries due to insert-remove pairs, replace-remove pairs, etc. We use a similar approach (cancel and eliminate optimizations) for removing redundancy from a sequence of schema evolution sequences. The focus of work is however, beyond simply condensing all changes into one change. In this work, we have shown that if one or more optimizations are applied, giving precedence to one over the other is immaterial as they all lead to the same minimal optimized sequence of operations. Segev et al. have applied similar pre-execution optimizations for updating distributed materialized views since data sequences of updates must be shipped from the base tables to the view [16].

3   Background - Taxonomy of Schema Evolution Primitives

The CHOP approach is based on the Object Model as presented in the ODMG Standard [4]. The ODMG object model encompasses the most commonly used object models and standardizes their features into one object model, thus increasing the portability and applicability of our prototype. Here we present a taxonomy of schema evolution primitives (Table 1) that we have defined for the ODMG model based on the other data models as O_2 or Itasca [18,3,14,10]. The taxonomy given in Table 1 is a **complete** set of schema evolution primitives such that it subsumes every possible type of schema change [1]. The taxonomy is the **essential** [19] set of schema evolution primitives, i.e., each primitive updates the schema and the objects in a unique way that cannot be achieved by a simple composition of the other primitives.

Table 1. The Taxonomy of Schema Evolution Primitives.

Term	Description	Capacity Effects
$add\text{-}class(c, \mathcal{C})$	Add new class c to $\mathcal{C}$ in schema S (AC)	augmenting
$delete\text{-}class(c)$	Delete class c from $\mathcal{C}$ in schema S if $subclasses(\mathcal{C}) = \emptyset$ (DC)	reducing
$rename\text{-}class(c_x, c_y)$	Rename class c_x to c_y (CCN)	preserving
$add\text{-}ISA\text{-}edge(c_x, c_y)$	Add an inheritance edge from c_x to c_y (AE)	augmenting
$delete\text{-}ISA\text{-}edge(c_x, c_y)$	Delete the inheritance edge from c_x to c_y (DE)	reducing
$add\text{-}attribute(c_x, a_x)$	Add attribute a_x to class c_x (AA)	augmenting
$delete\text{-}attribute(c_x, a_x)$	Delete the attribute a_x from the class c_x (DA)	reducing
$rename\text{-}attribute(a_x, b_x, c_x)$	Rename the attribute a_x to b_x in the class c_x (CAN)	preserving

4   Foundations of Schema Evolution Sequence Analysis

To establish a foundation for our optimization principles we have developed a formal characterization of the schema evolution operations, their impact on the schema, as well as their interactions within a sequence. Due to space constraints we only summarize these characterizations here. For more details please see [6].

Table 2 defines the various relationships that can exist in general between schema evolution operations. Table 3 applies these to the schema evolution operation presented in Table 1.

Table 2. Classification of Operation Properties.

Operation Relation	Description
same-operation-as	op1 is **same-operation-as** op2 if they both have the same operation name irrespective of the particular parameters they are being applied to.
inverse-operation-of	op1 is **inverse-operation-of** op2 if the effects of one operation op1 could be canceled (reversed) by the effects of the other operation op2.
super-operation-of	op1 is **super-operation-of** op2 if the functionality of op1 superimposes the functionality of op2, i.e., op1 achieves as part of its functionality also the effects of op2

Table 3. Classification of Operation Properties for the Schema Evolution Taxonomy in Table 1 (with **same** = **same-operation-as**, **inverse** = **inverse-operation-of** and **super** = **super-operation-of**).

	AC()	DC()	CCN()	AA()	DA()	CAN()	AE()	DE()
AC()	same	inverse	-	super	-	-	-	-
DC()	inverse	same	super	super	super	super	super	super
CCN()	-	-	same/inverse	-	-	-	-	-
AA()	-	-	-	same	inverse	-	-	-
DA()	-	-	-	inverse	same	super	-	-
CAN()	-	-	-	-	-	same	-	-
AE()	-	-	-	-	-	-	same	inverse
DE()	-	-	-	-	-	-	inverse	same

However, for optimization it is not sufficient to categorize the schema evolution operations based on just their functionality. It is important to also know the parameters, i.e., the context in which these operations are applied. Table 4 presents the schema element relationships.

Table 4. Classification of Schema Element Relations.

Schema Relation	Description
definedIn	gives the scope for all schema elements (from ODMG).
extendedBy	gives the inheritance relationship of schema elements of the type `Class` (from ODMG).
same-as	gives the identity of a class or a property based on unique name in given scope (CHOP extension).
aliasedTo	gives the derivation of a schema element from another element through a series of name modifications (CHOP extension).

While the *operation properties* (Table 2) and the *context properties* (Table 4) provide *necessary* criteria for when an optimization function can be applied, they are not always sufficient in the context of a sequence. Here we briefly summarize the relationships of operations in a sequence.

- **Schema-Invariant Order Property.** When operation op1 is **sameAs** op2, we identify the **schema-invariant-order** property as:
  - For two **capacity-augmenting** and **capacity-reducing** operations, op1 is in **schema-invariant-order** with op2 if the order of their parameters is the **same**.
  - For **capacity-preserving** operations, op1 is in **schema-invariant-order** with op2 if the order of their parameters is **reversed**.

- **Object-Invariant-Order Property** - op1 is **object-invariant-order**
  with op2, if op1 is **capacity-augmenting** and op2 is **capacity-reducing**
  and in the sequence of evolution operations the **capacity-augmenting** operation appears prior to the **capacity-reducing** operation. There is no specific **object-invariant-order** for the **capacity-preserving** operations.
- **Dependency Property** - The schema elements used as parameters by the
  two operations op1 and op2 being considered for optimization must not be
  referred to by any other operation which is placed between the two operations
  in the sequence.

5   The CHOP Optimization Functions

The integral component of the CHOP optimization algorithm are the optimization functions that can be applied to pairs of schema evolution operations within
the context of their resident schema evolution operation sequence. In this section we present the general description of an optimization function and three
instantiations of the optimization functions (*merge, cancel, eliminate*), that we
have formulated for the optimization of the primitive set of schema evolution
operations given in Section 3.

5.1   An Optimization Function

The crux of the CHOP optimization algorithm is an optimization function which
takes as input two schema evolution operations and produces as output zero or
one schema evolution operation, thereby reducing the sequence of the schema
evolution operations. Formally, we define an optimization function as follows:

Definition 1. *Given a schema evolution operation sequence Σ, op1, op2 ...
opn with op1 before op2 (i.e., if the index position i of op1 is less than the index
position j of op2 in Σ, index(op1) $= i < j =$ index(op2)), an optimization function F_Σ produces as output an operation op3 which is placed in the sequence Σ
at the index position i of the first operation, op1. The operation at index position j is set to a* no-op. *The operations op1, op2 and op3 can be either schema
evolution primitives as described in Table 1 or complex evolution operations as
defined in Section 5.2.*

A major requirement for the CHOP optimization is to reduce the number of
schema evolution operations in a sequence such that the final schema produced
by this optimized sequence is consistent and is the same as the one that would
have been produced by the unoptimized sequence for the same input schema.
Thus, an optimization function must not in any way change the nature of the
schema evolution operations or the order in which they are executed. Towards
that goal, any optimization function must observe several properties characterized below.

Invariant-Preserving-Output Operations. Schema evolution operations guarantee the consistency of the schema and the database by preserving the invariants defined for the underlying object model [1]. An important property of the optimization function therefore is for its output (any of its output operations) to also preserve the schema consistency by preserving the invariants defined for the object model.

Schema-State Equivalent. Above all an optimization function must guarantee correctness, i.e., the schema produced by output of the optimization function (optimized sequence) must be the same as the schema produced by the unoptimized sequence when applied to the same input schema. This property can in fact be proven formally. In [6] we provide a formal set of definitions and proofs for this.

Relative-Order Preserving. As discussed in Section 4, the order in which the schema evolution operations appear with respect to one another in a sequence is relevant to the application of an optimization function. This **relative order** of an operation op1 in a sequence is defined by its index, index(op1), with respect to the index of the other operations, e.g., index(op2), in the sequence. For example, if index(op1) < index(op2), then op1 is *before* op2 in the sequence, denoted by op1 < op2. Operations executed out-of-order can cause unexpected variance in the final output schema. For example, consider two operations in a sequence with the order as given here: < DA(C,a), AA(C,a) >. When executed in the order given the attribute a is first deleted from the class C and then re-added. However, all of the information stored in the attribute a is lost. Now, switching the order of execution of the two operations leads to a very different schema.

Thus, it is essential for an optimized sequence to preserve the **relative-order** of the input sequence.

Using the above stated properties, we now refine the definition of an optimization function as follows:

Definition 2 (Optimization Function.). *Any optimization function in CHOP defined as in Definition 1 must be* **invariant-preserving,** **schema-state-equivalence preserving** *and* **relative-order preserving**.

For the CHOP approach, we define three such optimization functions, Merge, Eliminate and Cancel.

5.2   The Merge Optimization Function

The time taken for performing a schema evolution operation is largely determined by the page fetch and page flush times [7]. In our proposed CHOP approach we amortize the page fetch and flush costs over several operations by collecting all transformations on the same set of objects and performing them simultaneously[1].

A collection of schema evolution operations for the same class which affect the same set of objects, i.e., it is possible to perform all the object transformations for these operations during the same page fetch and flush cycle, is called a **complex operation** denoted by $< op_1, \ldots op_k >$, with $k \geq 2$. For two complex operations, $op1 = < op_i \ldots op_j >$ and $op2 = < op_m \ldots op_n >$, the operation pairs (op_j, op_m) and (op_n, op_i) are termed **complex-representative pairs**.

Definition 3. Merge *is an optimization function (Definition 2) that takes as input a pair of schema evolution operations, either primitive or complex,* op1 *and* op2, *and produces as output a complex operation* op3 $= < op1, op2 >$. *If one or both of the input operations are a complex operation, e.g.,* op1 $= <op_i, op_j >$ *and* op2 $= <op_m, op_n >$, *then a relative order within the complex operations* op3 *is maintained such that the output operation* op3 $= <op_i, op_j, op_m, op_n >$. *The input operations* op1 *and* op2 *must satisfy:*

- **Context Property**
  - *If* op1 *and* op2 *are related by the* **same-operation-as** *property, then their context parameters must be* **definedIn** *in same scope.*
  - *If* op1 *and* op2 *are related by the* **super-operation-of** *property, then for the sub-operation the* **definedIn** *scope of the context must be the* **sameAs** *the context of the super-operation.*
  - *If* op1 *and* op2 *are related by the* **inverse-operation-of** *property, then the context of* op1 *must be* **sameAs** *the context of* op2 *and* **definedIn** *same scope.*
- **Dependency Property** *must hold.*

When one or both of the input operations op1 *and* op2 *are complex, then all the merge conditions given above must be satisfied by at least one pair of operations in the complex operation. This is the* **complex-representative pair***.*

For example, given an operation that adds a **name** attribute to a class called **Employee** and a subsequent operation that adds a **age** attribute to the same class **Employee**, we can merge the two operations they are related by the **same-operation-as** property and their context parameters are **definedIn** the same scope, i.e., **Employee** for both operations is in the same schema and the attributes **name** and **age** are being added to the same class **Employee**. Lastly, the **dependency** property holds as there are no operations between the index positions of the two operations.

A complex operation is thus a sub-sequence of schema evolution operations and other optimization functions (cancel and eliminate) can be applied on the primitive schema evolution operations inside of a complex operation. However, the merge optimization function itself cannot be applied inside of a complex operation as this can lead to infinite recursion.

---

[1] This merge of operations relies on the underlying OODB system to be able to separate the schema evolution operation into a schema change at the Schema Repository level and into object transformations at the database level.

5.3   The Eliminate Optimization Function

In some cases a further optimization beyond merge may be possible. For example, while it is possible to merge DA(Employee, name) and DC(Employee) the execution of DC(Employee) makes the prior execution of DA(Employee, name) redundant. Hence, some operations may be optimized beyond a merge by being completely **eliminated** by other operations, thus reducing the transformation cost by one operation.

Definition 4. Eliminate *is an optimization function as defined in Definition 2 that takes as input a pair of schema evolution primitives* op1 *and* op2 *and produces as output* op3, *such that* op3 = op1 *if* op1 = **super-operation-of** *(*op2*) or* op3 = op2 *if* op2 = **super-operation-of** *(*op1*). The input operations* op1 *and* op2 *must satisfy:*

  - **Operation Property** *such that either* op1 = **super-operation-of** *(*op2*) or* op2 = **super-operation-of** *(*op1*),*
  - **Context Property** *such that the* **definedIn** *scope of the sub-operation is* **sameAs** *the context parameter of the super-operation, and*
  - **Dependency Property** *must hold.*

5.4   The Cancel Optimization Function

In some scenarios further optimization beyond a merge and eliminate may be possible. Some schema evolution operations are inverses of each other, for example, AA(Employee, age) adds an attribute and DA(Employee, age) removes that attribute. A **cancel** optimization thus takes as input two schema evolution operations and produces as output a no-op operation, i.e., an empty operation that does nothing.

Definition 5. Cancel *is an optimization function as in Definition 2 which takes as input a pair of schema evolution primitives* op1 *and* op2 *and produces as output* op3, *where* op3 = no-op, *an empty operation, assuming the input operations* op1 *and* op2 *satisfy:*

  - **Operation Property** *such that* op1 *and* op2 *are related by the* **inverse-operation-of** *property,*
  - **Context Property** *such that* op1 *and* op2 *are* **definedIn** *the same scope and* op1 *is* **sameAs** op2,
  - **Schema-Invariant-Order Property** *for capacity-reducing operations must hold, and*
  - **Object-Invariant-Order Property** *must hold, and*
  - **Dependency Property** *must hold.*

6   CHOP Optimization Strategy

The CHOP optimization algorithm iteratively applies the three classes of optimization functions **merge**, **eliminate** and **cancel** introduced in Section 5 until the algorithm terminates and a minimal solution is found.

However, before we can address the issue of minimality it is necessary to examine two issues: (1) if one or more functions are applicable, is choosing the right function essential? and (2) when there are more than one pair of operations that can be optimized, is choosing the right pair essential?

Choosing the Right Optimization Function. We note that the conditions under which the **merge** optimization function can be applied is a *superset* of the conditions under which an **eliminate** or a **cancel** can be applied, while the conditions under which a **cancel** and an **eliminate** can be applied are mutually exclusive. Thus, often a **merge** can be applied to a pair of operations where either an **eliminate** or a **cancel** can be also applied. However, as these optimizations offer different degrees of reduction for a pair of schema evolution operations (with **merge** offering the least and **cancel** the most), choosing the optimization function that offers the most reduction is very desirable.

We can however formally show that doing a **merge** where a **cancel** or an **eliminate** is also applicable does not prevent the application of a **cancel** or an **eliminate** during the next iterative application of these functions. A formalization of this property and its proof can be found in [6].

Operation Dependencies and Optimization Functions. An important criteria for the successful application of any of the three optimization functions is that the *Dependency Property* as given in Section 4 must hold. That is, there must be no reference to the schema elements used as parameters in the two operations op_1 and op_2 being considered for optimization by any other operation which is placed between the two operations in the sequence. However, the order in which the pairs of operations are selected can have an effect on this dependency.

Consider a sequence of three operations op_1, op_2 and op_3. Consider that the pairs (op_1, op_2) and (op_2, op_3) can be immediately optimized while a successful optimization of the pair (op_1, op_3) requires removing the dependency operation op_2. In this case, there are two possibilities for applying the optimization functions on the pairs of operations. We could either apply the respective optimization functions on the pair (op_1, op_2) and then on the pair (op_2, op_3) [2] and not be concerned about the optimization possibility between op_1 and op_3. Or we could first apply the optimization function on the pair (op_2, op_3), reduce the dependency op_2 and then optimize the pair (op_1, op_3). However, as before our goal is to achieve the *maximum* optimization possible.

---

[2] Note that in some cases op_2 may not exist any more and hence optimizing (op_2, op_3) may no longer be possible.

We can formally show that the order of selection for pairs of schema evolution operations in a sequence for the application of one of the three optimization functions does not prevent the achievement of *maximum* optimization [6].

Confluence. While the main goal for the optimization is to achieve maximum optimization possible in an effort to reduce schema evolution costs, we also want to keep the overhead of optimizing to a minimal. However, there are multiple permutations and combinations of the optimization functions and the pairs of schema evolution operations that can potentially achieve the maximum optimization. Enumerating all the possible choices prior to selecting one for execution results in an exponential search space. This overhead from enumerating these choices alone would cancel any potential savings achieved by the optimization.

However, based on the function properties in [6], we can show that all possible combinations of optimization functions for a given sequence converge to one **unique minimal**, thereby eliminating the need to enumerate all the possible choices. The following states the theorem of confluence. We have formally and experimentally proven this result [6].

Theorem 1. [Confluence Theorem]: *Given an input schema evolution sequence, Σ_{in}, all applicable combinations of optimization functions f_i produce minimal resultant sequences Σ_i that are all exactly the same.*

7   Experimental Validation

We have conducted several experiments to not only evaluate the potential performance gains of the CHOP optimizer. Our experimental system, CHOP, was implemented as a pre-processing layer over the Persistent Storage Engine (PSE Pro2.0). All experiments were conducted on a Pentium II, 400MHz, 128Mb RAM running WindowsNT and Linux. We used a `payroll` schema (refer [6]). The schema was populated with 5000 objects per class in general or are otherwise indicated for each individual experiment. Due to lack of availability of a benchmark of typical sequences of schema evolution operations, the input sequences themselves were randomly generated sequences.

The applicability of CHOP is influenced by two criteria, the performance of the optimized vs the unoptimized sequence of schema evolution operations, and the degree of optimization achievable on average by the optimization functions of CHOP. Due to space limitations we only present a brief summary of our experimental observations. The details can be found in [6].

- The SE processing time for a sequence is directly proportional to the number of objects in the schema. Hence, for larger databases we can potentially have larger savings.
- The optimizer algorithm overhead is negligible when compared to the overall cost of performing the schema evolution operations themselves. Thus our optimization as a pre-processor offers a win-win solution for any system handling sequences of schema changes (Figure 1).

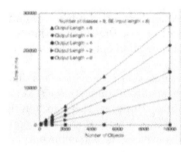

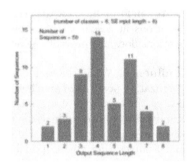

Fig. 1. Best and Worst Case Sequence Times w/o Algorithm Overhead for Input Sequences of Length 8 on the Sample Schema.

Fig. 2. Distribution: Number of Classes = Sequence Length

- The degree of optimization increases with the increase in the number of class-related operations in the sequence. Hence, depending on the type of sequence, major improvements are possible (Figure 2).
- A random application of the optimization functions on the same sequence resulted in the same final sequence of schema evolution operations.
- We have experimentally tested that on a small-sized database of 20,000 objects per class, even the removal of a single schema evolution operation on a class already results in a time saving of at least 7000 ms. This time savings is directly proportional to the number of attributes and the extent size of a class thus offering huge savings for today's larger and larger database applications.

8   Conclusions

In this paper, we have presented the first optimization strategy for schema evolution sequences. CHOP minimizes a given schema evolution sequence through the iterative elimination and cancellation of schema evolution primitives on the one hand and the merging of the database modifications of primitives on the other hand. Important results of this work are the proof of correctness of the CHOP optimization, a proof for the termination of the iterative application of these functions, and their convergence to a unique and minimal sequence. A version of this system along with the SERF system has been implemented and was presented as a demo at SIGMOD'99 [15]. We have performed experiments on a prototype system that clearly demonstrate the performance gains achievable by this optimization strategy. For random sequences an average optimization of about 68.2% was achieved.

Acknowledgments. The authors would like to thank students at the Database Systems Research Group at WPI for their interactions and feedback on this research.

References

1. J. Banerjee, W. Kim, H. J. Kim, and H. F. Korth. Semantics and Implementation of Schema Evolution in Object-Oriented Databases. *SIGMOD*, pages 311–322, 1987.
2. P. Bréche. Advanced Primitives for Changing Schemas of Object Databases. In *Conference on Advanced Information Systems Engineering*, pages 476–495, 1996.
3. R. Bretl, D. Maier, A. Otis, J. Penney, B. Schuchardt, J. Stein, E. H. Williams, and M. Williams. The GemStone Data Management System. In *Object-Oriented Concepts, Databases and Applications*, pages 283–308. ACM Press, 1989.
4. Cattell, R.G.G and et al. *The Object Database Standard: ODMG 2.0*. Morgan Kaufmann Publishers, Inc., 1997.
5. K.T. Claypool, J. Jin, and E.A. Rundensteiner. SERF: Schema Evolution through an Extensible, Re-usable and Flexible Framework. In *Int. Conf. on Information and Knowledge Management*, pages 314–321, November 1998.
6. K.T. Claypool, C. Natarajan, and E.A. Rundensteiner. Optimizing the Performance of Schema Evolution Sequences. Technical Report WPI-CS-TR-99-06, Worcester Polytechnic Institute, February 1999.
7. C. Faloutsos, R.T. Snodgrass, V.S. Subrahmanian, S. Zaniolo, C. Ceri, and R. Zicari. *Advanced Database Systems*. Morgan Kaufmann, 1997.
8. F. Ferrandina, T. Meyer, and R. Zicari. Correctness of Lazy Database Updates for an Object Database System. In *Proc. of the 6th Int'l Workshop on Persistent Object Systems*, 1994.
9. F. Ferrandina, T. Meyer, and R. Zicari. Implementing Lazy Database Updates for an Object Database System. In *Proc. of the 20th Int'l Conf. on Very Large Databases*, pages 261–272, 1994.
10. Itasca Systems Inc. Itasca Systems Technical Report. Technical Report TM-92-001, OODBMS Feature Checklist. Rev 1.1, Itasca Systems, Inc., December 1993.
11. Bo Kähler and Oddvar Risnes. Extending logging for database snapshot refresh. In Peter M. Stocker, William Kent, and Peter Hammersley, editors, *VLDB'87, Proceedings of 13th International Conference on Very Large Data Bases, September 1-4, 1987, Brighton, England*, pages 389–398. Morgan Kaufmann, 1987.
12. B.S. Lerner. A Model for Compound Type Changes Encountered in Schema Evolution. Technical Report UM-CS-96-044, University of Massachusetts, Amherst, Computer Science Department, 1996.
13. S. Marche. Measuring the Stability of Data Models. *European Journal of Information Systems*, 2(1):37–47, 1993.
14. Object Design Inc. *ObjectStore - User Guide: DML. ObjectStore Release 3.0 for UNIX Systems*. Object Design Inc., December 1993.
15. E.A. Rundensteiner, K.T. Claypool, M. Li, L. Chen, X. Zhang, C. Natarajan, J. Jin, S. De Lima, and S. Weiner. SERF: ODMG-Based Generic Re-structuring Facility. In *Demo Session Proceedings of SIGMOD'99*, pages 568–570, 1999.
16. A. Segev and J. Park. Updating Distributed Materialized Views. *IEEE Transactions on Knowledge and Data Engineering*, 1:173–184, 1989.
17. D. Sjoberg. Quantifying Schema Evolution. *Information and Software Technology*, 35(1):35–54, January 1993.
18. O₂ Technology. *O₂ Reference Manual, Version 4.5, Release November 1994*. O₂ Technology, Versailles, France, November 1994.
19. Z. Zicari. Primitives for Schema Updates in an Object-Oriented Database System: A Proposal. In *Computer Standards & Interfaces*, pages 271–283, 1991.

ODMQL: Object Data Mining Query Language

Mohamed G. Elfeky [1], Amani A. Saad, and Souheir A. Fouad

Computer Science and Automatic Control Department
Faculty of Engineering, Alexandria University, EGYPT
[1] is currently a Ph.D. student in Department of Computer Sciences, Purdue University, USA
mgelfeky@cs.purdue.edu, {amani, souheir}@alex.eun.eg

Abstract. Data mining is the discovery of knowledge and useful information from the large amounts of data stored in databases. The emerging data mining tools and systems lead to the demand of a powerful data mining query language. The concepts of such a language for relational databases are discussed before. With the increasing popularity of object-oriented databases, it is important to design a data mining query language for such databases. The main objective of this paper is to propose an Object Data Mining Query Language (ODMQL) for object-oriented databases as an extension to the Object Query Language (OQL) proposed by the Object Data Management Group (ODMG) as a standard query language for object-oriented databases. The proposed language is implemented as a feature of an experimental object-oriented database management system that is developed as a testbed for research issues of object-oriented databases.

1. Introduction

Data Mining means the discovery of knowledge and useful information from the large amounts of data stored in databases [12]. There is a lot of research that has been conducted on data mining in relational databases to mine a specific kind of knowledge such as [3, 10, 15, 17, 18, 19]. Also, there are some data mining experimental systems that have been developed for relational databases, such as DBMiner [9], Explora [14], MineSet [5], Quest [2], etc. The objective of such systems is to mine different kinds of knowledge by offering isolated discovery features. Such systems cannot be embedded into a large application and typically offer just one knowledge discovery feature [13]. The ad hoc nature of knowledge discovery queries in large applications needs an efficient query language much more general than SQL, and this query language is called Data Mining Query Language (DMQL). An example of such language in relational databases is found in [11].

Although the wide variety of advanced database systems relying deeply on the object-oriented data model, there is no data mining query language for object-oriented databases. This motivates us to propose such a language in this paper.

The rest of this paper is organized as follows. Section 2 describes the design principles of object data mining query languages. Section 3 introduces the main features of the proposed language. A formal and complete definition of the language

K.R. Dittrich et al. (Eds.): Objects and Databases 2000, LNCS 1944, pp. 128-140, 2001.
© Springer-Verlag Berlin Heidelberg 2001

is given in Section 4. Section 5 gives a large number of examples serving a wide variety of data mining requests. Section 6 discusses briefly the implementation of the language as a feature of ALEX object-oriented database management system [8, 16]. Section 7 summarizes the paper and presents different work to be done in the future.

2. Principles

The definition of data mining may imply that the two terms, Data Mining and Knowledge Discovery, have the same meaning. However, there are some trials to distinguish between those two terms since the first international KDD conference in Montreal in 1995. It was proposed that the term Knowledge Discovery in Databases (KDD) refers to the overall process of discovering useful knowledge from databases while Data Mining refers to a particular step in this process. This step considers specific algorithms for extracting specified patterns from data. The additional steps in the KDD process, which are essential before the step of data mining, are data selection, data preparation and data cleaning. Also, there is an additional step after data mining. That is the proper interpretation of the results of data mining algorithms.

Data Selection means to select the set of data in relevance to the knowledge discovery process. *Data Preparation* prepares the background knowledge helping in the data mining step. *Data Cleaning* applies some basic operations, such as the removal of noise and handling missing data fields, on data. *Interpretation* of the mined patterns involves the proper representation of the mined patterns to what may mean knowledge. It may involve visualization and/or evaluation. Hence, the main principle in designing a data mining query language is to support the specifications of four main primitives:

1. the set of data in relevance to the knowledge discovery process,
2. the background knowledge,
3. the justification of the interestingness of the knowledge (thresholds), and
4. the kind of knowledge to be discovered.

The first primitive can be specified in a way similar to that of an object query used to retrieve a set of objects from the database. The second primitive is a set of concept hierarchies which assist data mining process. The third primitive can be specified through a set of different mining thresholds depending on the kind of knowledge to be discovered, that is the fourth primitive, that can be specified by stating explicitly the type of knowledge to be mined in the current knowledge discovery process. In the next sub-sections, each one of these primitives, except the first, will be discussed in more detail.

2.1 Concept Hierarchies

A concept hierarchy defines a sequence of mappings from a set of concepts to their higher-level correspondences. Concept hierarchies represent necessary background knowledge to control the generalization process that is a preliminary step in most data mining algorithms. Generalization of an attribute means to replace its value by a higher one based on a concept hierarchy tree. For example, a person's address can be generalized from a detailed address, such as the street, into a higher leveled one, such as a district, a city, a country, etc. based on the concept hierarchy tree shown in Figure 1. Hence, generalization of an object means to generalize one or more of its properties using a pre-specified concept hierarchy tree for each property. The trees shown in Figures 1 show different levels of concepts. Note that the word *"ANY"* is a reserved word for the root of the tree. Using concept hierarchies, the knowledge mined from the database can be represented in terms of generalized concepts and stated in a simple and explicit form.

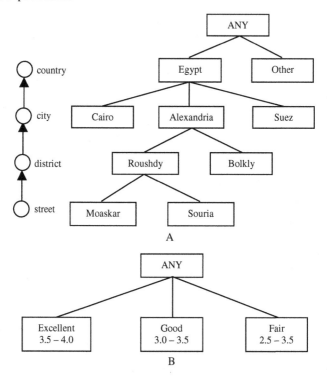

Fig. 1. (A) A concept hierarchy tree for the attribute "address".
(B) A concept hierarchy tree for the attribute "gpa".

2.2 Rules

The extracted patterns may be represented in many forms according to the data mining method used. Some of those forms are classification trees, neural networks, multidimensional regression, or more generally *rules*. An example of such rules represented in first-order predicate calculus is

x.diagnosis = "Heart" And x.sex = "Male" ==> x.age > 50 [1200 , 0.70]

indicating that there are 1200 male persons with heart attack and that 70% of them are over 50.

A rule is composed of a Body, a Consequent, a Support, and a Confidence. The *Body* of the rule is the part before the implication operator representing the examined data. The *Consequent* is what follows the implication operator representing a discovered property for the examined data. The *Support* is the value representing the number of records in the whole data satisfying the *body* clause. The *Confidence* is the value representing the percentage of the records satisfying both the *body* and the *consequent* clauses to those satisfying only the *body* clause.

There are different types of knowledge to be discovered. Hence, there are so many types of rules including Characteristic, Discriminant, Classification, Association, Data Evolution, and Deviation rules according to the data mining method applied. The literature contains so many algorithms and techniques for mining these different kinds of rules from different kinds of databases. It is beyond the scope of this paper to refer to those algorithms. However, those different kinds of rules will be defined.

A *characteristic rule* is an assertion that characterizes the concepts satisfied by all or most of the objects in the set of relevant data. For example, the symptoms of a specific disease can be summarized by a *characteristic rule*. Another example characterizing graduate students is

x.status = "Graduate" ==> (x.nationality = "Egyptian" And x.gpa > 3.5 [0.75])
x.status = "Graduate" ==> (x.nationality = "Foreign"   And x.gpa > 3.0 [0.25])

indicating that *a graduate student is either Egyptian with an excellent GPA (with 75% probability) or foreign with a good GPA (with 25% probability).* The *body* of a *characteristic rule* contains the specification of the set of relevant data being characterized, while the *consequent* contains the characterizing attribute values.

A *discriminant rule* is an assertion that discriminates concepts of two contrasting sets of data. For example, to distinguish one disease from another, a *discriminant rule* should summarize the symptoms that discriminate this disease from the other. Another example discriminating graduate students from undergraduate ones is

x.nationality = "Foreign"   And x.gpa > 3.5 ==> x.status = "Graduate" [1.00]
x.nationality = "Egyptian" And x.gpa > 3.0 ==> x.status = "Under"   [0.90]

indicating that *a foreign student with an excellent GPA is certainly a graduate, and an Egyptian student with a good GPA is an undergraduate with 90% probability.* The *consequent* of a *discriminant rule* contains the specification of one of the two contrasting sets, while the *body* contains the discriminating attribute values.

A *classification rule* is a set of rules, which classifies the set of relevant data according to one or more specific attributes. For example, a *classification rule* can classify diseases into classes and provide the symptoms of each. Another example classifying students is

x.status = "Graduate" ==> x.nationality = "Egyptian" [0.60] Or x.nationality = "Foreign"   [0.40]
x.status = "Under"   ==> x.nationality = "Egyptian" [0.85] Or x.nationality = "Foreign"   [0.15]

indicating that *regarding the status and nationality, students are either graduates (60% Egyptians and 40% foreign) or undergraduates (85% Egyptians and 15% foreign).* Each distinct value of the attribute, according to which the data is classified, must appear in the *consequent* of a rule. The *body* contains the classifying attribute values for each distinct value.

An *association rule* describes association relationships among the set of relevant data. For example, an *association rule* may discover a set of symptoms frequently occurring together. Another example is the one given in the beginning of this section.

Each attribute of the relevant set of data being examined can appear either in the *body* or in the *consequent* of the *association rule* according to its role in the rule.

A *Data Evolution Rule* reflects the general evolution behavior of the set of relevant data. Clearly, this kind of rules is valid only in time-related (temporal) data. For example, a *data evolution rule* can describe the major factors that influence the fluctuations of stock values through time. Another example is

x.term = "Previous" And x.nationality = "Egyptian" ==> x.gpa > 3.5 [0.80]
x.term = "Current" And x.nationality = "Egyptian" ==> x.gpa > 3.5 [0.70]

indicating that *in the previous term, 80% of the Egyptian students had excellent GPA, but in the current term, only 70% of the Egyptian students have excellent GPA*. A *data evolution rule* may be a characteristic rule describing the general behavior of a set of data fluctuating with time, just like the above example, or a discriminant rule comparing the behaviors of two different sets of data changing with time.

2.3 Thresholds

There are many kinds of thresholds that should be specified to control the mining process. The a*ttribute threshold* is the maximum number allowed of distinct values for an attribute in the generalized objects. It is specified independent of the kind of rules since it is considered in the generalization step before considering the kind of rules to be mined. The other kinds of thresholds depend on the specified type of rules being mined. For example, mining *association rules* should specify a *support threshold* that is the minimum support value of a rule, and a *confidence threshold* that is the minimum confidence value of a rule. Also, mining *classification rules* should specify a *classification threshold* such that further classification on a set of classified objects may become unnecessary if a substantial portion (no less than the specified threshold) of the classified objects belong to the same class.

3. Features

The proposed ODMQL allows the user (data miner) to write data mining queries and specify each primitive presented above in a an OQL-like syntax. The following sub-Sections discuss the main features of the proposed language.

3.1 Kind of Rules

The proposed ODMQL supports the specification of the kind of rules to be extracted in the current query. Certainly, the specification should include the name of this kind and some other specifications according to the specified kind. For example, mining *discriminant rules* should specify the two contrasting classes. The kinds of rules supported are *characteristic, discriminant, classification* and *association*. There is no need to support explicitly *data evolution* rules since they can be considered as any other kind of rules with the specification of one or more time-related attributes in any part of the data mining query.

Note that in the following examples, the **bold** and *italic* words indicate keywords of the language. **Bold** ones must be written, while *italic* ones are selected from alternatives. The complete syntax will be discussed in Section 4.

Example 1:   mine for *Characteristic* rules

Example 2:   mine for *Discriminant* rules
                      contrasting x.status = "Graduate" with x.status = "Under"

Example 3:   mine for *Classification* rules
                      according to x.term

3.2 Relevant Data

The set of relevant data is specified in the proposed ODMQL just like the way in OQL replacing the word "*select*" with "*with relevance to*" to follow the meaning of the data mining query.

Example 4:   mine for *Characteristic* rules
                      with relevance to x.nationality , x.gpa
                      from Student x
                      where x.status = "Graduate"

3.3 Thresholds

The proposed ODMQL supports the specification of the previously discussed thresholds. Note that each attribute could have a different *attribute threshold*. Mentioning just one *attribute threshold* means that this threshold is applied for all the attributes.

Example 5:   mine for *Association* rules
                      with relevance to x.store, x.product, x.date
                      from Sales x
                      where x.date.year = "1998"
                      with thresholds (*Attribute* = 4 , *Support* = 0.35 , *Confidence* = 0.25)

Example 6:   mine for *Characteristic* rules
                      with relevance to x.nationality , x.gpa
                      from Student x
                      where x.status = "Graduate"
                      with thresholds (*Attribute* = 3 , *Attribute* = 4)

3.4 Concept Hierarchies

The proposed ODMQL allows the user to specify concept hierarchies for the attributes of the schema. The specification includes both defining a new hierarchy, and modifying a pre-defined one. Note using the object type name before the attribute to distinguish that attribute.

Example 7:   define hierarchy for Student.major :
ANY -> { Science, Art } ,
Science -> { Biology, Chemistry, Computer } ,
Art -> { Music, Literature , ... } ,
Chemistry -> { Analytical, Biochemistry, ... } ,
Music -> { Rock, Pop, Arabic, ... }

Example 8:   define hierarchy for Student.gpa :
ANY -> { Excellent , Good , Fair } ,
Excellent -> [3.5 .. 4.0] ,
Good -> [3.0 .. 3.5] ,
Fair -> [2.5 .. 3.5]

Example 9:   modify hierarchy for Student.gpa :
delete ANY -> Fair ,
insert ANY -> { Average , Poor } ,
insert Average -> [1.5 .. 2.5] ,
insert Poor -> [0.0 .. 1.5] ,
update Good -> [2.5 .. 3.5]

Since object-oriented data model defines more data types other than numerical and string, such as collections and structures, the proposed ODMQL should allow the user to define concept hierarchies for such attributes. In the next two examples, "hobbies" is a collection attribute, and "address" is a structure attribute that has a member called "street".

Example 10:   define hierarchy for Student.hobbies :
ANY -> { Sport , Music , ... } ,
Sport -> { Football , Tennis , ... } ,
Music -> { Pop , Rock , ... }

Example 11:   define hierarchy for Student.address.street :
ANY -> { Egypt , Other } ,
Egypt -> { Cairo , Alex , Suez } ,
Alex -> { Roushdy , Bolkly } ,
Roushdy -> { Moaskar , Souria }

One of the concepts of the object-oriented database model is the *inheritance* [4], that is, a class (object type), called sub-class, can inherit the attributes and the methods of another class, so called super-class. The inheritance hierarchy describes the inheritance relationships between object types. Therefore, the inheritance hierarchy can be considered as the concept hierarchy of the entire object model. The proposed ODMQL, similar to the OQL, allows the user to reference the object itself same as an attribute. In this case, the inheritance hierarchy is automatically viewed as the concept hierarchy of this object without the need that the user defines this concept hierarchy. See Example 7 in Section 5.2.

4. Syntax

The proposed ODMQL syntax is given in an extended BNF grammar using the following notations:

- {symbol} represents zero or more occurrences of this symbol.
- [symbol] represents zero or one occurrence of this symbol.
- keyword represents a terminal of the grammar.
- <symbol> represents a non-terminal of the grammar.
- symbol1 | symbol2 represents either the first symbol or the second.

Note that in this grammar, any non-terminal without definition stands for a non-terminal of the OQL BNF presented in [6].

Grammar

```
<ODMQL> ::= <data_mining_query> | <concept_hierarchy_query>
<data_mining_query> ::= mine for <rule_specification>
                        with relevance to <projection_attributes>
                        from <variable_declaration> {, <variable_declaration>}
                        [where <query>]
                        [with threshold[s] ( <threshold> {, <threshold>} )]
<rule_specification> ::= Characteristic rules | Association rules |
                         Discriminant rules contrasting <query> with <query> |
                         Classification rules according to <projection_attributes>
<threshold> ::= <threshold_type> = <numerical_value>
<threshold_type> ::= Attribute | Support | Confidence | Classification
<concept_hierarchy_query> ::= <define_hierarchy> | <modify_hierarchy>
<define_hierarchy> ::= define hierarchy for <projection> :
                       ANY -> <concept _set> {, <concept_definition>}
<modify_hierarchy> ::= modify hierarchy for <projection> :
                       <modification> {, <modification>}
<modification> ::= delete <concept> -> <concept> |
                   insert <concept_definition> |
                   update <concept_definition>
<concept_definition> ::= <concept> -> <concept_set>
<concept_set> ::= { <concept> {, <concept>} } |
                  [ <numerical_value> .. <numerical_value> ]
<concept> ::= ANY | <string_literal>
<numerical_value> ::= <integer_literal> | <float_literal>
```

5. Examples

In this Section, we try to develop extensive examples to show the various capabilities of the proposed ODMQL. The examples presented here are grouped into two subsections, one for the *concept hierarchy* queries, and the other for the *data mining* queries.

5.1 Concept Hierarchy Queries

Example 1 shows how to define the concept hierarchy shown in Figure 1(A) for a member of a structure attribute.

Example 1:   define hierarchy for Student.address.street :
ANY -> { Egypt , Other } ,
Egypt -> { Cairo , Alex , Suez } ,
Alex -> { Roushdy , Bolkly } ,
Roushdy -> { Moaskar , Souria }

Example 2 shows how to define a concept hierarchy for a numerical attribute. Example 3 shows how to modify that previously created concept hierarchy by insertion of new concepts, deletion of pre-existing ones, and updating the values of pre-existing ones. Figure 2 shows the concept hierarchy tree before and after the modification.

Example 2:   define hierarchy for Employee.salary :
ANY -> { Low , Big } ,
Low -> [0 .. 1500] ,
Big -> [1500 .. 5000]

Example 3:   modify hierarchy for Employee.salary :
insert ANY -> { Medium , High } ,
delete ANY -> Big ,
update Low -> [0 .. 500] ,
insert Medium -> [500 .. 2000] ,
insert High -> [2000 .. 5000]

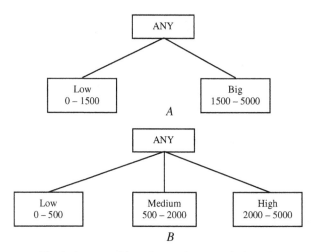

Fig. 2. A concept hierarchy tree for the attribute "salary".

5.2 Data Mining Queries

Example 4 shows a query to mine the *characteristic rules* related to the attributes "*nationality*" and "*gpa*" of the graduate students. Each attribute has its own *attribute threshold*.

Example 4:   mine for Characteristic rules
with relevance to x.nationality , x.gpa
from Student x
where x.status = "Graduate"
with threshold (Attribute = 3 , Attribute = 4)

Example 5 shows a query to mine the *discriminant rules* contrasting graduate students with undergraduates in the computer science department according to the attributes "*nationality*" and "*gpa*".

Example 5:   mine for Discriminant rules
contrasting s.status = "Graduate" with s.status = "Under"
with relevance to s.nationality , s.gpa
from Student s
where s.into.name = "cs"
with threshold (Attribute = 5 , Confidence = 0.90)

Example 6 shows a query to mine the *classification rules*, related to the attribute "*nationality*", which classify the graduate students according to their departments. Note using a path expression *s.into.id* in the *according to* clause since it is supported in the object-oriented data model. This path expression means the *department id* of this *student* since *s.into* refers to an object of the class *department* and *id* is an attribute of that class.

Example 6:   mine for Classification rules
according to s.into.id
with relevance to s.nationality
from Student s
where s.status = "Graduate"
with thresholds (Attribute = 4 , Classification = 0.85)

Example 7 shows a query to mine the *association rules*, related to the attributes "*hobbies*", "*age*" and the object identifier of the department class, considering only the graduate students. Note using two classes in the *from* clause and an explicit join condition in the *where* clause. Note also the possibility to use a set-valued attribute "*hobbies*" and a method "*age*" which calculates the age from the attribute "*birth_date*". Note also that mentioning the object itself in the relevance attributes means the object identifier that is generalized using the inheritance hierarchy.

Example 7:   mine for Association rules
with relevance to s.hobbies , d , s.age ( )
from Student s , Department d
where (s.status = "Graduate") And (s.into.id = d.id)
with thresholds (Attribute = 4 , Support = 0.75 , Confidence = 0.85)

Example 8 shows a query to mine the *discriminant rules* contrasting the sales performed in 1998 with those performed in 1997 according to the attributes "*store*" and *"product"*. Those rules may be considered as *data evolution rules* comparing the behaviors of some data in two contrasting times.

Example 8:   mine for Discriminant rules
contrasting x.date.year = "1998" with x.date.year = "1997"
with relevance to x.store , x.product
from Sales x
with threshold (Attribute = 5)

6. Implementation

The proposed Object Data Mining Query Language (ODMQL) is a simple language used to mine knowledge from object-oriented databases. Integration of such language into the ALEX object-oriented database management system [8] makes it possible to examine this language and extract knowledge from object-oriented databases. ALEX is a continuous research project whose objective is to build an OODBMS that follows the standards put forward by the Object Data Management Group (ODMG) to be used as a testbed for developing and evaluating different query processing algorithms, indexing techniques, clustering techniques, and data mining tools for Object-Oriented Databases.

The ALEX system enables the user to define the object database model through an Object Definition Language (ODL), and to build queries about the data through an Object Query Language (OQL). Also, the system enables the user to write the object methods code using the *C++* language, and to call these methods through the OQL.

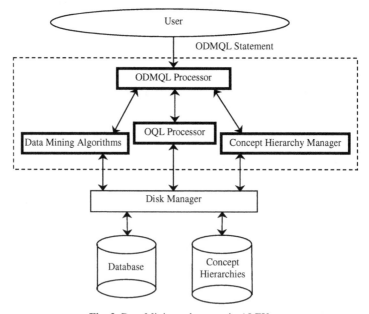

Fig. 3. Data Mining subsystem in ALEX.

The proposed language is integrated into ALEX by implementing an ODMQL processor that executes the data mining statements (Figure 3). The ODMQL processor includes a parser that parses the statements, a concept hierarchy manager that manipulates the concept hierarchies, and data mining techniques to mine the different kinds of rules supported. The ODMQL processor uses the OQL processor to retrieve the set of relevant objects that will participate in the current data mining process.

7. Conclusion and Future Work

In this paper, a new query language for mining object-oriented databases is proposed. The concepts and features of this language are outlined, and its syntax grammar is presented. Also, some examples of queries written in that language are encountered. Finally, the implementation of this language is discussed.

This language can be extended to support other kinds of knowledge that can be discovered from databases such as data deviations and clusters.

Other kinds of databases such as spatial databases, multimedia databases and video databases must be examined to discuss the design of data mining query languages for them.

References

1. R. Agrawal, T. Imielinski, and A. Swami. Mining Association Rules between Sets of Items in Large Databases. In *Proceedings of 1993 ACM-SIGMOD International Conference on Management of Data*, pages 207-216, May 1993.
2. R. Agrawal, M. Mehta, J. Shafer, R. Srikant, A. Arning, and T. Bollinger. The Quest Data Mining System. In *Proceedings of 1996 International Conference on Data Mining and Knowledge Discovery (KDD'96)*, pages 244-249, Portland, Oregon, August 1996.
3. R. Agrawal and R. Srikant. Fast Algorithms for Mining Association Rules. In *Proceedings of 1994 International Conference on Very Large Databases*, pages 487-499, Santiago, Chile, September 1994.
4. E. Bertino and L. Martino. *Object-Oriented Database Systems*. Addison-Wesley, 1994.
5. C. Brunk, J. Kelly, and R. Kohavi. MineSet: An Integrated System for Data Mining. In *Proceedings of Third International Conference on Data Mining and Knowledge Discovery (KDD'97)*, pages 135-138, Newport Beach, California, August 1997.
6. R.G.G. Cattell. *The Object Database Standard: ODMG-93 (Release 1.2)*. Morgan Kaufmann, 1996.
7. U. Fayyad, G. Piatetsky-Shapiro, and P. Smyth. From Data Mining to Knowledge Discovery: An Overview. In U. Fayyad, G. Piatetsky-Shapiro, P. Smyth, and R. Uthurusamy, editors, *Advances in Knowledge Discovery and Data Mining*, pages 1-34. AAAI / MIT Press, 1996.
8. S.A. Fouad, A.A. Saad, and M.G. Elfeky. ALEX Object-Oriented Database Management System. Published in *ICCTA'99 International Conference on Computers: Theory and Applications*, Alexandria, Egypt, August 1999.

9. J. Han, J. Chiang, S. Chee, J. Chen, Q. Chen, S. Cheng, W. Gong, M. Kamber, G. Liu, K. Koperski, Y. Lu, N. Stefanovic, L. Winstone, B. Xia, O.R. Zaiane, S. Zhang, and H. Zhu. DBMiner: A System for Data Mining in Relational Databases and Data Warehouses. In *Proceedings of CASCON'97*, Toronto, Canada, November 1997.
10. J. Han and Y. Fu. Discovery of Multiple-Level Association Rules from Large Databases. In *Proceedings of 1995 International Conference on Very Large Databases*, pages 420-431, Zurich, Switzerland, September 1995.
11. J. Han, Y. Fu, W. Wang, K. Koperski, and O. Zaiane. DMQL: A Data Mining Query Language for Relational Databases. *1996 SIGMOD'96 Workshop on Research Issues on Data Mining and Knowledge Discovery (DMKD'96)*, Montreal, Canada, June 1996.
12. J. Han, S. Nishio, H. Kawano, and W. Wang. Generalized-Based Data Mining in Object-Oriented Databases Using an Object Cube Model. In *Data and Knowledge Engineering*, 25(1-2), pages 55-97, 1998.
13. T. Imielinski and H. Mannila. A Database Perspective on Knowledge Discovery. In *Communications of the ACM*, No. 11, pages 58-64, November 1996.
14. W. Klösgen. Explora: A Multipattern and Multistrategy Discovery Assistant. In U. Fayyad, G. Piatetsky-Shapiro, P. Smyth, and R. Uthurusamy, editors, *Advances in Knowledge Discovery and Data Mining*, pages 249-271. AAAI / MIT Press, 1996.
15. M. Mehta, R. Agrawal, and J. Rissanen. SLIQ: A Fast Scalable Classifier for Data Mining. In *Proceedings of 1996 International Conference on Extending Database Technology*, Avignon, France, March 1996.
16. A.A. Saad and G.M. Badr. The ALEX Object Manager. In *Proceedings of ISCC'97 Second IEEE Symposium on Computers and Communications*, pages 200-204, Alexandria, Egypt, July 1997.
17. R. Srikant and R. Agrawal. Mining Generalized Association Rules. In *Proceedings of 1995 International Conference of Very Large Databases*, pages 407-419, Zurich, Switzerland, September 1995.
18. L. Winstone, W. Wang and J. Han. Multiple-Level Data Classification in Large Databases. Submitted for publication, March 1996.
19. T. Zhang, R. Ramakrishnan, and M. Livny. BIRCH: An Efficient Data Clustering Method for Very Large Databases. In *Proceedings of 1996 ACM-SIGMOD International Conference on Management of Data*, Montreal, Canada, June 1996.

Benefits of an Object-Oriented Multidimensional Data Model

Alberto Abelló[1], José Samos[2], and Fèlix Saltor[1]

[1] U. Politècnica de Catalunya (UPC), Dept. de Llenguatges i Sistemes Informàtics
{aabello,saltor}@lsi.upc.es
[2] U. de Granada (UGR), Dept. de Lenguajes y Sistemas Informáticos
jsamos@ugr.es

Abstract. In this paper, we try to outline the goodness of using an O-O model on designing multidimensional Data Marts. We argue that multidimensional modeling is lacking in semantics, which can be obtained by using the O-O paradigm. Some benefits that could be obtained by doing this are classified in six O-O-Dimensions (i.e. Classification/Instantiation, Generalization/Specialization, Aggregation/De-composition, Behavioural, Derivability, and Dynamicity), and exemplified with specific cases.

Keywords: Object-Oriented Data Model, Semantics, Multidimensionality, Data Marts

1 Introduction

Data warehousing is a relatively new research area. W. Inmon is considered the father of the "Data Warehouse" (DW), whose definition can be read in [7]: "A data warehouse is a subject oriented, integrated, non-volatile, and time variant collection of data in support of management's decisions". Note that the definition does not refer to the size of the warehouse. However, if it is integrated and we assume that its scope is the whole corporation, it will contain a huge volume of data. Smaller storage systems, called "Data Marts" (DMs), with the same characteristics but devoted to satisfy the needs of a reduced set of users, are defined in order to improve response times. The DMs are customized to obtain good query performance (most of times by means of a query-driven design).

Closely related to the DMs are OLAP (On-Line Analytical Processing) applications, which, as said in [10], are intended for "Fast Analysis of Shared Multidimensional Information" by using the data contained in DMs. Multidimensionality is just a design technique that separates the information into facts (what we want to analize) and dimensions (what we use to analize the facts). It gives rise to schemas with star shape (like that one depicted in figure 1(a)), having the abstraction representing the facts in the middle, and the analysis dimensions around it. The fact in a multidimensional schema is the entity containing the measures to be analyzed (mainly numeric attributes). The analysis dimensions

K.R. Dittrich et al. (Eds.): Objects and Databases 2000, LNCS 1944, pp. 141–152, 2001.

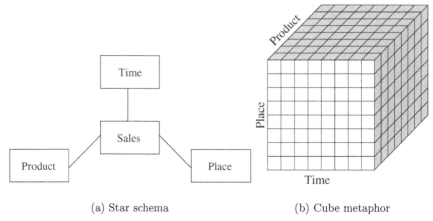

(a) Star schema   (b) Cube metaphor

Fig. 1. Multidimensional modeling

are the points of view that will be used to analyze the fact, and mainly contain descriptive attributes that describe it. Frequently, the "Data Cube" metaphor (depicted in figure 1(b)) is used to explain multidimensionality. Each cell in the cube represents a unit of data (for instance, in the example above, *Sales* as the intersection of a *Product*, *Place*, and *Time*). A given position in every analysis dimension, by defining a position in the space, allows you to select exactly one of those cells. This kind of representation is close to the analysis concepts, and eases the usage of the data by final users.

Multidimensional modeling tries, on the one hand, to make the data schemas understadable to final users, and on the other hand, to improve query performance. The way to do it is by simplifying the data schemas, so that they only contain the essential things (i.e. a fact to be analyzed and its analysis dimensions). These schemas are close to the analysts conception of data, and suggest a specific kind of queries, so that the system can be easly customized to solve them with good response times.

One of the main focus of data warehousing and OLAP literature is on improving query response times. Always having performance on mind, the direct design of logical (usually Relational) schemas, skipping conceptual modeling, is well accepted. A survey of logical models is in [16]. Very few publications recognize the importance of conceptual design in this area. The existence of one fact table related by foreign keys to other flat, denormalized tables (one for each analysis dimension) is encouraged in the literature (see [8]). By denormalizing the dimension tables, unnecessary joins are avoided, adding a little redundancy (with regard to the size of the fact table). However, other people argue for some kind of conceptual modeling (usually by means of E/R, like [5], [13], [15]). Others even propose the usage of semantically richer models (e.g. description logics in [6], or O-O in [4], [14]).

Leaving aside the importance of performance, and paying special attention to conceptual design, in [2], we proposed a seven layers conceptual schemas architecture to integrate the DW in a federation of databases. It allowed us to see everything in a different context. Since [12] found O-O models as good "Canonical Data Models" for a federation (from a semantic point of view), we suggested the usage of a multidimensional O-O model to conceptually design the DMs. In next sections, we go further discussing the advantages of using the O-O paradigm in multidimensional design. In this paper, we are not proposing a new multidimensional model. The aim is just to outline how the O-O paradigm could be used to help multidimensional modeling by giving some examples.

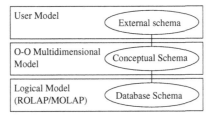

Fig. 2. Three-level schemas

In figure 2, it can be seen the level where the discussion is located. We are not interested neither in the best user model, nor the best kind of database to use (either ROLAP -Relational OLAP-, MOLAP -Multidimensional OLAP-, or even O3LAP -Object Oriented OLAP- presented in [3] could be good). What we want is to present the benefits of an O-O data model to integrate the different multidimensional views and keep the semantics of the data at the conceptual level. If the user wishes to use a different one, it could always be translated to the desired model (maybe due to the tools being used). The same can be said about the internal level, the usage of an O-O multidimensional model does not imply we are storing the data in an O-O database.

Probably, the most important advantage of conceptualizing (multidimensionaly or not) the Universe of Discurs (UoD) by means of an O-O model is that the result is closer to the user conception. It reflects people's way of thinking. Every object or class modeled will have a correspondence with some UoD entity, making it quite easy to be understood. We can find other, not that abstract, benefits in the O-O paradigm, like the usage of Object Identifiers (OIDs), that solves the identification problem of being using keys; the allowance to use Non-First Normal Form (NF^2), which means the design of objects containing non-atomic values; semantics, an Object-Oriented model is semantically richer than others (for instance E/R or Relational); or even its proximity to Object-Oriented Software Engineering, which, for instance, eases some specific tasks like designing a Distributed Object System.

This paper is structured as follows: in section 2, six O-O-Dimensions (i.e. Classification/Instantiation, Generalization/Specialization, Aggregation/Decomposition, Behavioural, Derivability, and Dynamicity) are presented, and their usage in multidimensional modeling, one by one, is exemplified; the paper ends with some conclusions, acknowledgements, and references.

2   Benefits by O-O-Dimension

"Expressiveness" or "Semantic Power", as it is defined in [12], is the degree to which a model can express or represent a conception of the real world. It measures the power of the structures of the model to represent conceptual structures, and to be interpreted as such conceptual structures. The most expressive a model is, the better it represents the real world, and the more information about the data gives to the user.

In [11], there were enumerated six O-O-Dimensions (i.e. Classification/Instantiation, Generalization/Specialization, Aggregation/Decomposition, Behavioural, Derivability, and Dynamicity). Each one of these O-O-Dimension adds a little of Semantic Power to a data model. We are going to see how each one of them helps multidimensional modeling, by allowing to represent different relationships among data.

Along these sections, we call nexus any relationship (tagged or not) between two objects. Usually, it is graphically represented by arrows. The nexus are specialized for every one of the O-O-Dimension to obtain the different meanings.

2.1   Classification/Instantiation

This O-O-Dimension distinguishes between the occurrences and the schema. Every instance is related to, at least, a class in the schema by nexus in this O-O-Dimension. All instances sharing some attributes, and representing related concepts are grouped into a given class. In the same way, all elements in a schema (i.e. classes, nexus, ...) representing related concepts in a data model are grouped into a metaclass. To finish the recurrence, all metaclasses can be grouped into exactly one metametaclass, which is instance of itself. Of special interest in this dimension, present in all data models in one way or another, is the dynamic and multiple classification, explained in [9].

Dynamic classification refers to the ability of the instances to change the class they belong to. If we want to analize the sales depending on the goodness of our clients, and we have them classified into different classes, it is a matter of time we want to move a given client from a class to a different (hopefully better) one. We cannot delete the instance of the client in the database and create a new one in the new desired class because we would get a new identity (OID) for it. That is not what we want to represent, we did not lose a client and found a new one. It was just our consideration (classification) about a client what actually changed, and that is exactly what the data model should be able to represent.

On the other hand, multiple classification refers to the possibility of having an instance classified in more than one class (not related by Generalization/Specialization nexus) at the same time. For instance, it is absolutely possible to have a client as provider at the same time. Since there is not any relationship between the *Clients* and *Providers* classes, we need to have the same instance classified at both of them (multiply classified).

These characteristics are always desirable. Specifically in the field of data warehousing, the words "non-volatile" and "time variant", together with the OLAP need of analyzing relatively long periods of time, emphasizes their importance. Dynamic and Multiple Classification are really interesting due to the flexibility needed to represent the big amount of changes present along the long period of time that uses to be taken into account in analysis tasks.

2.2   Generalization/Specialization

Another O-O-Dimension is that of Generalization/Specialization relationships. The nexus in this O-O-Dimension relate two classes (or metaclasses). One of those classes has a more specific meaning than the other. The more general class is called "Superclass" with regard to the specific one, referred as "Subclass". As a consequence of this kind of nexus, we obtain inheritance. That is, the Subclass inherits the properties and methods of its Superclass (or Superclasses). If it is allowed to have more than one Superclass, we gain multiple inheritance (a class inherits from all its Superclasses at a time). Every class will have (besides its own attributes) the attributes and relationships of each one of its Superclasses. Note this is absolutely different from Multiple Classification where an instance is classified in multiple classes.

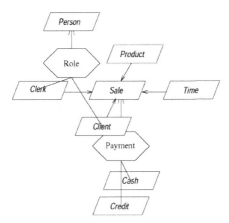

Fig. 3. Sales example

In figure 3, we can see an example of a multidimensional schema[1]. It has *Sales* as fact, and *Clerk, Time, Product,* and *Client* as analysis dimensions. Thus, the subject of analysis is *Sales,* and we want to analyze it depending on the clerk who sold, the moment it was done, the product sold and the client who bought. Besides that basic information, other details are also represented by means of nexus in this O-O-Dimension:

- the *Sales* fact is specialized in two different facts (i.e. *Cash,* and *Credit*) depending on the kind of payment, and
- two analysis dimensions (i.e. *Clerk,* and *Client*) are related by generalizing them in the same class (*Person*).

Specializing facts, you can generate new data cubes (if they contain any different data), or, at least, show a criteria to select the facts involved in the analysis. In our example, if *Sales* would have different attributes depending on the kind of payment, we would obtain three different cubes to be analyzed i.e. two containing the measures specific to each kind of payment, and another one with those measures shared by both of them. Conversely, if it would not have any other attribute but those common to both kinds of payment, we could analyze the *Sales* cube depending on whether the payment was done by cash, or by credit card. This could also be achieved by just adding an attribute to the facts, but it would give a slightly different tint.

With regard to relating two analysis dimensions, it shows a common domain between them, so that it is allowed to compare the classes, or restrict both at the same time. In the example, the analyst could formulate queries comparing instances of *Client* and *Clerk,* because the data schema shows both as Subclasses of the same class (i.e. *Person*). Moreover, we can consider the possibility of class *Person* being used in a different multidimensional schema, which would become directly related to that of *Sales* by means of the generalization nexus between the analysis dimensions. This would point out the relationship between facts, easing the navigation through the data.

2.3   Aggregation/Decomposition

By means of this O-O-Dimension, it is possible to build new objects as result of the aggregation of others, which in turn can be aggregations, as well. We distinguish two different nexus belonging to it. Attending to their strength, a nexus in the Aggregation/Decomposition O-O-Dimension can denote:

Composition, if the new object is conceived as composed by others, which are its parts. This is called "Part-Whole Relation" by some authors, and implies an existence dependency between both sides of the nexus (i.e. the whole cannot exists without its parts).

---

[1] The syntax used in the example schemas along this paper is that of BLOOM99, and can be found in [1]

Simple Aggregation, if the aggregating objects are just characteristics of the new one. They could have an existence dependency too, but it is not an implication of the existence of the nexus itself.

The usage of this O-O-Dimension in multidimensional design is mandatory. It helps to represent some of the most common situations, and other maybe not so common:

- Firstly, it helps to define the analysis dimension hierarchies by means of Composition links. A dimension hierarchy must be a lattice with the class corresponding to the maximum level of detail in the facts at the bottom, and a class representing the whole set of points in the dimension at the top. In between, we have other levels corresponding to different data granularities. For instance, if we collect data hourly, the time analysis dimension would have *Hours* class at the bottom, which would compose *Days* above it, which would give raise to *Weeks* and *Months*, and so forth. The lattice would be closed at the top by an *Eternity* class containing exactly one instance representing all time points in the database. These hierarchies are used to roll-up the data in the database, augmenting its granularity. Moving a query up (e.g. rolling-up from days to months) or down (e.g. drilling-down from months to weeks) along a hierarchy we obtain more or less detail in the data.
- On the other hand, using any kind of aggregation, we can relate either analysis dimensions classes or facts classes to their attributes. These attributes will be used to ease the selection of facts to be considered in a given analysis by allowing to group them depending on the values.
- Nexus between the facts class and the bottom classes in every dimension hierarchy are aggregation nexus, as well. They can be Composition or Simple Aggregation nexus, but whether denoting composition or not, a fact will be identified by exactly one object at each linked analysis dimension (or more than one if the dimension has more than one nexus with the facts class). Thus, the nexus with the analysis dimensions will form the class-key of the facts, and that is what really distinguishes them from other attributes. In figure 3, we associate a sale with a point in the 4-dimensional space defined by dimensions *Clerk*, *Time*, *Product*, and *Client*. Therefore, *Sales* functionally depends on those four dimensions.
- Finally, Composition relationships can be found between facts classes. By reflecting them in the schema, we will allow the navigation between them.

The example in figure 4 depicts two facts classes, sharing some analysis dimensions, and related by a Composition nexus. The first facts class is that of *Flight*. We are interested in analyzing each flight depending on the time it takes place, the airline company that owns the plane, and its origin and destination airports (it is related to the corresponding analysis dimensions by Simple Aggregation nexus). At the same time, we want to analyze the sequences of flights that give rise to whole trips sold by travel agencies. *Trip* and *Flight* being connected by a composition nexus represents the fact that an instance of *Trip* is composed of a set of instances of *Flight*. *Trip* is also connected to the corresponding analysis dimensions by Simple Aggregation nexus. Moreover, it is important to

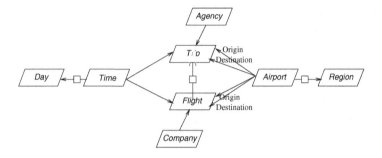

Fig. 4. Traveling example

notice that two of those dimensions contain more than one class, connected by Composition nexus. A *Region* is composed of a set of *Airport*s, in the same way that a *Day* is a set of *Time*s.

In order to keep it simple and understandable, the example does not contain the nexus representing the attributes of the facts and dimension classes, which would belong to the Aggregation/Decomposition O-O-Dimension, as well. Because of the same reason, the four classes at the top of each one of the analysis dimension hierarchies are not depicted (i.e. in the time dimension, the *Eternity* class mentioned above). These classes always exist and contain exactly one instance corresponding to the whole set of instances in the lowest granularity level of the dimension. Therefore, one can infer them.

2.4   Behavioural (Caller/Called)

In O-O, the objects interchange messages. A class accepts certain kinds of messages from instances of other classes, which trigger the execution of methods (i.e. queries, updates, calculations, etc.). The nexus in this Behavioural O-O-Dimension, also known as "Caller/Called", show when a class is allowed to invoke a given method in another class.

As pointed out in [4], Relational entities represent tables, purely passive containers for data, and since they are not real objects, are independent of behaviours. The inclusion of methods in the data model helps to model the behaviour together with the data. It looks like a bad idea to have two different, separated models for statics and dynamics. Specifically, in multidimensional modeling, by associating operations to a domain, we will be able to know which aggregation functions can be used on a given fact measure. For instance, as explained in [5], we can find semi-additive attributes (those that are not additive along one or more dimensions), or non-additive attributes (which are additive along no dimension). *Temperature* should be marked as non-additive (nobody could call an additive method on it), and *Inventory level* as semi-additive, since it cannot always be added (e.g. along *Time* dimension). It does not imply that other aggregation operations could be applied on those measures. Therefore, we need to show the applicability of every different operation.

Moreover, methods facilitate the implementation of complex aggregate functions. In an analysis environment, it is important to keep track of the way the measures are obtained. It is not advisable to allow the users to implement their own ad hoc functions. It is error prone, and drive to misunderstandings. O-O concepts such as inheritance, polymorphism, or encapsulation look really nice at this point. For instance, suppose we would like to obtain the delay of a flight, defined as the difference between the expected and real durations (actually, not a complex function). The problem could arise if the expected duration of the flight were kept as a time interval. If this is the case, the difference could be done by subtracting the minimum, maximum, or even midpoint expected duration, which result in completely different values. Probably, it does not matter how it is obtained, but we must ensure it is always calculated in the same, easy to change way to be able to compare the obtained values among different users or even sessions.

Leaving those considerations aside, this O-O-Dimension is also important because of security reasons, but that is completely out of the scope of this paper.

2.5 Derivability

"Semantic Relativism" of a data model is defined in [12] as the degree to which the model can accommodate not only one, but many different conceptions. It is really important because since different persons perceive and conceive the world in different ways, the data model should be able to capture all of them.

The Derivability O-O-Dimension, also known as "Point of View", helps to represent the relationships between abstractions in different conceptions of the UoD. The database does not need to physically keep all those conceptions, but only their definitions and different relationships among them. In general, it is not good to store derived data (unless because of performance reasons, not considered in this paper). What we do really need to store is that derived data exists and how it is obtained. Here is the importance of this O-O-Dimension. Derivation mechanisms can be used to easily restructure the schemas to show them in the way the user wants, in order to be closer to his/her thoughts. Summing up, it is used to define derived data.

Some analysts do not mind whether a data is atomically stored in the database or not. In this sense, it is desirable that either derived or atomic measures are treated equally. However, others would like to know how measures are obtained. Therefore, the definition of the derived measures should be in the schema of the database, as Relational views are. It allows either to hide the complexity, or to know where something comes from, depending on the user needs. At the same time, as in the Behavioural O-O-Dimension, this also makes possible that groups of users have available the same definitions.

In multidimensional modeling, it is specially important to have the powerful possibilities offered by this O-O-Dimension. When a fact is being analyzed, what really matters is to be able to see it from as many points of view as possible. Therefore, it is crucial to have the mechanisms to define those different views of the data. For instance, all summarized data is related to its detail data by a nexus in this O-O-Dimension. If we did not have it, we would not have any kind of summarized data.

Going back to our example in figure 4, we can see that the *origin* of a *Trip* would be derived from the *origins* of the *Flights* that compose it, by taking the first one; *destination* would be defined in the same way; the duration of a *Trip* would be function of the duration and taking off times of the different *Flights*; and so on.

2.6   Dynamicity

This O-O-Dimension refers to changes along time. We consider these changes at three different levels:

Object Objects are created, deleted, and also updated. Keeping the history of those updates is often referred as "Versioning".

Class As well as the objects, the data schema can be updated, too. New classes are created, old ones are deleted, and others just modified in what is called "Schema Evolution".

Metaclass In the same way we can modify classes, we can add new metaclasses (notice we can neither modify nor delete them). This means having an "Extensible Data Model".

If we just wanted to represent the current reality, we would not need to consider Dynamicity O-O-Dimension. However, it is common to need past states. Therefore, changes need to be kept, and often stamped with some kind of time tag to know when they happened.

In multidimensional analysis tasks, time is an omnipresent dimension. Moreover, to worsen it, analysts frequently consider a scale of years. If we add how fast things change nowadays, we can see the importance of this O-O-Dimension for multidimensional modeling. It is almost impossible to find a business that has not changed at all in the last three or five years, and those changes must be reflected in the corresponding information system. Leaving aside changes in metaclasses, we want to see the need of considering the other two kinds of changes (i.e. those in objects and classes).

The importance of user requirements makes Schema Evolution an important issue. When the user requirements or conceptions change, it is advisable to change the data schema in accordance with them. A change in a class or nexus should be shown in the schema by connecting the old an the new version with a Dynamicity nexus. By doing it, the analist can easily see the available data, and the meaning of the results he is obtaining. For instance, when the definition of a derived measure changes, the analyst is able to compare the results using the new and the old definitions. Moreover, if some attribute is not kept any more, or a new one is added, the analist can know whether it can be queried or not at a given point in time.

The problem of changes in the data is referred in [8] as "Slowly Changing Dimensions". It arises when attributes in analysis dimension classes are modified. The old values must be kept, because the facts previous to the change are probably still related to them, while the new ones will be referred by the facts occurring from now on. However, both instances represent the same entity in reality, and it has to be outlined by a nexus between them. Clearly, if an airport increases its number of tracks, it would be incorrect to analyze the air traffic previous to the enlargement with regard to the new number of tracks. Therefore, we need to have two instances of the same airport related by a Dynamicity nexus showing that they represent the same object.

3   Conclusions

Along the paper we have introduced the problematic of multidimensional modeling. Probably because of the interest of the industry in the subject, it is being mainly developed in a specially commercial way. This means stressing performance, and passing over semantics and conceptual modeling. Multidimensional semantics are really important because of their proximity to the inherent structure of the problem domain, but they are not the only ones to be represented. Other semantics should not be forgotten. It is not enough having an isolated multidimensional schema reflecting how the user will access the information, leaving aside the representation of other data relationships.

We have shown the applicability of six O-O-Dimensions (i.e. Classification/ Instantiation, Generalization/Specialization, Aggregation/Decomposition, Behavioural, Derivability, and Dynamicity) to semantically enrich multidimensional schemas, by exemplifying how they could be used to interelate and integrate some of those schemas. This is a really important point since most people consider isolated star schemas composed by a central fact table, and different flat, denormalized dimension tables arranged around it, each one related to the central table by a foreign key. That is not a bad idea at all, but we are sure there is much more information about the data subject of analysis that the schema could contain, which would be really useful to the analysts, users of the system.

For the sake of simplicity and understandability, the stars use to be represented in an isolated manner. We have tried to stress the necessity of providing an overall view of the data. Multidimensional analysis is used in decision making processes. Therefore, the most global view is provided, the more the schema helps the users. It is really important to offer an integrated vision of the business or subject of analysis, in order to give the analist a unified set of data instead of lots of puzzle pieces. We have proposed to relate the puzzle pieces by means of nexus in the different O-O-Dimensions.

As a future work, we plan to add multidimensional semantics to a semantically rich data model (i.e. BLOOM, which syntax is described in [1], and has been used along this paper). Previously, the role of the O-O-Dimensions in multidimensional design has to be studied in more depth. Moreover, it would be interesting to find patterns in a semantically rich data schema that suggest the possibility of a multidimensional analysis.

Acknowledgements. This work has been partially supported by the Spanish Research Program PRONTIC under projects TIC99-1078-C02-01 and TIC99-1078-C02-02, as well as the grant 1998FI-00228 from the Generalitat de Catalunya.

References

1. A. Abelló, M. Oliva, E. Rodríguez, and F. Saltor. The syntax of BLOOM99 schemas. Technical Report LSI-99-34-R, Dept. Llenguatges i Sistemes Informàtics, Universitat Politècnica de Catalunya, 1999.
2. A. Abelló, M. Oliva, J. Samos, and F. Saltor. Information System Architecture for Secure Data Warehousing. In *Proceedings of the Third Int. Workshop on Engineering Federated Information Systems (EFIS'2000)*, Dublin (Ireland), June 2000.
3. J. W. Buzydlowski, I. Song, and L. Hassell. Framework for Object-Oriented Online Analytical Processing. In *Int. Workshop on Data Warehousing and OLAP (DOLAP)*, 1998.
4. J. M. Firestone. Object–Oriented Data Warehousing. Technical report, Executive Information Systems, Inc., 1997. White Paper No. Five.
5. M. Golfarelli, D. Maio, and S. Rizzi. Conceptual Design of Data Warehouses from E/R Schemes. In *Proceedings of the Hawaii Int. Conference On System Sciences*, 1998.
6. Mohand-Saïd Hacid and Ulrike Sattler. An object-centered multi-dimensional data model with hierarchically structured dimensions. In *Proceedings of the IEEE Knowledge and Data Engineering Workshop, Newport Beach, CA, USA*, pages 65–72. IEEE Computer Society, November 1997.
7. W. H. Inmon. *Building the Data Warehouse*. John Wiley & Sons, second edition, 1996.
8. Ralph Kimball. *The Data Warehouse toolkit*. John Wiley & Sons, 1996.
9. J. Martin and J. Odell. *Object-Oriented Methods: Pragmatic Considerations*. Prentice-Hall, 1996.
10. N. Pendse. The OLAP report. Bussiness Intelligence Ltd., 1999. http://www.olapreport.com/fasmi.htm.
11. F. Saltor. Semántica de datos. In *Panorama Informático*, pages 39–64. Federación Española de Sociedades de Informática (FESI), 1996.
12. F. Saltor, M. Castellanos, and M. García-Solaco. Suitability of Data Models as Canonical Models for Federated DBs. *ACM SIGMOD Record*, 20(4):44–48, 1991.
13. C. Sapia, M. Blaschka, G. Hoefling, and B. Dinter. Extending the E/R Model for the Multidimensional Paradigm. *Lecture Notes in Computer Science*, 1552:105–116, 1999. ER Workshops 1998.
14. J. C. Trujillo and M. Palomar. An Object-Oriented Approach to Multidimensional Database Conceptual Modeling. In *Int. Workshop on Data Warehousing and OLAP (DOLAP)*, 1998.
15. N. Tryfona, F. Busborg, and J. Christiansen. starER: A Conceptual Model for Data Warehouse Design. In *Int. Workshop on Data Warehousing and OLAP (DOLAP)*, pages 3–8, 1999.
16. P. Vassiliadis and T. Sellis. A Survey of Logical Models for OLAP Databases. *ACM SIGMOD Record*, 28(4):64–69, December 1999.

The NODS Project: Networked Open Database Services

Christine Collet

ENSIMAG-INPG, LSR-IMAG Lab,
BP 72 38402 Saint-Martin d'Hères, France.
Christine.Collet@imag.fr,
http://www-lsr.imag.fr/Les.Personnes/Christine.Collet

Abstract. This paper introduces the NODS project been currently conducted at the LSR-IMAG laboratory, Grenoble – France. NODS aims at defining an open, adaptable, evolutionary architecture that can be extended and customized on a per-application basis. A database system is seen as an infrastructure comprised of co-operating adaptable and extensible services from which applications can build their customized NODS database components. Furthermore, services or database systems configuration can be adapted at runtime (e.g., add new services, change services internal policies), according to environmental changes.

1 Introduction

1.1 Motivations

Large-scale distributed information systems with petabytes of data and thousands of users are now a reality. Such systems access large sources of structured, semi-structured or non-structured data under several formats (digitalized, multimedia). Data of different sizes are stored in databases, files or devices (clocks, radio, television, cell phones, heat control, etc.) all around the world. Applications are built from distributed components accessing and manipulating these data. Some applications manage quite small sets of data (databases!) included in Personal Information Systems, and do not want to pay the overhead of a full database system, while others should be able to handle (at the same time) from petabytes to yottabytes (10^{24}) of data and numerous connections including mobile ones. Thus, to be usable as highly distributed components, database systems should be able to adapt and scale themselves to several kinds of data, different sizes of databases, amounts of queries and complex environments.

The classical client-server architectures are not anymore suitable. Applications now follow the three-tier architecture (thick middleware). The software running at the server level (the database system) and the one running in the middle tier have to process a huge number of interactions/operations with data sources and users with very high availability, security and fault tolerance. Mobile bases will be connected to "control" servers. So, there will be hundreds of

K.R. Dittrich et al. (Eds.): Objects and Databases 2000, LNCS 1944, pp. 153–169, 2001.
© Springer-Verlag Berlin Heidelberg 2001

thousands of servers (of data and applications) and clients that cooperate. Also clients may play the role of (thin) servers.

To summarize, flexible and reactive networked information systems require infrastructures for making tools, services, software components and database functions inter-operate. Inter-operation should be efficient, with timely responses and it must preserve components autonomy. Programming such systems also needs specific environments and tools.

From the database point of view, we claim that future database software (i.e., applications, systems) can no longer be monolithic. Database technology is evolving towards cooperation and integration. Having database components that inter-operate, being self-tuned, scalable, highly available, adaptable and extensible is a new challenge. Such components should be implemented taking into account advances on hardware (RAID disks), operating systems (extensible and adaptable, 64-bit addressing), networks (high speed, with QoS) and parallel architectures (SMP machines).

1.2   Objectives

Capitalizing on our previous experiences on object-oriented, active and multi-media systems [42,23,2,61,24,30] we define the NODS project whose major goal is to investigate the construction of future database systems from Networked and Open Distributed Database Services (NODS services). As suggested in [57] we propose to (i) unbundling database systems for providing services of various granularities, and (ii) consider how such services can co-operate on a middleware.

Instead of proposing a "one-size-fits-all" set of software modules or services (communication and concurrency protocols, persistence, replication policies, etc.), NODS aims at defining an open, adaptable, evolutionary architecture that can be extended and customized on a per-application basis. We see a database system as an infrastructure comprised of co-operating adaptable and extensible NODS services from which one can build its customized NODS database components.

Thus, services have to be seen more as specifications of database components. Implementation of the components may either be done specifically for a given information system or integrating existing technologies (for example database systems, persistent storage systems, already existing implementations of our services, etc.). Thus, information systems will not be developed anymore with a database system as the center of communication, integration and exchange of data. Applications will use customized database services as other components. With such an approach they may "build" their own database systems. Furthermore, services/system configuration can be adapted at runtime (e.g., add new services, change services internal policies), according to environmental changes.

The following sections describes current aspects of the project. Section 2 overviews the NODS services and discusses their properties. Then, Section 3 describes some on-going research on specific services. Finally, Section 4 concludes the paper.

2   NODS Overview

Our research mainly concerns the design of a software framework and the integration of the different infrastructure services as detailed in the next section while maintaining architectural consistency between them. Services/components can be tailored and combined according to specific needs of applications. The architectural support and the infrastructure rely on object-oriented technologies.

2.1   Services

As we have already said the main idea in NODS is not to see a database system as a closed software dedicated to data management, but rather as an open platform comprised of cooperating, adaptable and extensible services. The services we are currently working on are:

- services for storing and accessing distributed bases of data and code: persistence, replication, transactions and access (queries). The persistence service will provide mechanisms or components that can be combined and specialized for managing bindings and translations (typing) between persistent objects on disks and their distributed images in memories and caches, and also for grouping of objects on persistence storage (organization strategies). The replication service will be in charge of managing replicated data (coherency, synchronization, etc.) and replicated tasks/code (dispatching, coordination, etc.). It is the basic component for high-availability of data and code, improving also efficiency of applications. Aspects related to transactions (locking, logging, concurrency, etc.) may be included within the persistence / replication services as they can be used for other things than transactions management. These aspects may also define services. Basic object access mechanisms on which can be defined high-level associative queries should be provided. It is clear that all these services will share mechanisms and it might be difficult for example to isolate persistence functions from replication and access mechanisms to distributed data. Research on theses aspects is at its beginning (see Section 3.3).
- services for supporting novel programming and execution environment that facilitate the structuring and cooperation of heterogeneous components. We are currently investigating on event and reaction services [61] for the generation of adequate distributed active systems comprised of event listeners and rule managers that can be easily deployed on the network [62](see Sections 3.1 and 3.2). The possible use of such components has been demonstrated [51]. As shown in [1] such event listeners and rule managers are basic components to support electronic commerce applications. [19] also shows that business rules can be used for changing statically and dynamically views of Web sites. Such rules can be processed with event managers at the client level and rule managers at the Web server level.

2.2   Architectural Support

Database cooperating components require to use mechanisms for managing distribution, synchronization, communication, localization, information sharing, access, etc. Industrial and research activities are currently being carried to develop suitable tools and related runtime infrastructures for supporting distributed component-based systems (with databases or not). Middleware has emerged as an important architectural component in supporting such distributed frameworks. The architectural support for our service infrastructure is the JONATHAN object bus (http://www.objectweb.com), developed at France Télécom R&D. Such a communication component will allow our services to inter-operate via different personalities (CORBA/IIOP, RMI, DCOM, etc.). For the time being we chose the CORBA personality to unify components of our framework. We will use an extension of the CORBA interface definition language (IDL) to specify interfaces of NODS services. Research on a dynamic database object naming and localization support for distribution is done in collaboration with France Télécom R&D, ASR department.

2.3   Originality of the Approach

The originality of the NODS approach comes from the extensibility and adaptability properties given to its services and to the (generated) networked information systems it may support. To reach this objective the services are:

- reusable: it is a basic property, inherent to the notion of service;
- adaptable: a service should be able to adapt statically and dynamically to some characteristics coming from the application and the environment;
- extensible: the service can be extended without losing its properties.

Adaptability and extensibility are achieved thanks to meta-programming and reflection techniques. Reflection is the capability of a computation system to reason about and act upon itself: it distinguishes what an object does (its base level) from the way it does it (its meta-level) [43]. Meta-programming defines different models that can be used to build reflective systems. Program characteristics can be instantiated –reified– created and modified by meta-programs. The use of reflection and meta-programming techniques to specify dynamic reconfigurable platforms is not new. Architectures have already been proposed [26,41] that support the development and execution of distributed applications. OpenCorba [41] is a reflexive ORB enabling users to adapt dynamically the representation and the execution policies of the software bus. Reflection is ensured by providing a set of meta-classes and a protocol for dynamically changing meta-classes allowing runtime evolution of systems. DART (Distributed Adaptive Run-Time) [52] proposes a software runtime which allows application programmers to develop distributed software without dealing with the details of distribution technology. The runtime is configurable to application requirements, to the system and to the networking environment using a reflective architecture.

NODS will share with these adaptive middleware approaches the ability to extend the internal characteristics of the platform and services with meta-classes to enable runtime adaptability. However, different to existing works, we do not add runtime adaptability and extensibility to applications using wrapping techniques.

Going back to the late 80s and beginning of the 90s, several research projects (e.g., EXODUS[15], GENESIS[9], SHORE[16], PREDATOR[10]) had for objective to provide open database management systems. Also there have been recent propositions for designing and building componentized database systems over an open infrastructure [57,34,36]. NODS shares such a generation and componentization approach with these projects, allowing developers to build adequate database technologies needed for a given class of applications. From services, one can build adequate NODS systems. NODS is different from extensible database systems because of the context and technologies have changed (internet, object brokers, components, etc.) and the properties and characteristics we want for the services.

3   Some Ongoing Research

3.1   Event Service

An event service is an architectural component that observes the occurrence of events or combinations of them and consequently notifies all the components that have declared their interest. Our event service compiles event processing strategies that are spread out in existing products and proposals (subscription, filtering) from different domains such as active databases [51,20], networks (communication protocols) [53,14,39], distributed systems [50] and middle-ware [50, 31,46]. Event processing with rich semantic can be tailored to different application needs.

Figure 1 depicts our service framework to specify, generate and execute event managers. Using the Specification Interface of the service one can define an Event Manager Schema (em-schema) that associates a set of event types definitions (structure and operations or semantics) with a management model: $\mathcal{S}_{evt} : \varepsilon\tau \rightarrow \varepsilon\mu$. Such a schema ($\mathcal{S}_{evt}$) is used for generating adaptable event managers for a group of applications sharing a set of event type definitions ($\varepsilon\tau$), instances of the Event Type Meta Model. An event management model ($\varepsilon\mu$) is an instance of the Event Management Meta Model that restricts domains of the proposed dimensions. The following introduces the two meta models on which is based our event service. More details are given in [60].

1. The Event Type Meta Model provides concepts for describing primitive event types (names and contexts) that concern specific application domains, as well as composition operators semantics. An event type has the following meta-structure: (instant (EventTypeName, [s_v,e_v]) [with delta] [where mask]))
   instant represents the granularity of the observed situation. An event type can either represent a whole process or the fact that a process will be or

has been executed. The validity time interval is denoted by $[s_v, e_v]$ where s_v and e_v represent respectively the starting and ending points in a logical time line. This interval can also be specified as a period (i.e., every two seconds). The delta contains context information about the situation represented by the event type. The mask is a filter expressed in terms of conditions including predicates and temporal expressions that events must satisfy.

Note that event types are defined in a parametric way. Once adopted by applications (i.e., consumers, producers) the instant of detection, the validity time interval, the delta and the mask are instantiated according to an event management model.

2. The Event Management Meta Model proposes a set of dimensions to characterize event processing: detection, production and notification. More information on these dimensions can be found in [60].

Detection dimensions describe the conditions in which events are detected and how they are recognized. They specify the observation granularity; properties such as scope (e.g., events concern the same object, they are produced within the same transaction); possible intervals during which events can be recognized. Production dimensions specify how to order and compute events production instants (with respect to a global reference, under which time representation); how to build events contexts using information contained in delta structures; how to combine events to produce composite events. Notification dimensions concern information delivery, filtering (visibility) and event life-span. Events can be delivered to consumers at different instants and with different degrees of visibility.

Finally, detection and notification dimensions describe interaction protocols depending on producers and consumers characteristics. In general, events can be detected (notified) under pull and push protocols. Both operations can be executed with (a)synchronous modes. The synchronous (asynchronous) mode implies that producer (consumer) executions are (not) interrupted by the detection (notification) mechanism.

Em-schema example. Let us consider a financial application example involving three actors: a financial trader, a stock exchange vendor, and a federation of bank agencies. Each actor has various views of data (e.g., a trader can only see his/her own purchase operations and banking information) and has specific access rights. Furthermore, each actor has different information needs (i.e., information is notified at different instants, with various reliability degrees). For example, traders need to be notified automatically as soon as stock exchange events are detected (e.g., *actions upward trend, the stock exchange session is closed*) while they can wait until the end of a stock exchange session to receive a summary of their banking information.

For this application example, we can define the em-schema $\mathcal{S}_{evt} : \varepsilon\tau_1 \rightarrow \varepsilon\mu_1$ with the set of event types $\varepsilon\tau_1 = \{$E$_1$: *Actions upward trend*, E$_2$: *the Dow Jones changed by 20%*, E$_3$: *The stock exchange session is closed*, E$_4$: *a purchase transaction has been completed*, E$_5$: *Update of an account*$\}$ and $\varepsilon\mu_1$ that defines different management policies taking into account sources and traders characteristics and needs. For instance, traders need to be notified automatically as soon as stock exchange events are detected while information sources can wait until the end of a session. Similarly, the trader can receive purchase and bank account events. An event manager can retrieve events from the bank server and notify them once atomic operations are completed. A valid definition of E_1 is: (after, ActionsUpwardTrend, [9:00, 17:00] with delta(company: string, domain: string, price: real, country: string) representing Upward trend of actions of a company of a country in a given domain domain. Event of this type will be detected after an update of the action's price occurring during stock exchange sessions ([9:00,17:00]).

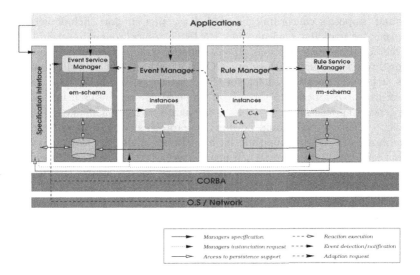

Fig. 1. Event and Rule services

Event managers. process events according to schema instances (internal functionalities) and offer mechanisms to control and execute adaption operations. Applications and other services such as rule service, transaction service, persistence service, Internet services, etc. use event managers to i) produce/consume events; and ii) to adapt managers (i.e., modify instances) according to their internal states and to the environment evolution[1]. They can also interact with the specification interface to define and generate event managers.

Schemas can be updated on explicit demand of applications and according to changes stemming from the execution environment (e.g., network traffic, platform, connectivity). The Event Service Manager is responsible for observing such events. It also controls schema updates with respect to consistent execution of managers and to the administration of associated schema versions (see Figure 1). The Event Service Manager creates a new schema version and signals changes to the

---

[1] Each application can only modify its own instances.

corresponding event managers that consequently adapt themselves. Adaptation depends on the type of changes and it is executed at different points of event processing (as soon as they are produced, when a new instance is subscribed, at a particular checkpoint, etc.).

Figure 1 also shows that the object oriented environment CORBA has been chosen to unify components of our event service framework. CORBA interface definition language (IDL) is used to specify interfaces between event managers, event producers/consumers. The CORBA Event Service is used as a underlying "low level" communication infrastructure for event managers.

3.2   Rule Service

Existing proposals concerning distributed reaction support include active mechanisms for workflow environments [45,18,33], asynchronous reaction support for relational database systems [37], parametric wrappers enabling rule engines tailored to specific applications in a CORBA platform [40], and single reaction-event managers constructed for specific database environments [32]. Our Rule Service can be compared to these later proposals. It can be used for specifying and generating rule managers able to cooperate with event managers (through specific events, detection and notification protocols) and to execute reactions (conditions and actions) upon specific execution models. Reactions are executed within application frameworks and may concern database systems. Specifying a rule manager mainly corresponds to define a Rule Manager Schema ((rm-schema) in Figure 1) that couples a rule definition model (for defining specific kind of rules) with a rule execution model, and the rule model with a cooperation one. Rule definitions concern EA or ECA rules. A rule execution model is an instance of the Rule Execution Meta Model that restricts domains of the proposed dimensions. A cooperation model is an instance of the Cooperation Meta Model that provides cooperation contracts (i.e., one per event, transaction or rule manager). The following introduces our rule meta models. More details can be found in [62].

1. The Rule Definition Meta Model provides concepts for specifying rules of the form : <behavior> ON <EventType> [IF<Condition>] DO <Action>
   <behavior> describes the way i) a rule is executed with respect to event notification; and ii) how to couple its execution within application execution (e.g. transactions). <EventType> describes operations executed by (database) systems and applications, users or situations that happen within the execution context. <Condition> is optional and it can be a predicate on database states expressed in a query language, or on information contained in the event context. <Action> is a sequence of operations that can concern multiple applications, database systems, operating systems and services.

2. The Rule Execution Meta Model provides dimensions to characterize different aspects of rule execution such as event consumption, execution mode, transaction mode, multiple rule policies [54].
   Rule triggering policies specify how to handle an event that has triggered a rule. For rule execution events are considered during their validity time interval.

An event can be taken into account either for one execution of the rule or for several executions after its notification until the end of its validity time interval. Rules can be triggered every time their triggering event is notified or only once for a set of triggering events. Furthermore, one can specify whether the net effect must be taken into account or not, for the execution of each rule. The net effect is the result of executing a sequence of operations on the same data (or object).

Reaction execution has to be coupled with the underlying transaction model of a database system (local, federated), a specific transaction service or an application execution. Rule execution can start either immediately after the notification of its triggering event or it can be deferred, for example to the end of the global triggering transaction[2]. A rule is executed either as a new transaction that belongs to the same global triggering transaction or as a separate global transaction. In addition, the global transaction in which a rule is executed can be dependent or independent of the global triggering transaction. Clearly, coupling aspects imply that the rule service has both sufficient access over global transactions to be informed of their execution status, and influence to abort, block and restart them according to rule behavior properties.

Table 1. Cooperation with event managers

1	ActivateEM $\rightarrow$ connection(IdEM)
2	ActivateEvType(EvType) $\rightarrow$ subscribe(EvType)
3	DisactivateEvType(EvType) $\rightarrow$ unsubscribe(EvType)
4	reception(EvType(ev)) $\rightarrow$ trigger_rules(ev)
5	DisActivateEM $\rightarrow$ disconnection(IdEM)

3. The **Rule Cooperation Meta Model** provides generic contracts describing the way a rule manager cooperates with other components such as event, transaction or other rule managers. Cooperation contracts are given as production rules.

   Table 1 gives rules characterizing the cooperation between a rule manager and an event manager. Once connections are established (1 in Table 1) a rule manager subscribes the set of event types (2) to be processed by event managers. Later, it receives event instances of subscribed event types (4). Rule managers unsubscribe a given event type (3) when there are no rules triggered by such an event because rules were either deleted or deactivated.

   Production rules describing the way a rule manager may cooperate with a transaction manager or another rule manager can be found in [24,62].

---

[2] The triggering transaction is the transaction within which events are produced; a triggered transaction is the one that executes a triggered rule.

Rm-schema example. Actors of our application example can execute their activities either on explicit demand or automatically using active rules. Let us consider that the Telecom actions upturn will probably continue. A trader can therefore define the RTelecom rule (see Figure 2) to automatically buy such actions, every time their price raises. For other type of actions (e.g. Oil companies actions) traders prefer to decide and eventually to buy actions explicitly at the stock exchange site. Furthermore, purchase transactions are authorized by a bank only if the bill does not exceed the trader global credit (see rule RPurchase in Figure 2). The system keeps local credits below a specific threshold. Thus, money is transfered automatically from one account to another. This is also ensured using rules. Note that banking operations are executed within global transactions, consequently banking events are detected within such transactions ([GTbegin, GTend]).

Rule RTelecom

CONSUMPTION consume
E_PROCESSING instance
NET EFFECT off
COUPLING immediate, independent, separate
ON after ActionsUpwardTrend, [9:00, 17:00]
    with delta(company: string, domain: string,
        price: real, country: string)
    where domain = 'Telecom'
DO /** get_object purchase object **/
purchase.buy(company, price, myaccount.number)

Rule RPurchase

CONSUMPTION consume
E_PROCESSING set_oriented
NET EFFECT off
COUPLING deferred_before, dependent, same
ON before UpdateAccount, [GTbegin, GTend]
    with delta(accountId: string, amount: real)
IF select account from account in Accounts
    where account.accountId = accountId
DO abort

Fig. 2. Rule RTelecom and RPurchase

For our financial application example we can define the rm-schema $\mathcal{S}_{rule}$: $r\delta_1 \rightarrow r\varepsilon\mu_1$; $r\varepsilon\mu_1 \rightarrow coop\mu_1$ where $r\delta_1 = \{$ RTelecom ; RPurchase$\}$ and $r\varepsilon\mu_1$ specifies different execution policies taking into account application needs. For instance, since purchases are in general timely operations, RTelecom (triggered by instances of type ActionsUpwardTrend) must be executed immediately as separate independent operations. In contrast, RPurchase (triggered by instances of type UpdateAccount) execution is coupled with global transactions execution performed by the **bank federation mediator**. Since the rule implements an integrity constraint concerning accounts credit it must be executed as a dependent transaction within the same global triggering transaction (**GTT**). Also its execution can be deferred with respect to the **prepare phase** of GTT and it is executed for a set of events (**event processing *set oriented***). Finally, cooperation policies are specified by $coop\mu_1 = \{$em-coop contract, tm-coop contract, rm-coop contract$\}$.

Considering $\mathcal{S}_{rule}$ and $\mathcal{S}_{evt}$ a valid instance of em-coop contract is shown in Table 2. $r\delta_1$ contains two rules triggered by events of type E_1 and E_5. So, instances of production rules of Table 1 are created only for these event types. This shows that an instance of rule is created for every couple rule-event managers. Note also that for event subscription and reception a production rule is created for every event type associated to the rule manager.

Table 2. Event manager cooperation instance

1	ActivateEM → connection($IdEM$)
2	(Dis)ActivateEvType(E_1) → (un)subscribe(E_1)
3	(Dis)ActivateEvType(E_5) → (un)subscribe(E_5)
4	reception(E_1(ev)) → trigger_rules(ev)
5	reception(E_5(ev)) → trigger_rules(ev)
6	DisActivateEM → disconnection($IdEM$)

3.3 Persistence Service

Persistence of data [4], meaning the seamless management of data that outlives computations, has motivated a lot of work in several research communities. The database research community has been largely concerned by the problem of providing persistence of data. Relational systems dominates since the early 70s. However, they have been considered as inappropriate for orthogonal persistence systems because of the dichotomy between database support (set-oriented manipulation of data, transactions, concurrency, recovery, etc.) and programming languages. Object-oriented database systems [8] have been proposed to unify database and programming language concerns. Database programming languages have been an attempt to embed databases capabilities into programming languages, but the data type orthogonality and the persistent independence properties have been thrown away. This means, that persistence has been integrated into the programming language with a weak level of transparency. Proposed database programming languages include Pascal/R [56], DBPL [44], ADAPLEX [58], TAXIS [48] and Galileo [3].

At the same time, the idea of having orthogonal persistent programming languages has been introduced [4]. The idea was to add persistence to programming languages in a way that persistent data are seamlessly managed with respect to transient data. Persistence is integrated into the programming language with high level of transparency. Representative projects include PS-Algol [5,4], Napier88 [28], and PJama [6].

In the early 80's, Stonebraker pointed out the poor operating systems' support for database management systems requirements [59]. Representative projects having taken into account such requirements include the work on Mach's external mapers [65], single address space operating systems such as Angel [47], Opal [21] and Mungi [63], persistent virtual shared memories such as ARIAS [29] and RVM [55], reflective operating systems such as Apertos [64], orthogonal persistent operating systems such as Grasshoper [27] and Charm [38].

Projects trying to provide toolkits for the construction of database management systems can be put also in that category as they needed to identify the basic modules/functions of a database system that have to be developed or adapted from some tools offered by existing operating systems or memories supports. Approaches to making database systems extensible were very interesting. The approach taken at Wisconsin was to provide a general storage manager, as well as some tools (e.g. query compiler generators) in order to build a specific, *ad-hoc* system. This manager provides the basic storage functions, and a set of well-defined interfaces used by the database system programmer in case he/she has to add a functionality that is not included in the basic storage manager. In fact, both Exodus [15] and Shore [16] systems have been used for prototyping a large amount of systems. The other approach called "database compilers" was to give to the database system programmer a set of software components which have to be assembled following a given specification. Such a specification can be thought as a program describing the database management system architecture. The prototype proposed in the Genesis project [9] allowed the construction of mono-user and mono-transaction database management systems.

To conclude, there has been a lot of work related to persistence in several domains. Categorizing and comparing them is not easy and it is sometimes not simple to have a global view of what should be a distributed persistence support. Although the development of orthogonal persistence has led the unification of language and database concerns, the challenge remains to construct (and apply) orthogonally persistent systems providing full database facilities such as transactions, recovery, concurrency, distribution, and scalability.

Designing and building such persistent systems is an effort that should be shared by several communities. One way to do it is to provide what we called a persistence service, i.e. a framework capitalizing the best technologies in operating system supports, transaction management, cache management, concurrency control, recovery techniques, etc. and that allows the construction of customized data and application servers, i.e. persistent systems.

Toward a flexible persistence service. We accumulated knowledge on the design and development of data servers and transaction systems [42] and noticed that current persistent systems architecture is not flexible enough to serve applications built as cooperating components dealing with large set of distributed data and users. The proposed supports (storage managers or database servers) are often black boxes that impose specific execution environment even if they can be customized. They cannot easily cooperate or reuse services proposed for the construction of complex distributed systems such as the Persistent State Service 2.0 [49] and Java Data Objects [35]. These proposals provide a well defined framework to access the services requiered to integrate persistence into applications. However, their interfaces have been mostly oriented to resolve problems of interoperability and heterogeneity of the persistence underlying infrastructure. The standard definitions for the persistence services do not include hooks to tune the persistence to application's needs and to include database facilities mainly transactions, caching and concurrency.

Our current work includes the design and development of a framework providing basic mechanisms to access and manage resources that can be used to implement any resource management policy. Therefore, implementing a persistent system "only" consists in implementing the policies but not the mechanisms. We have already defined some key mechanisms that will serve our framework or persistence service. Such mechanisms can be classified into three main categories. Their are (1) those that help in managing the distributed main memory, (2) those that allow access to the distributed permanent memory and (3) those that help in distributing the execution of the mechanisms. In order be able to define it's own policies, a "resulting" persistent system must control the supplied mechanisms. Therefore, our service provides adaptable and extensible mechanisms based on an open architecture. To implement efficient persistent systems, these mechanisms are well integrated within the operating system, take into account the distribution of the resources and are distributed themselves.

4   Conclusion

NODS is a long-term research project that revisits extensible database technologies and combines them with other technologies coming from outside the classical database area. Our main research trends are:

- adopt a plug-and-play approach: this means to identify which interface(s) should be provided for our services – assuming their extensibility and adaptability properties;
- consider techniques and tools for programming with components and provide services to support them;
- make the services and the architectural support cooperate for application programming and execution;
- experiment our services in data warehouse management [11], querying and browsing the Web of information [22], providing persistence and high-availability to distributed virtual worlds and games (IST Ping project number IST-1999-11488).

As we already said the originality of our approach comes from the extensibility and adaptability properties given to our services and to the NODS generated (information) systems comprised of instances of these services.

With the NODS approach we should be able to contribute to the database research issues suggested in [25,12,7,36,13]: build database systems using a plug-and-play approach, federate millions of database systems (mediation), offer concepts (workflow, component) and tools (trigger) for making application logic a first class citizen.

Acknowledgments. Thanks to the NODS project members: Michel Adiba, Pierre Habraken, Claudia Roncancio, Elizabeth Perez Cortes, Edgard Benitez-Guerrero, Luciano Garcia-Banuelos, Helena Grazziottin-Ribeiro, Olivier Guyotot, Olivier Lobry, Tanguy Nedelec, Khalid Belhajme, Patricia Serrano-Alvarado, Genoveva Vargas, Jose-Luis Zechinelli. Thanks also to colleagues of France Télécom R&D working with us on the architectural support for NODS services and systems: Thierry Coupaye, Stéphane Drapeau, Pascal Déchamboux and Alexandre Lefebvre.

References

1. Serge Abiteboul, Bernd Amann, Sophie Cluet, Adi Eyal, Laurent Mignet, and Tova Milo. Active Views for Electronic Commerce. In *Proceedings of 25th International Conference on Very Large Data Bases*, Edinburgh, Scotland, UK, September 7-10 1999. Morgan Kaufmann.
2. M. Adiba and J. L. Zechinelli-Martini. Spatio-Temporal Multimedia Presentations as Database Objects. In *Proc. of DEXA'99, 10th International Conference on Databases and Expert Systems Applications*, Florence - Italy, August - September 1999.
3. A. Albano, G. Ghelli, and R. Orsini. Galileo: A strongly-typed, interactive conceptual language. *ACM Transactions on Database Systems*, 10(2):230–260, 1985.
4. M.P. Atkinson, P.J. Bailey, K.J. Chisholm, P.W. Cockshott, and R. Morrison. An Approach to Persistent Programming. *The Computer Journal*, 26(4):360–365, 1983.
5. M.P. Atkinson, K.J. Chisholm, and P.W. Cockshott. PS-Algol: an Algol with a persistent heap. *ACM SIGPLAN Notices*, 17(7):24–31, 1982.
6. M.P. Atkinson, L. Daynès, M.J. Jordan, T. Printezis, and S. Spence. An Orthogonally Persistent Java. *ACM SIGMOD Record*, December 1996.
7. Roger Bamford, Rafiul Ahad, and Angelo Pruscino. A scalable and highly available networked database architecture. In *Proceedings of 25th International Conference on Very Large Data Bases*, Edinburgh, Scotland, UK, September 7-10 1999. Morgan Kaufmann.
8. F. Bancilhon and D. Maier. Multilanguage Object-Oriented Systems: New answers to old database problems. In K. Fuchi and L. Kotti, editors, *Future Generation Computers II*. North Holland, 1989.
9. D. Bartory, J.R. Barnett, J.F. Garza, K.P. Smith, K. Tsukuda, B.C. Twichell, and T.E. Wise. GENESIS: An Extensible Database Management System. *IEEE Transactions on software engineering*, 14(11):1711–1729, November 1988.
10. D. Batory and J. Thomas. P2: A Lightweight DBMS Generator. Technical Report TR-95-26, University of Texas at Austin, June 1995.
11. Edgard Benitez-Guerrero, Christine Collet, Tuyet-Trinh Vu and Michel Adiba. Data Warehouses and XML: Opportunities and Limitations. *Submitted*, 2000.
12. Phil Bernstein, Michael Brodie, Stefano Ceri, David DeWitt, Mike Franklin, Hector Garcia-Molina, Jim Gray, Jerry Held, Joe Hellerstein, H. V. Jagadish, Michael Lesk, Dave Maier, Jeff Naughton, Hamid Pirahesh, Mike Stonebraker, and Jeff Ullman. The Asilomar Report on Database Research. *SIGMOD Record*, 18(1), september 1998. Asilomar meeting of 1998.
13. Michael L. Brodie and Surajit Chaudhuri. Issues in network management in the next millennium. In *Proceedings of 25th International Conference on Very Large Data Bases*, Edinburgh, Scotland, UK, September 7-10 1999. Morgan Kaufmann.
14. M.R. Cagan. The HP SoftBench environment: an architecture for a new generation of software tools. *Hewlett-Packard Journal: technical information from the laboratories of Hewlett-Packard Company*, 3(41), June 1990.
15. M.J. Carey, D.J. DeWitt, G. Graefe, D.M. Haight, J.E. Richardson, D.T. Schuh, E.J. Shekita, and S.L. Vandenberg. The EXODUS Extensible DBMS Project: An Overview. In S. Zdonik and D. Maier, editors, *Readings in Object-Oriented Databases*. Morgan-Kaufman, 1990.
16. M.J. Carey, D.J. DeWitt, J. Naughton, and M. Salomon. Shoring Up Persistent Applications. In *Proceedings of the 1994 ACM SIGMOD Conference*, May 1994.

17. F. Casati, S. Ceri, B. Pernici, and G. Pozzi, *Deriving active rules for workflow enactment*, Proc. of the 7th Int. Conf. on Database and Expert Systems Applications (DEXA) (Zurich, Switzerland), Lecture Notes in Computer Science, no. 1134, Springer-Verlag, 1996, pp. 94–110.

18. S. Ceri, P. Grefen, and G. Sanchez, *Wide - a distributed architecture for workflow management*, Proceedings of Reserch Issues in Data Engineering (RIDE'97) (Birmingham, England), IEEE, March 1997, pp. 76–79.

19. Stefano Ceri, Piero Fraternali, and Stefano Paraboschi. Data-driven, one-to-one web site generation for data-intensive applications. In *Proceedings of 25th International Conference on Very Large Data Bases*, Edinburgh, Scotland, UK, September 7-10 1999. Morgan Kaufmann.

20. S. Chakravarthy, R. Le, and R. Dasari. ECA Rule Processing in Distributed and Heterogeneous Environments. In *Proceedings of the Fourteenth International Conference on Data Engineering*, Florida, USA, February 1998. IEEE Computer Society Press.

21. J.S. Chase, H.M. Levy, M.J. Feeley, and E.D. Lazowska. Sharing and protection in a single address space operating system. *ACM Transactions on Computer Systems*, 12:271–307, November 1994.

22. B. Chidlovskii, C. Roncancio, and M-L. Schneider. Semantic Cache Mechanism for Heterogeneous Web Querying. *Computer Networks*, 31:1347–1360, 1999.

23. C. Collet. NAOS. In Norman W. Paton, editor, *Active Rules in Database Systems*, chapter 15, pages 279–294. Springer Verlag, March 1998.

24. C. Collet, G. Vargas-Solar, and H. Grazziotin-Ribeiro. Open Active Services for Data-Intensive Distributed Applications. In *Proceedings of the International Database Engineering and Applications Symposium, IDEAS'2000*, Yokahama-Japan, september 2000. IEEE.

25. Presidents Information Technology Advisory Committee. PITAC Report to the President. Technical report, http://www.ccic.gov/ac/, February 1999.

26. F.M. Costa, G.S Blair, and G. Coulson. Experiments with reflective middleware. In *ECOOP'98 Workshop on Reflective Object-Oriented Programming and Systems*, Brussels-Belgiun, July 1998.

27. Alan Dearle, Rex di Bona, James Farrow, Frans Henskens, Anders Lindström, John Rosenberg, and Francis Vaughan. Grasshopper: An arthogonally persistent operating system.

28. A. Dearly, R. Conner, F. Brown, and R. Morrison. Napier88 – A database programming language? In R. Hull, R. Morrison, and D. Stemple, editors, *Proceedings of the second international Workshop on Database Programming Languages*, pages 179–195. Morgan Kaufmann, 1989.

29. P. Déchamboux and A. Knaff. Reliable Support for a Persistent Distributed Shared Memory. Technical report, INRIA Rhône-Alpes, 1997.

30. Stephane Drapeau, Claudia L. Roncancio, and Edgard Benítez-Guerrero. Generating Association Rules for Prefetching. April 2000.

31. Flanagan, editor. *JAVA in a nutshell*. O'Reilly, 1997. O'Reilly andssociates, Inc.

32. H. Fritschi, S. Gatziu, and K. Dittrich, *FRAMBOISE-an Approach to Framework-Based Active Database Management System Construction*, Proceedings of the 1998 ACM 7th International Conference on Information and Knowledge Management (CIKM) (Washington USA), November 3 - 7 1998, pp. 364–370.

33. A. Geppert, M. Kradolfer, and D. Tombros, *Realization of cooperative agents using an active object-oriented database management system*, Proceedings of the 2nd Workshop on Rules in Databases (RIDS'95) (Athens, Greece), Lecture Notes in Computer Science, no. 985, Springer, September 1995, pp. 327–341.

34. A. Geppert and K. R. Dittrich. Bundling: Towards a New Construction Paradigm for Persistent Systems. *Networking and Information Systems*, 1(1), June 1998.
35. Java Data Objects Expert Group. Java^{TM} Data Objects version 0.8, Public Review Draft. Technical report, Sun Microsystems, June 2000.
36. James Hamilton. Networked data management design points. In *Proceedings of 25th International Conference on Very Large Data Bases*, Edinburgh, Scotland, UK, September 7-10 1999. Morgan Kaufmann.
37. E.N. Hanson and S. Khosla, *An introduction to the triggerman asynchronous trigger processor*, Tech. Report TR-97-007, CISE Department, University of Florida, United States, April 1997.
38. D. Hulse and A. Dearle. Trends in Operating System Design: Towards a Customisable Persistent Micro-Kernel. Technical Report Pastel RT1R4, University of Stirling, 1998.
39. A.M. Julienne and B. Holtz. *ToolTalk and open protocols, inter-application communication*. Prentice-Hall, New Jersey, 1994.
40. A. Koschel, R. Kramer, G. von Bultzingsloewen, T. Bleibel, P. Krumlinde, S. Schmuck, and C. Weinand, *Configurable active functionality for corba*, Proc. of the 11th European Conference on Object-Oriented Programming (ECOOP'97) Workshop 7 (CORBA: Implementation, Use and Evaluation), Finland, June 1997.
41. T. Ledoux. *Réflexion dans les systèmes répartis : application à Corba et Smalltalk*. PhD thesis, Ecole de Mines de Nantes, Nantes-France, 1998.
42. O. Lobry, C. Collet, and P. Déchamboux. The VIRTUOSE Distributed Object Store. In *Proc. of DEXA'97 workshop*, Toulouse - France, September, 2-5 1997.
43. P. Maes. Concepts and experiments in computational reflection. In *Proceeding of the ACM Conference on Object-Oriented Programming Systems, Languages and Applications (OOPSLA)*, 1987.
44. F. Matthes and J.W. Schmidt. The type system of DBPL. In R. Hull, R. Morrison, and D. Stemple, editors, *Proceedings of the second international Workshop on Database Programming Languages*, pages 219–225. Morgan Kaufmann, 1989.
45. J. Mylopoulos, A. Gal, K. Kontogiannis, and M. Stanley, *A generic integration architecture for cooperative information systems*, Proceedings of the 1st IFCIS International Conference on Cooperative Information Systems (CoopIS'96) (Brussels, Belgium), IEEE, June 1996, pp. 208–217.
46. *MOMA Educational Information: A Middleware Taxonomy*. Message Oriented Middleware Association, http://www.moma-inc.org/, 1998.
47. K. Murray, A. Saulsbury, T. Stiemerling, T. Wilkinson, P. Kelly, and P. Osmon. Design and implementation of an object-oriented 64-bit single address space microkernel. In *Proceedings of the 2nd USENIX Symposium on Microkernels and other kernel architectures*, pages 96–99, September 1993.
48. J. Mylopoulos, P.A. Bernstein, and H.K.T. Wong. A language facility for designing database-intensive applications. *ACM Transactions on Database Systems*, 5(2):185–207, 1980.
49. Object Management Group. Persistent State Service 2.0, Joint Revised Submission. OMG, August 1999.
50. OMG, editor. *The Common Object Request Broker Architecture and Specification*. 1997. Object Management Group.
51. N. Paton. *Active Databases*. Springer Verlag, 1998.
52. P-G. Raverdy and R. Lea. Dart: A distributed adaptive run-time. Technical report, Sony Computer Science Lab and Sony Distributed Systems Lab, Tokyo, 1999.
53. S. Reiss. Connecting tools using message passing in the field environment. *IEEE SOftware*, July 1990.

54. G. Ribeiro-Grazziottin and C. Collet. Behavior of Active Rules within Multi-Database Systems. In *Proceedings of the XIV Symposium on Databases*, Florianopolis-Brazil, October 1999.

55. M. Satyanarayanan, H.H. Mashburn, P. Kumar, D.C. Steere, and J.J. Kistler. Lightweight Recoverable Virtual Memory. *ACM Transactions on Computer Systems*, 12(1), February 1994.

56. J.W. Schmidt. Some high level language constructs for data of type relation. *ACM Transactions on Database Systems*, 2(3):247–261, 1977.

57. A. Silberschatz and S. Zdonik. Database Systems – Breaking out the Box. *SIGMOD Record*, 26(3), September 1997.

58. J.M. Smith, S. Fox, and T. Landers. *ADAPLEX: Rationale and Reference Manual*. Computer Corporation of America, Cambridge Mass., 2nd edition, 1983.

59. M. Stonebraker. Operating system support for database management. *Communications of the ACM*, 24(7):412–418, July 1981.

60. G. Vargas-Solar and C. Collet. A Flexible Event Service for database co-operating components. Technical Report RR-1031-I-LSR-13, LSR - IMAG , Grenoble - France, july 2000. 18 pages.

61. G. Vargas-Solar, C. Collet, and H. Grazziotin-Ribeiro. Active Services for Federated Databases. In ACM, editor, *Proceedings of the 14th. Annual Symposium of Applied Computing:SAC 2000*, Como-Italy, March 2000.

62. G. Vargas-Solar, C. Collet, and H. Grazziotin-Ribeiro. Open Active Services for Data-Intensive Distributed Applications. In *Proceedings of the 16èmes Journées Bases de Données Avancées, BDA'2000*, Blois-France, October 2000. Long version of [24].

63. J. Vochteloo, S.Russell, and G. Heiser. Capability-based protection in the Mungi operating system. In *Proceedings of the 3rd International Workshop on Object Orientation in Operating Systems*, pages 108–115. IEEE, December 1993.

64. Y. Yokote. The Apertos Reflective Operating System: The Concept and Its Implementation. In *Proceedings of the OOPSLA'92*, pages 414–434. ACM, October 1992.

65. M. Wayne Young, A. Tevanian, R.F. Tashid, D.B. Golub, J.L. Eppinger, J. Chew, W. Bolosky, D.L. Black, and R.V. Baron. The Duality of Memory and Communication in the implementation of a Multiprocessor Operating System. In *Proceedings of the Eleventh Symposium on Operating System Principles*, pages 63–76. ACM, November 1987.

Pointwise Temporal Object Database Browsing

Marlon Dumas[1], Chaouki Daassi[1,2],
Marie-Christine Fauvet[1], and Laurence Nigay[2]

[1] LSR-IMAG, Univ. of Grenoble, BP 72
38402 St-Martin d'He-'res (France)
`Marlon.Dumas@imag.fr`
[2] CLIPS-IMAG, Univ. of Grenoble, BP 53
38041 Grenoble Cedex 9 (France)
`Laurence.Nigay@imag.fr`

Abstract. Visual object database browsers are essentially based on two
kinds of interactions: navigation within a collection of objects, and navigation between objects by the way of their relationships. These two interactional operators have proven to adequately support the main user task
addressed by these tools, that is, exploring the states of a set of related
objects. In temporal object databases, visual browsing tools should addi-
tionally support users tasks such as examining a snapshot of a collection
of objects at a given instant, or detecting changes within object states.
In this paper, we show that the two interactional operators supported
by classical object browsers do not adequately address these tasks. We
consequently propose an interactional operator dedicated to navigation
through time, and we study how it may be orthogonally integrated with
the above two.

Keywords: temporal databases, object databases, user interface, data
browsing

1   Introduction

Three main tasks involving intensive user interaction are classically identified in
the context of database management: schema definition, query formulation, and
data visualization. Accordingly, three kinds of visual interfaces have been designed and are currently provided by most commercial DBMS: schema browsers
and editors, visual query languages, and data visualization tools (see [3] for a
survey).

In this paper, we focus on a family of data visualization interfaces for object
databases, known as *object browsers* [12,5,7,4]. The underlying principle of such
interfaces is to provide a visual representation of the data residing within objects,
and to offer visual operators for navigating through related objects. Two kinds
of interactions are commonly supported by object database browsers: navigation
within a collection of objects, and navigation between objects by the way of their
relationships.

K.R. Dittrich et al. (Eds.): Objects and Databases 2000, LNCS 1944, pp. 170–184, 2001.
© Springer-Verlag Berlin Heidelberg 2001

In the context of a database modeling the evolution of a set of objects and their relationships over a period of time (i.e. a *temporal object database*), the user interface must integrate additional interactional paradigms. Indeed, within such databases, time is a dimension of objects *per se*, orthogonal to their other components. Data visualization tools in this setting must therefore support time-dependent tasks, such as detecting and analyzing changes of object attributes and relationships over time, or exploring a snapshot of the database at a fixed instant. To illustrate these tasks, let us consider a database storing historical data about workers, supervisors and pieces of equipment in a factory's assembly lines. Examples of users tasks are:

- Analyze data about an assembly line at a given date (including its supervisor, workers, equipment and productivity parameters).
- Compare at different dates, a given worker's wage with respect to that of the supervisor of the assembly line to which he is assigned.
- Find out whether the composition of a given assembly line (equipment plus workers) considerably changes when its supervisor does.

In this paper we advocate that existing object database browsers do not adequately support the above tasks, and consequently propose a technique addressing them, namely *pointwise temporal object browsing*. The basic idea of this technique is to display a snapshot at a fixed instant, of a set of path expressions stemming from a given object or collection. The user interacts with this representation, either by navigating through related objects as in classical object browsers, or by modifying the instant with respect to which the visualization is performed. The resulting interface naturally stresses simultaneity by focusing on one instant at a time, but also supports change observation, by providing operators for "jumping" to the next/previous instant where a change occurs in a given visualized path expression.

The structure of the paper is as follows. First, we provide an overview of existing object database browsers and highlight their limitations with regards to temporal databases. We then describe our browsing technique, stressing important aspects such as support for null-valued and collection-valued properties. Lastly, we present the browser's implementation and sketch some future work.

2   Problem Description and Related Works

2.1   Object Database Browsers

Most object database browsers, e.g. ODEVIEW [7], SUPER [5] and PESTO [4], rely on the concept of *synchronous navigation*. Basically, the browsing interface of these systems consists of a canvas containing a set of forms[1], each of them denoting either a single object or a collection of objects. A form denoting a single object is structured into lines, one per property attached to that object. If

---

[1] SUPER offers a graph-based visualization mode in addition to the form-based one. However, the underlying principles of both visualization modes are the same.

a property's type is atomic, its value is directly displayed on the corresponding line. Otherwise, if a property's type is a class or a collection, a clickable button stands in place of its value. When the user clicks on such button, a new form displaying the referenced object or collection is added to the canvas.

A collection is displayed in the same way as a single object, except that the corresponding form contains a couple of arrow-labeled buttons. At any time, this form displays the contents of one of the objects within the collection. Clicking on either of the arrow-labeled buttons allows the user to switch to the next or the previous object in the collection. As in the case of a single object, whenever the value of a property is a complex object or a collection, a button is used to denote its value, and clicking on this button opens a new form.

When a form F2 is opened from another form F1, F2 is said to be *dependent* upon F1. This dependency relationship defines a tree structure over the set of forms displayed on the canvas. The term *synchronous navigation* refers to the way dependent forms are semantically linked. Indeed, a form F2 directly dependent upon another form F1, is expected to reflect the value of one of the properties of the object displayed by form F1. Now, if F1 displays a collection of objects instead of a single one, the property values displayed by this form may vary as the user navigates through the objects of the collection. Hence, when the user clicks on the "Next" or "Previous" buttons of form F1, F2 is updated accordingly (in order to maintain the visual consistency between F1 and F2). This principle is then applied to all forms directly dependent upon F2, and subsequently to all forms transitively dependent upon F1.

As a working example, consider the ODMG [2] database schema in figure 1.

| class Employee (extent Employees) {
    attribute string name;
    attribute float wage;
}
class Worker extends Employee
            (extent Workers) {
    attribute AssemblyLine worksIn;
} | class Supervisor extends Employee
                (extent Supervisors) {
    attribute set<AssemblyLine> supervises;
}
class AssemblyLine (extent AssemblyLines) {
    attribute string lineNumber;
    attribute Supervisor supervisor;
    attribute set<Worker> workers;
} |

Fig. 1. ODMG schema of a non-temporal database.

Figure 2(a) depicts a "synchronized" visualization obtained by starting from the collection Workers and successively clicking on the properties worksIn, supervisor and workers. Notice that the forms dedicated to collections, contain two buttons at the top left corner that enable the user to navigate from one object to another. Figure 2(b) depicts the displayed forms after the user has selected the right arrow in the form entitled Workers.

Object database browsers not based on the concept of synchronous navigation include O_2Look [12] (a component of the O_2 DBMS). A visualization in O_2Look

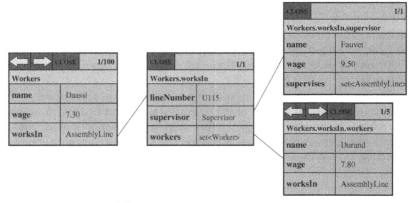

(a) Visualization of the first worker

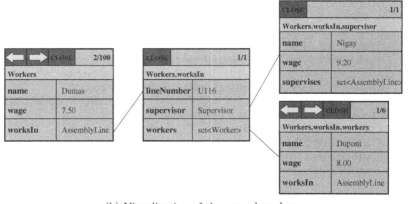

(b) Visualization of the second worker

Fig. 2. Synchronous navigation as defined in PESTO and ODEVIEW.

is made up of a set of forms, each one denoting an object, a tuple or a collection. Forms denoting objects and tuples are similar to those depicted in figure 2. A form denoting a collection is composed of buttons denoting object references (one button per object in the collection). When a button within a form denotes an object reference, the user may invoke any method on this object, and in particular a predefined method for visualizing it, namely display. By default, this method opens a new form displaying the referenced object. Unlike ODEVIEW and PESTO, forms opened during a session are not explicitly linked.

2.2   Applying Object Database Browsers to Temporal Data

We define a temporal object database as one whose schema includes *temporal classes and properties*. A class is said to be temporal if at least one of its properties is temporal. A property is temporal, if its value denotes the evolution of an object characteristic over a period of time. The value of a temporal property is a *history*. At an abstract level, a history models a function from a finite set of instants to a set of objects of a given type. For the sake of simplicity, we consider that a history is simply a collection of instant-timestamped or interval-timestamped objects, although there are many other ways of representing a history [6].

Figure 3 describes the schema of our working temporal database, which is actually a "temporal" variant of the schema presented in figure 1. All classes in this schema are temporal. Property AssemblyLine::production is an example of a temporal property whose history is represented through an instant-timestamped collection of objects, while the history of property Employee::wage is represented using intervals. Note that all histories are observed at the granularity of the day, since instants are modeled through the ODMG type Date.

```
typedef struct { Date lb; Date ub; } Interval;
typedef struct { Supervisor value; Interval timestamp; } TimestampedSupervisor;
typedef struct { set<Worker> value; Interval timestamp; } TimestampedWorkers;
typedef struct { long value; Date timestamp; } TimestampedProduction;
typedef struct { float value; Interval timestamp; } TimestampedWage;
typedef struct { AssemblyLine value; Interval timestamp; }
                                        TimestampedAssemblyLine;
typedef struct { set<AssemblyLine> value; Interval timestamp; }
                                        TimestampedAssemblyLines;
class AssemblyLine (extent Lines, key lineNumber) {
   attribute string lineNumber;
   attribute set<TimestampedSupervisor> supervisor;
   attribute set<TimestampedWorkers> workers;
   attribute set<TimestampedProduction> production;
}
class Employee (extent Employees, key name) {
   attribute string name; attribute set<TimestampeWage> wage;
}
class Worker extends Employee (extent Workers) {
   attribute set<TimestampedAssemblyLine> worksIn;
}
class Supervisor extends Employee (extent Supervisors) {
   attribute set<TimestampedAssemblyLines> supervises;
}
```

Fig. 3. ODMG schema of a temporal database.

Since histories are assimilated to collections, the concept of synchronous navigation may be applied to browse them. However, the resulting navigation approach is not suitable to explore a snapshot of a set of related temporal objects at a given point in time. Indeed, in the synchronous navigation paradigm, two forms corresponding to two distinct histories do not necessarily display data items with overlapping timestamps, even if one of the forms is dependent upon the other (see for instance figure 4). Therefore, if the user wishes to visualize synchronous states of two temporal properties, he must establish this synchronization by hand.

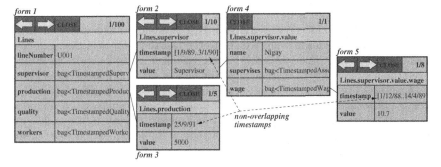

Fig. 4. Applying synchronous navigation to temporal object browsing. Notice that forms 2, 3 and 5 do not display synchronous data (i.e. their validity timestamps do not overlap).

In PESTO, this limitation can be partially circumvented using the concept of *synchronizer*, that is, a predicate semantically linking the values displayed by two forms. In the example of figure 4, synchronizers may be used to force the browser to choose the elements displayed by forms 2, 3 and 5, in such a way that the displayed timestamps overlap. In this way, the user always visualizes data with overlapping periods of validity. However, with respect to the task of exploring object attributes and relationships at fixed instants, the resulting navigation mode has two drawbacks:

- Synchronizers should explicitly be introduced each time that a new form is opened.
- Navigation through the objects composing a collection is not orthogonal to navigation through time. For instance, let us consider the example of figure 4 augmented with synchronizers. Suppose that while analyzing data about a given assembly line as of 1/10/1990 (i.e. the timestamps of forms 2, 3 and 5 all three contain or are equal to this date), the user asks to visualize the next object in the collection of assembly lines (i.e. he clicks on the "Next" button of form 1). Although the resulting visualization is such that forms 2, 3 and 5 necessarily have overlapping timestamps (thanks to the synchronizers), there is no guarantee that these timestamps contain or are equal to instant 1/10/1990. Therefore, in order to view the data of the newly displayed assembly line as of this date, the user must furtherly interact with the "Next" and "Previous" buttons of forms 2, 3 and 5.

2.3   Other Related Works

In the previous section, we show that it is possible to use classical object browsers for temporal database exploration, by simply considering a history as a collection of timestamped objects. Nevertheless, this approach does not fit several important user tasks, such as observing a snapshot of a set of related objects at a given point in time. Before describing our approach to this problem, we present some existing temporal database visualization tools, and discuss to what extent they address the above issue.

Data visualization has received little attention within the temporal database research domain[2] . This is probably due to the fact that efforts in this area have mainly focused on relational models, where visualization tools are often simple, given the flat structure of relations and the lack of explicit links between them.

A notable exception to the above remark is [14], which specifies a 3D interface for browsing temporal relational databases. In this approach, a temporal relation is represented as a sequence of time-indexed planes, each one displaying a snapshot of the browsed relation. Although the interface is not detailedly described, it seems that the interactional devices are limited to two scroll-bars: one for browsing through the records of a relation snapshot, and the other for navigating across the time dimension. This interface therefore integrates the concepts of "navigation through a collection" and "navigation through time", but it does not support the concept of "navigation through object relationships" which is fundamental in the context of object databases.

In the setting of information visualization, many techniques for graphically displaying temporal data have been considered [1,16]. Contrarily to our work which aims at designing a technique for browsing any kind of temporal data, these techniques are specifically oriented towards *quantitative time series* (i.e. periodical series of numerical data items).

[13] adapts some concepts developed in [16] to design an interface for visualizing legal and medical personal records involving non-quantitative data such as texts and complex objects. However, this work does not address the issue of comparing the states of two complex objects at a given point in time, nor the issue of navigating through object relationships.

3   Pointwise Temporal Object Database Browsing

3.1   Overview

The pointwise browser interface is composed of two parts: a time-line and a tree of form-structured windows (called *snapshot windows*). A snapshot window displays either a non-temporal object[3] or a snapshot of a temporal object at a given instant. The internal structure of a snapshot window is the same as that of the forms of classical database browsers presented in section 2.1. For the time being, we restrict our examples to snapshot windows displaying single objects or object snapshots. We will discuss afterwards how collections are accommodated.

---

[2] On the contrary, several visual query languages for temporal databases have been proposed (e.g. [10]). We do not discuss them since the functionalities addressed by these proposals are beyond the scope of the present paper

[3] An object is *temporal* if it owns at least one temporal property and *non-temporal* otherwise.

The instant with respect to which the object snapshots are determined is the same for all the windows in the tree, and is subsequently called the *reference instant*. The reference instant is constrained to reside within a given interval called the *temporal browsing range*.

The role of the time-line window is to fix the reference instant. At the beginning of a session, the reference instant is at the middle of the temporal browsing range. Its position varies thereafter according to the user interactions with the sliders and buttons composing the time-line window. In its simplest form, the time-line window is composed of a slider (called the *main slider*) and four buttons placed at the ends of this slider. Two of the buttons (labeled by simple arrows), allow the user to move the reference instant forward or backward by one unit. The other pair of buttons (labeled with double-arrows) are used to move the reference instant to the next/previous instant where the value of a given navigation path (called the *visualized path*) changes. The instants at which the value of the visualized path changes are called *change instants*. Change instants are visually represented as vertical marks lying within a horizontal line just beneath the main slider.

In figure 5, the visualized path is Workers.worksIn.supervisor and the change instants are those when the supervisor of the worker named "Daassi" changes, whether this change is due to the fact that the worker is assigned to a new assembly line possessing a different supervisor, or to the fact that the supervisor of the assembly line to which this worker is assigned, changes.

In addition to the main slider, the time-line window may contain several *granular sliders*, which allow the user to move the reference instant with different "steps" according to a calendar. For instance, if the reference instant is a date, and that the user specifies the calendar Year/Month/Day (as in figure 5), three granular cursors appear in the time-line window: the first one allows the user to move the reference instant with a step of a year, the second one with a step of a month, and the third one with a step of a day (within the limits of a month).

Snapshot windows are structured as forms containing one line per property of the visualized object or object snapshot. Each line is composed of two boxes: one labeled with the name of the property, and the other labeled with its value at the reference instant[4]. The value of a non-temporal property is always the same regardless of the reference instant. The value of a temporal property at a given instant is equal to the value of its history at that instant, which is itself defined as follows:

- The value at instant I, of a history represented as an instant-timestamped collection of objects, is equal to the object within this collection whose timestamp is equal to I. If no such object exists, the history's value is null.
- The value at instant I, of a history represented as an interval-timestamped collection of objects, is equal to the object within this collection whose timestamp contains instant I. If no such object exists, the history's value is null.

---

[4] If the value of a property at the reference instant is not "printable", the name of its class is used as its label.

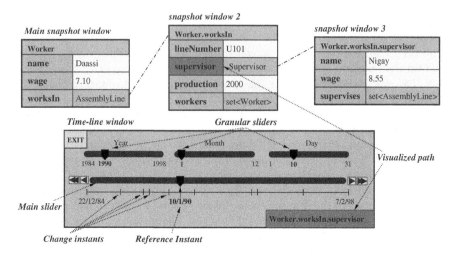

Fig. 5. The pointwise browser interface.

An outcome of this definition is that the pointwise browser displays temporal properties in the same way as it displays non-temporal ones. For this reason, there is a slight difference between the apparent schema of an object visualized through the pointwise browser, and its actual one. For instance, the schema of the database visualized in figure 5 is the one described in figure 3, and not the one of figure 1 as it may appear at first glance (e.g. the actual type of property Worker::wage is bag<TimestampedWage> instead of float).

All the boxes within a snapshot window are clickable buttons, except those which denote literal values (i.e. integers, reals, string, and characters). For instance, in figure 5 all the boxes within the snapshot windows are clickable, except the white-colored ones.

At the beginning of a session, there is a single snapshot window. Other snapshot windows are incrementally added to the tree as the user clicks on the buttons denoting object references. The object displayed by a given snapshot window other than the main one, is equal to the object referenced by the button from which this window was opened. For instance, the configuration shown in figure 5 is obtained by displaying the worker named "Daassi" and successively clicking on the buttons labeled AssemblyLine and Supervisor.

The user may also click on the buttons labeled with property names (i.e. the buttons on the left column of a form). The semantics of this interaction is that the selected property becomes the visualized path expression and the set of "change instants" attached to the time-line window are updated accordingly. For instance, clicking on the button labeled production on window 2 of figure 5, sets the visualized path to be Worker.worksIn.production.

A whole sub-tree of windows can be removed from the screen by clicking on the button from which the root of this sub-tree was opened. For instance, in figure 5, window 2 was opened by clicking on the button denoting the value of property Worker::worksIn. Therefore, clicking on this button again closes windows 2 and 3. The main snapshot window is closed when the time-line window does.

Whenever the user modifies the reference instant by interacting with the time-line window, the new reference instant is notified to the main snapshot window. Upon receiving this notification, the main window computes the snapshot at the new reference instant, of the object that it displays, and updates itself so as to reflect this new snapshot. During this process, if the value of a temporal property changes, the new value is transmitted to its dependent window if any. Finally, the main window propagates the notification of the new reference instant to all its dependent windows, and the above process is carried out recursively.

Figure 6 shows the result of modifying the reference instant over the example of figure 5.

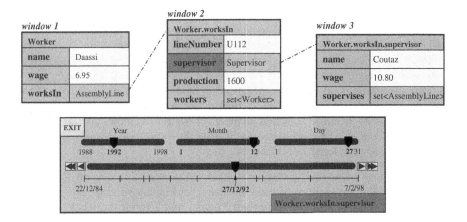

Fig. 6. Modification of the reference instant upon the configuration given in figure 5.

As stated before, the reference instant ranges through an interval called the temporal browsing range. This range is chosen so as to cover all the instants where at least one of the temporal properties of the object displayed by the main snapshot window (called the *main object*) is defined. In other words, the temporal browsing range is taken to be the smallest interval containing all the timestamps within the temporal property histories of the main object. For instance, if the main object is a worker (say W) such that:

W.salary = set(struct(VT: [1..4], VS: 10.0), struct(VT: [6..9], VS : 12.0)) and
W.worksIn = set(struct(VT: [2..4], VS: X), struct(VT: [6..8], VS : Y)).

(where X and Y are two assembly lines), then the temporal browsing range is taken to be interval [1..9]. This definition entails that the main object is temporal, since otherwise, the browsing range would be empty.

3.2   Pointwisely Browsing in the Presence Null-Valued Properties

Heretofore, we have implicitly assumed that all properties displayed within snapshot windows have non-null values. However, null-valued properties within a snapshot window may arise in two cases:

- The value of the property at the reference instant was actually set to "null" through an update (this can occur whether the property is temporal or not).
- The history of a temporal property is not defined at the reference instant, in which case we consider that its value is null. This situation can occur in the middle of a pointwise browsing session, since the temporal browsing range may include instants at which some of the temporal properties of the main object are defined while others are not.

As in O_2Look, we visually denote a null value through a black rectangle. However, this does not solve all the problems arising from nulls. Indeed, suppose that the worker displayed in figure 6 is not assigned to any assembly line at instant 1/5/97 (i.e. there is no element in its history whose timestamp contains this date). If the reference instant is set to this date, the value of property worksIn becomes null, and therefore something has to be done with the forms of the sub-tree stemming from this property (i.e. windows 2 and 3 in figure 6).

In our approach, if further a modification of the reference instant, one of the properties displayed by a snapshot window becomes null, and if this property has a snapshot window attached to it, then all the windows in the sub-tree stemming from this property become *inactive*. Inactivity of a snapshot window can be visually rendered in at least two ways:

- Hide the window (and redisplay it when it becomes active again).
- Modify the appearance of some elements within the window, e.g. by graying out the labels denoting property names and erasing the labels denoting property values.

We believe that the second approach is to be preferred, since hiding and redisplaying windows goes against the screen stability ergonomic principle.

3.3   Pointwisely Browsing Collections of Temporal Objects

To accommodate collections, we augment the pointwise browser with the synchronous navigation concept that we described in section 2.1. As illustrated in figure 7, the user can, as a result of this augmentation, navigate through a collection of objects using the arrow-labeled buttons. This new type of navigation is orthogonal both to the navigation via object relationships (which is carried out using the buttons within the right columns of the snapshot windows) and to the navigation through time (which is carried out using the time-line). For instance, in figure 7, when the user clicks on the right-labeled button of the main snapshot window, the next object in the collection of workers is displayed, while the reference instant remains unchanged.

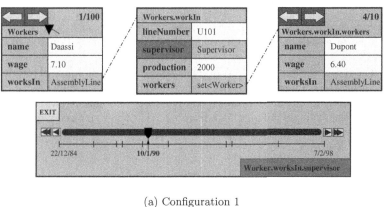

(a) Configuration 1

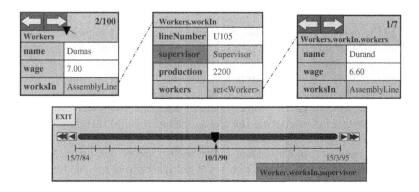

(b) Configuration 2

Fig. 7. Pointwisely browsing a collection of temporal objects. Configuration 2 is the result of clicking on the right arrow of the main snapshot window in configuration 1. Notice that the value of the reference instant remains unchanged, although the time-line is redrawn.

As before, the temporal browsing range is defined with respect to the object visualized by the main snapshot window. Therefore, when this object changes, the browsing range is recomputed. This is the reason why the time-line is redrawn when transitioning from configuration 1 to 2 in figure 7. Notice also from figure 7, that the change instants are recomputed when transitioning from one object to another within a collection.

3.4   Implementation Issues

We have prototyped the pointwise browsing technique on top of TEMPOS [6], a temporal extension of the ODMG's standard implemented on top of the O_2 DBMS.

The response time of the prototype is acceptable for all kinds of interactions, except for the computation of the change instants. Indeed, under some circumstances this computation involves a relatively large amount of data. For instance, consider the example of figure 5 and suppose that the visualized path expression is Worker.worksIn.supervisor.wage. Computing the change instants involves the following histories:

- The history of the employee's assembly lines.
- The histories of the supervisors of each assembly line in which the visualized employee has ever worked.
- The histories of the wages of each supervisor appearing within any of the histories referenced in the previous item.

In the current version of the prototype, we use a naive algorithm to compute the change instants. Under some situations, the execution of this algorithm takes about half a second. This leads to some undesirable interactional discontinuities, especially when the main snapshot window displays a collection of objects. Indeed, the change instants have to be recomputed each time that the user clicks on the Next or the Previous button of the main snapshot window. Designing an efficient technique for computing the change instants would therefore considerably improve the current implementation.

The generation of the visual interfaces is carried out using XForms[5], an Xlib-based toolkit providing a rich set of graphic objects such as texts, buttons, sliders and menus. The choice of XForms was guided by its simplicity, efficiency, and adequacy regarding the design of form-structured windows. Thanks to these features, the implementation of the browser's presentation module required less than 800 lines of C source code.

4   Conclusion and Future Work

We have presented a new technique for browsing temporal object databases. This technique orthogonally supports three kinds of navigation: (i) navigation through time, (ii) navigation via object relationships, and (iii) navigation within the elements of a collection. Our approach to navigation through time is based on the idea of systematically displaying synchronous values of attributes, relationships, and more generally, arbitrarily complex path expressions involving temporal properties.

In temporal database research, synchronization of temporal attributes and relationships has usually been associated with querying (e.g. SQL/Temporal's *sequenced queries* [15] and TempOQL's *pointwisely generalized operators* [8]).

---

[5] http://world.std.com/~xforms

With respect to these works, our contribution has been to demonstrate the need to integrate this synchronization at the browsing level, and to propose a browsing technique to this end.

As a future work, we aim at extending the pointwise browser into a visual query language. A seamless approach towards this goal is to exploit the concept of "query in place" developed in PESTO. This concept allows one to transform a form-based interface designed for object browsing, into a query formulation tool. Another seamless approach to extend the pointwise browser into a visual query interface, is to integrate its underlying principles into the visual interface to ODMG's OQL reported in [9].

Data contained in a temporal database may either be timestamped so as to reflect the evolution of the modeled reality (valid-time), or to reflect the time when it was inserted/deleted into/from the database (transaction-time). In the former case, the database is said to be *historical*, while in the latter case it is said to be *rollback* [11]. In some situations, it is necessary to timestamp data both with respect to the modeled reality and the database evolution, leading to *bitemporal databases*. Up to now, we have limited ourselves to temporal databases managing a single dimension of time, whether valid-time or transaction-time. Extending our work to bitemporal databases could constitute another interesting perspective, provided that concrete applications requiring interactive browsing in this context are exhibited.

References

1. J. Bertin. *Graphics and Graphic Information Processing.* Walter de Gruyter & Co, Berlin, 1981.
2. R.G.G. Cattell and D. Barry, editors. *The Object Database Standard: ODMG 3.0.* Morgan Kaufmann, January 2000.
3. T. Catarci, M. Costabile, S. Levialdi, and C. Batini. Visual query systems for databases: a survey. *Journal of visual languages and computing*, 8(2), 1997.
4. M. Carey, L. Haas, V. Maganty, and J. Williams. PESTO : an integrated query/browser for object databases. In *Proc. of the Int. Conference on Very Large Databases (VLDB)*, Mumbai, India, August 1996.
5. Y. Dennebouy, M. Andersson, A. Auddino, Y. Dupont, E. Fontana, M. Gentile, and S. Spaccapietra. SUPER: visual interfaces for object + relationship data models. *Journal of visual languages and computing*, 6(1):27 – 52, 1995.
6. M. Dumas, M.-C. Fauvet, and P.-C. Scholl. TEMPOS: A Temporal Database Model Seamlessly Extending ODMG. Research report 1013-I-LSR-7, LSR-IMAG, Grenoble (France), March 1999.
7. S. Dar, N.H. Gehani, H.V. Jagadish, and J. Srinivasan. Queries in an object-oriented graphical interface. *Journal of visual languages and computing*, 6(1):27 – 52, 1995.
8. M.-C. Fauvet, M. Dumas, and P.-C. Scholl. A representation independent temporal extension of ODMG's Object Query Language. In *proc. of the French Conference on Advanced Databases (BDA)*, Bordeaux, France, October 1999.
9. L. Fegaras. VOODOO : a visual object-oriented database language for ODMG OQL. In *Proc. of the ECOOP Workshop on Object-Oriented Databases*, Lisbon, Portugal, June 1999.

10. S. Fernandes, U. Schiel, and T. Catarci. Visual query operators for temporal databases. In *Proc. of the 4th Int. Workshop on Temporal Representation and Reasoning (TIME)*, May 1997.
11. C.S. Jensen and C.E. Dyreson (Eds). The consensus glossary of temporal database concepts – February 1998 version. In O. Etzion, S. Jajodia, and S.M. Sripada, editors, *Temporal Databases: Research and Practice*. Springer Verlag, 1998.
12. D. Plateau, P. Borras, D. Leveque, J.C. Mamou, and D. Tallot. Building user interfaces with Looks. In F. Bancilhon, C. Delobel, and P. Kanellakis, editors, *The story of O₂*. Morgan Kaufmann, 1992.
13. C. Plaisant, B. Milash, A. Rose, S. Widoff, and B. Schneiderman. LifeLines: Visualizing Personal Histories. In *proc. of the ACM CHI conference*, Vancouver, Canada, April 1996.
14. P. Papapanagiotou and B. Theodoulidis. ERT/vql: A visual environment for querying and manipulating temporal database applications. Technical Report TR-94-5, Timelab, UMIST, 1994.
15. R.T. Snodgrass, M. Bo Transitioning temporal support in TSQL2 to SQL3. In O. Etzion, S. Jajodia, and S.M. Sripada, editors, *Temporal Databases: Research and Practice*. Springer Verlag, 1998.
16. E. Tufte. *The visual display of quantitative information*. Graphics Press, 1984.

Towards a Unified Query-by-Example (UQBE): UML as a Basis for a Generic Graphical Query Language

Miguel A. Sicilia Urbán [1], Elena García Barriocanal [2] , and
Juan M. Dodero Beardo [1]

[1] Carlos III University, Madrid, Computer Science Department, DEI Laboratory, Avda.
Universidad, 30, 28911 Leganés, Madrid, Spain
{msicilia, dodero}@inf.uc3m.es
[2] Alcalá de Henares University, Computer Science Department, Escuela Politécnica,
Campus Universitario, 28871 Alcalá de Henares, Madrid, Spain.
elena.garciab@uah.es

Abstract. A generic graphical query language for ODMG-compliant object
databases – called Unified Query By Example (UQBE) – is proposed, based on
the ideas of Zloof's Query-By-Example, and using UML-like diagrams as
schema notation. Both ease of learning for users coming from the relational
world and support for non object-oriented data sources are also considered as
design goals. The overall layout and some important features of the query
language are described, along with its relationship with the UML repository
architecture and several ODMG OQL translations of sample UQBE queries.

1. UQBE: A Simple Graphical Query Language for Object Databases

Query-By-Example (QBE) is a graphical query language for relational databases
developed decades ago at IBM by Moshe Zloof [1][2]. QBE is a complete domain
calculus language [3] and its expressive power is proved to be equivalent to that of
SQL [4]. Although it has been included in a variety of commercial products, ranging
from mainframe character-terminal programs (like IBM OS/390 Query Management
Facility [5]) to personal database engines (like Borland's Paradox [6]), it was
originally designed to be used "sitting at a terminal". Modern Visual Query Languages
(like Visual Query Builder, included in Borland's Delphi) can also be considered as
descendants of the QBE philosophy, but they're adapted to modern workstation
bitmapped user interfaces. In this paper, we present our initial results in the effort of
designing a graphical query language for object databases, called *Unified Query By
Example* (UQBE), based on the underlying ideas of QBE, but designed specifically
for a modern graphical user interface (GUI). Unlike other QBE-inspired languages for
the object world, like OOQBE [7], we have devised a generic language, capable of
supporting non object-oriented data sources and concepts as well (although we do not
cover this point in detail in this paper).

K.R. Dittrich et al. (Eds.): Objects and Databases 2000, LNCS 1944, pp. 185-196, 2001.

We have focused on usability and simplicity and not on expressive power, and therefore our current UQBE definition lacks many advanced features compared to other visual query languages. Our ultimate aim was an "entry-level" query language, and as a consequence, UQBE design goals were the following:

> UQBE should be standards-based.
> UQBE should be simple and intuitive (just the way QBE is).
> UQBE should be strongly GUI-based.
> UQBE should be easy to learn to object database users, and also to users coming from the relational world (and it should be capable of querying relational sources).

The rest of this section describes the relationship between UQBE and other standards and the overall appearance of UQBE. Section 2 describes UQBE queries on single classes, and Section 3 does the same for queries that involve association traversal. Section 4 describes some additional features of the language and conclusions are provided in Section 5.

1.1. Related Standards

QBE queries are constructed by filling "table skeletons" extracted from a relational database schema. We have selected a similar approach by showing class diagrams, extracted from the object database schema, and letting the user fill some information to build his/her query. Given that the *Unified Modeling Language* (UML) is becoming mainstream in the software industry, we have selected UML-like diagram elements as the UQBE notation, trying to respect UML notation [8] as much as possible, but adding the needed user interface elements for querying. On the other hand, ODMG version 2 *Object Query Language* (OQL), a textual language based on SQL92 among other influences [9], is the only non-vendor-specific or non-system-specific query language for object databases. The work presented here focuses only on UQBE definition, ignoring most implementation issues, and therefore, our current implementation translates UQBE queries to OQL text that can be used with commercial object databases.[1] From here, we assume to be making queries on a database that supports ODMG 2.0 (or some equivalent model), and therefore we will use ODMG object model concepts.

---

[1] Due to the generic nature of UQBE, we also support other kinds of data sources through the use of SQL queries via Microsoft's ActiveX Data Objects (ADO) interfaces on OLEDB data sources or JDBC libraries on ODBC data sources. We consider relational schemas as restricted versions of object schemas, but details are not described in this paper.

1.2. UQBE Graphical Interface

User interface design for UQBE is a mixture of QBE and existing modeling tools like *Rational Rose*. In fact, UQBE would ideally be packaged with a modeling tool capable of importing object database schema. Figure 1 sketches UQBE overall screen layout.

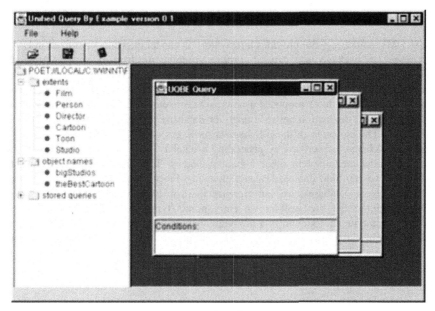

Fig. 1. UQBE interface layout

When UQBE starts, the user is prompted for the database to be queried (a relational data source or an object database). Then, a tree view on the left side of the main UQBE window shows the available database-scope navigation entries for the database, namely, extents and object names. The user opens the schema and can "drag-and-drop" some of them from the tree-view to one of the windows in the right pane, originating UML-like class boxes to be displayed, along with its associations. The user can form several independent queries at a time, each of them in a separate window (note the *Multiple Document Interface* appearance in the right pane).

Object names can refer to any single object, literal, or collection contained in the database. We indicate the kind (single element or collection) of each entry point with two UML stereotypes (in UML-like class boxes): «collection» or «singleton», since queries are different for each of them (note that extents are always collections). In the case of a relational data source, tables extracted from the schema will be shown as extents.

Class boxes represent the class of the single object or the base class of the collection (collection type is irrelevant in declarative languages). Attributes of object type are showed via UML associations with the corresponding type, and attributes of literal type are showed as UML attributes, in order to draw a clear distinction between querying elements inside an object or elements reachable by link traversal. In addition, the user can type expressions on the "conditions" part of the query windows regarding schema elements. Finally, the result of a query can be an object or literal,[2] or a collection of them, which would be showed in a separate window.[3]

1.3. UQBE Relationship with the UML Architecture

Any UML modelling tool provides a repository of model elements organized in UML *packages*. A package is a general-purpose grouping mechanism, and therefore all query-related elements can be stored in a package. Since packages can be specialised at design time through standard mechanisms (namely, stereotypes, constraints and tagged values), we have proposed a new package stereotype (called <<Schemata>>) to draw a clear distinction between query or database elements and the rest of model elements. The elements in those Schemata packages could be obtained by reading a database schema, or perhaps by generating a database schema from a subset of the design model contained in other logical packages. Therefore, inside an Schemata package, we can hold database-related elements. From the point of view of a query tool for object databases, we can organize them in two sub-packages: Extents and Object Names, the two well-known entry points types in ODMG databases. Our UQBE prototype shows them in a tree-view form similar to existing modelling tools, as we saw in Figure 1. Figure 2 shows an example of the described package structure (a dependency is shown from Object Names to Extents since object names refer to instances whose class usually has an associated extent).

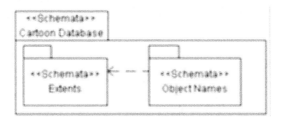

Fig. 2. Package structure for object names and extents

The notion of an Extent can be used to model relational tables (without polymorphism semantics, of course). Both extents and object names are bound to a class stored in the database schema. The difference is that the type associated to an object name can change when a different object is bound to that object name.

---

[2] An ODMG literal differs from an object in that it has not object identifier (OID); we only deal with atomic literals rather than collection or structured ones.

[3] Similar to spreadsheet-like navigable interface for instances that can be found in commercial tools like ObjectStore's *Object Inspector* or *POET Developer*.

The sub-package organization just presented can be extended to model other non-ODMG kinds of database entry points like, for example, ObjectStore's *OSReferences*, and to store previously defined queries, as we'll see later.

From the viewpoint of the UML metamodel, there's an important semantic difference between UQBE diagrams and normal class diagrams: UML class diagrams are views on the UML repository (and so, each class is stored only once in it), but UQBE class boxes need to store query-specific information and therefore, each time we put a class in a UQBE diagram, a separate repository model element needs to be stored for it.

2. Simple Queries

Let's first describe queries that don't involve navigation traversal. UML-like class boxes, called UQBE class boxes, are made up of query-specific elements (like the controls on the left of the upper image in Figure 3) and a UML class representation (the right part of Figure 3). Query-specific elements can be hidden (collapsed) to make the diagram appear as a standard UML diagram. On a class box we can specify the following query criteria:

> We can mark an attribute's checkbox to select it (equivalent to 'P.' QBE command), or the class name's checkbox to show all the attributes. Checking the class name (the checkbox is not showed in the figures) will query for a collection of database objects, since the query will return entire objects with identity, while checking attributes will give as a result a collection with query-generated literals.
> We can type comparison expressions following attribute names. The type of the attributes is showed in the tree-view or via "tool tips".[4]
> We can specify collating order by typing numbers in "spin edit" controls and selecting order from a combo box (ASC, DESC or none).

The images that follow are screen-shots for the current UQBE prototype. We have used also an equivalent simplified representation closer to UML that hides some of the details showed in screenshots. We have used the plus and minus signs that denote visibility in UML tools for the selection of attributes and/or methods (the function of checkboxes in the screen-shots) in that simplified form. Figure 3 shows the same query in both views.

The results of the query will show only the selected attributes of the object instances that satisfied the specified criteria, with a tabular representation. Given a database with an extent on class *Cartoon*[5] (see Figure 3), we could select attribute *title*, type a condition on attribute *year* (to obtain films between 1950 and 1980) and another on *title* (to obtain films whose title begin with "An"), and select primary and secondary sorting criteria. The generated OQL for that query would be the following:

---

[4] Small labels that appear when the mouse pointer is paused over a user interface element.

[5] A sample database extracted from POET 6 OODBMS Trial Edition.

```
select x.title
from    CartoonExtent x
where   x.year > 1950 and x.year < 1980
and x.title like "An*"
order by x.year DESC, x.title
```

We will obtain a collection of string literals as result.

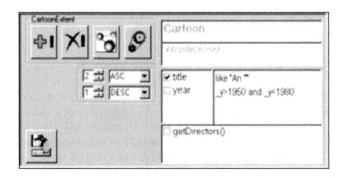

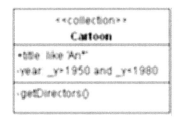

Fig. 3. An UQBE query on a single class[6] and its equivalent in simplified representation.

Note that we have defined variables by typing identifiers on the attributes (like _y in Figure 3), and used them in expressions. Conditions that affect multiple attributes of a class must be typed in the separate *Conditions* list-box, as it's done in QBE conditions table. The semantics are the same as those of QBE *domain variables*, and we have used the same notation: the identifiers must start with an underscore. For example, we are forced to type a condition if we want to specify the logical operator *or* between two attributes, overriding the described default conjunctive semantics.

We can also put one of the OQL aggregation operators (*count, sum, min, max, avg*) on an attribute to obtain a single literal with the corresponding summary data.

---

[6] Note insert, delete, hierarchy and run buttons in the upper left corner and "save query" button in the bottom.

3. Navigating Associations

Associations between classes are showed by default in UQBE diagrams. Since we execute queries only on entry point elements, other classes reachable from it via association traversal are automatically included in the query (if the user marked something on them). The OQL query will be generated by building a path expression from that class to any other class selected in the query, using schema information. Figure 4 shows an UQBE query equivalent to the following OQL sentence:

```
select film.title
from FilmExtent AS film, film.directors AS director
where director.Name = "Avery, Tex"
```

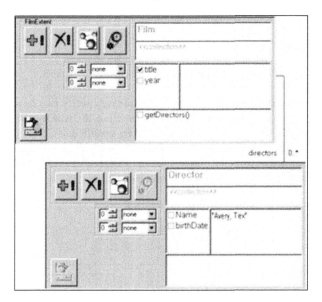

Fig. 4. An UQBE query involving association traversal

Figure 5 shows the simplified diagram for the query in Figure 3.

Expressions in *conditions* list allow the user to build more complex queries. For example, if we want to build a query to retrieve name and year of the films which have an associated director with the same name (for example, a film called "Almodovar" from famous film director Pedro Almodovar), we'd have to do the following:

check *title* and *year* attributes from *Film* UQBE box.

type a domain variable in *title* attribute of *Film*, for example, _t .

type another domain variable in *Name* attribute of *Director*, for example, _d.

type the condition _d = _t in one of the lines of the query window's *conditions* section.

The generated OQL would be the following:

```
select film.title, film.year
from FilmExtent AS film, film.directors AS director
where director.Name = film.title
```

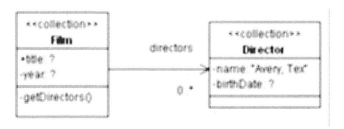

Fig. 5. UML diagram for UQBE query in Figure 3.

To compute a join in an object oriented database we specify two or more potentially unrelated collections in the from clause and then use the where-predicate to specify joining criteria. In UQBE, those criteria should be specified as Conditions in the query window (showed as UML notes attached to classes in our simplified representation). Figure 6 shows a join example corresponding to OQL query (extracted from [9]) that retrieves people whose first name is a flower's name:

```
select p
from Persons p, Flowers f
where p.firstname = f.name
```

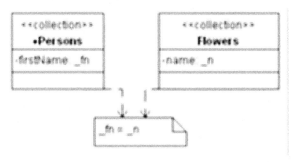

Fig. 6. Example of join operation in UQBE.

4. Additional Features

4.1 Schema and Instance Update

Inserting an object in QBE is as simple as writing values on the corresponding class box and clicking on the insert button. This works also for association implicit collections, and can be translated to OQL construction expressions. For example, if we take a blank diagram with *Film* and *Director* classes, we can type some values for *name* and *birthDate* attributes in *Director* box and click its insert button. UQBE will build an OQL type name constructor expression like:

```
Director(Name: "John Ford",
         birthDate: date '1973-2-26')
```

The insertion of the newly created element in *directors* collection is done by obtaining the collection through a *select* query and then inserting the new director. Of course, this kind of update is done through ODMG language mapping code (Java in our prototype) and not through a single OQL sentence.

Insertion can be done also in association implicit collections. To insert in association implicit collections we have to select an UQBE path and then click insert button in the class box that represent the class of the instance/s to be created. The example in Figure 7 shows in simplified representation how we can add a member to Financial Department (this time the plus and minus signs of attributes and methods do not imply any query semantics). As OQL does not support explicitly that kind of update, we have used OQL+ expressions – an proposed extended version of OQL – to describe it in an SQL-like form:

```
insert into
         Depts[name="Financial"].members
         values set(Employee(name:"Jim",
                             age:42,salary:30000))
```

In a similar way, we can delete instances on an entry point by specifying a query and clicking delete button (instance deletion doesn't have a direct OQL translation). We have decided to leave general updates on individual objects as a responsibility of the separate result window (the object browser) for now, since OQL lefts instance update to be done via method execution, following a common assumption: explicit updates should be carried out by operations defined on classes.

We have left unimplemented also schema definition and update, because these manipulations are better handled from a separate modelling tool, and imply some administration criteria (like schema and instance evolution).

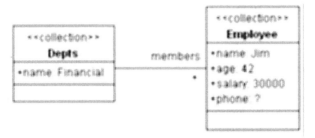

Fig. 7. Insertion in association implicit collection

Methods are supposed to guarantee object state postconditions, as is explicit in the Eiffel language. Since we are using alternative ways of updating the database, object state can become invalid. And we also need to address the problem of non-deterministic updates. Insertion and deletion can break database consistency in subtle ways, so the conclusion is that we need some kind of declarative ("outside- of-the-methods") integrity checking facility (one of the best choices for this purpose could be the use of UML *Object Constraint Language* to specify predicates).

4.2. Nested Queries and Method Invocation

To keep UQBE diagrams simple we have adopted a compositional approach for nested queries. UQBE allows the user to save a query and associate a name with it (these named queries are showed in the UQBE *tree view*, under the "stored queries" folder, see Figure 1). After that, the user can *drag and drop* that query on the right pane, and a class box representing the results of the query will appear (a single instance or collection). The user can then make a query on the result of the previous one, just like he/she does on an entry point. The result is a nested OQL query. In a similar way, method invocations that return a collection (like *getDirectors()* in Figure 3) or a single instance can be saved as a named query, and additional queries can be defined for them. The point is that method invocation's result and query executions are treated as entry points, since they ultimately are defined from one of them.

A query like the prior one can be stored (by clicking a button) and associated with a name. Stored queries are hold in a separate schemata package. A stored query can be reused in other UQBE diagrams, and its type is the type of the result of the query in represents. Another class stereotype like <<Query>> can be used to differentiate persistent queries from other model or UQBE elements within the UML repository.

4.3. Filtering Collections

Any UQBE collection defined on a base class C can also hold instances of any subclass of C, following the well-known semantics of polymorphism. Filtering (sometimes called *dowcasting* as in [10]) is a very common operation on collections that returns a new collection, with one of the subclasses of the original collection as the base class. Filtering is implemented in UQBE through hierarchy buttons on collection class boxes. When we click one of these buttons, a separate window shows us the inheritance hierarchy of the base class of the collection, letting us to select one of the classes (called the filtering class, whose name appears as a "tool tip" on the hierarchy button). Actual filtering is done by the UQBE program code, and it's not translated to an OQL query.

5. Conclusions and Future Work

Our work establishes the basis for a simple graphical query language based on UML that follows a different approach to object visual queries provided in languages that use flow notation (a relevant example is Kaleidoquery [11]) or a graph-based complex notation, like Quiver [12]. UQBE is simpler, easier to implement, and better suited for integration with existing modelling or database administration tools.

In our first Java prototype, tested only on Windows platform, we have only covered a small portion of the complex OQL syntax (we have used POET OQL to test our prototype, and it only supports a simplified version of the ODMG OQL *select* clause). Therefore, much work remains to be done, but we believe that a restricted implementation like the one described here brings some important benefits for the object database market:

UQBE is a good choice for simple interactive queries, whenever the user is novice or comes from the relational world.

UQBE can be used as a tool for teaching object database or object modelling basics.

Object database and modelling tool vendors would be able to offer a common visual query language, improving their user and administration suites.

A simplified version of UQBE can be used for relational databases, making joins between collections by marking the foreign key of a table (represented as a class) and the key in the parent table with the same attribute variable (just like in QBE). This generic design follows the spirit of some "relational-compatible" ODMG constructs like *tables, keys* and *joins*, and facilitates transition from the relational paradigm. The prototype presented here has grown from the feedback of a group of relational developers, and we'll continue UQBE evolution based upon those "relational compatibility" criteria.

UQBE must be extended and refined with additional constructs to cover the rich OQL syntax, adding optional advanced features to those described here (current prototype for UQBE lacks support for important OQL constructs like *group by* clauses.). As simplicity is one of UQBE's design goals, the addition of advanced features should be carried out along with associated usability inspection processes (techniques can be found, for example, in [13]).

An important future improvement for UQBE is the integration with some kind of object navigational browser. Good starting points could be PESTO [14], an integrated query/browser user interface for object databases, which follows a similar approach to that of UQBE for specifying queries, and *Inspector*, a spreadsheet-based browser for *ObjectStore* databases with support for queries.

Current UQBE definition is informal, and support for both object and relational sources has only been tested in a set of common queries on simple schemas. Formalization of UQBE is currently in progress, based on VQL foundation [15], but trying to integrate additional UML standard constructs. For example, the use of domain variables, borrowed from UQBE, could be replaced by using some subset of UML *Object Constraint Language* (OCL).

References

1. Zloof, M.: Query By Example, NCC, AFIPS, 44 (1975)
2. Zloof, M.: QBE: A Language for Office and Business Automation. Computer (1981) 13-22
3. Ullman, J.D.: Principles of Databases Systems, Second Edition. Computer Science Press (1982) 207-209
4. McLeod, D.: The translation and compatibility of SEQUEL and Query By Example. In: Proc. Intl. Conf. Software Engineering, San Francisco, CA (1976)
5. IBM: Using QMF Version 3 Release 3. Document Number SC26-8078-01. Appendix 1.1.10. (1997)
6. Prestwood, M.: Corel Paradox 9 Power Programming. Osborne/McGraw-Hill (1999) c. 11
7. Staes F., Tarantino, L.: OOQBE: An Intuitive Graphical Query Language with Recursion. In: Salvendy, G., (ed.): Human-Computer Interaction: Software and Hardware Interfaces. Vol. 19B, Elsevier (1993)
8. Object Management Group (OMG): Unified Modelling Language Specification, Version 1.3. (June 1999), available at http://www.omg.org/
9. Cattell, R. (Editor) *et al*: The Object Database Standard: ODMG 2.0. Morgan Kaufmann Series in Data Management Systems, Morgan Kaufmann Publishers (1997)
10. Blaha, M. and Premerlani, W.: Object-Oriented Modeling and Design for Database Applications. Prentice Hall (1997), p.101
11. Murray, N.: Kaleidoquery: A Visual Query Language for Object Databases. In: Proc. of Advanced Visual Interfaces, L'Aquila, Italy (1998) 25-27
12. Chavda, M., Wood, Peter T.: Towards an ODMG-compliant Visual Object Query Language. In: Proc. 23th Intl. Conf. on Very Large Databases, Athens, Greece (1997)
13. Nielsen, J. and Mack, R. (*editors*): Usability Inspection Methods. John Wiley & Sons, New York (1994)
14. Carey, M., Haas, L., Maganty, V., Williams, J.: PESTO: An Integrated Query/Browser for Object Databases. In: Proceedings of the 22nd International Conference on Very Large Data Bases, September 3-6, Bombay, India (1996)
15. Vadaparty, K., Aslandogan, Y., Ozsoyoglu, G.: Towards a Unified Database Visual Access. ACM-SIGMOD Conference (1993) 357-366

Concluding Remarks

Klaus R. Dittrich[1], Giovanna Guerrini[2], Isabella Merlo[2],
Marta Oliva[3], and M. Elena Rodríguez[4]

[1] Dept. of Computer Science, University of Zurich, Zurich, Switzerland
dittrich@ifi.unizh.ch
[2] Dipt. di Informatica e Scienze dell'Informazione, Universita' di Genova, Italy
{guerrini, merloisa}@disi.unige.it
[3] Dept. d'Informàtica i Enginyeria Industrial, Universitat de Lleida, Lleida, Spain
oliva@eup.udl.es
[4] Dept. Llenguatges i Sistemes Informàtics, Univ. Politècnica de Catalunya, Spain
malena@lsi.upc.es

This ending section briefly summarizes the remarks, impressions, and ideas that came out from the panel session held at the end of the symposium.

The discussion started from the fact that Object Oriented Database Management Systems (OODBMSs) have not achieved the success that they promised when they were launched. The first commercial products appeared in the middle eighties and after fifteen years they are still a market niche out of the competition with the very big Relational Database Management Systems (RDBMSs). Starting from this remark, the discussion went on in two directions. First, we discussed the possible motivations for this, trying to understand why the object-oriented technology, that has emerged in several fields - as an example let us recall the "Java boom" in the programming language field-, has not been able to compete with the relational technology in the database area. The second part of the discussion was mainly devoted to sketch what can be done to make OODBMs a successful technology, devising its strengths and its lacks.

Why are OODBMSs still in the shadow of RDBMSs? This is a very good question and, of course, to which there is not a single answer, but many. Surely the fact that database management systems, in general, deal with data which have to last for years played a main role in this. Indeed, many systems, which are now called legacy systems, were based on relational technology and to migrate all these data would imply an enormous effort in terms of money and time, thus the ratio efforts/benefits did not motivate the change. By contrast, OODBMSs presented, at least in the early years, drawbacks, such as the lack of declarative query languages, access control support, transactional mechanisms, and integrity constraints, whose support had determined the success of relational databases. Finally, the fact that the ODMG (Object Data Management Group) standard itself did not have an impact in the development of OODBMs comparable to the one of SQL (Structured Query Language) in RDBMSs came out from the discussion as another proof of the hegemony of relational technology in the management of data.

K.R. Dittrich et al. (Eds.): Objects and Databases 2000, LNCS 1944, pp. 197–198, 2001.

It would be obvious to think that, coming up with these conclusions would lead people at the symposium to a very pessimistic mood, but this was not the case! Do not forget, for instance, that theoretical foundations of the relational model date back to the seventies, but relational databases were successful in the nineties. The reaction was: try to find out what we can do as researchers to improve the current status of OODBMSs in order to make them more and more competitive with respect to RDBMSs. Surely, we can say that an SQL-like query language should be developed to get data from OODBMSs as easy and as quick as RDBMSs. Then, integrity constraint enforcement is another big issue to cope with and which has been completely neglected so far by current products.

Finally, we would like to underline that frequently things are so different depending on the point of view one looks at them. Now, we do not speak any more of pure RDBMSs, rather we speak of Object-Relational Database Management Systems (ORDBMSs). Indeed, most RDBMSs vendors have incorporated in their systems object-oriented features, such as the capability of defining abstract data types (classes), encapsulation, polymorphism, and inheritance. ORDBMSs are just at the beginning and we believe that in next generation systems more and more object-oriented features will be included. This fact by itself can be regarded as a success of object-oriented databases and as the proof of their usefulness. Looking at the future, we want to believe that next generation systems would support a peaceful coexistence of the two data models, the relational and object-oriented one, in a unique system, giving born to very powerful systems. These systems should be capable to capture complex data relationships effectively, as well as provide the performance, reliability and scalability that most of current applications need.

Author Index

Lecture Notes in Computer Science

For information about Vols. 1–1910
please contact your bookseller or Springer-Verlag

Vol. 1941: A.K. Chhabra, D. Dori (Eds.), Graphics Recognition. Proceedings, 1999. XI, 346 pages. 2000.

Vol. 1942: H. Yasuda (Ed.), Active Networks. Proceedings, 2000. XI, 424 pages. 2000.

Vol. 1943: F. Koornneef, M. van der Meulen (Eds.), Computer Safety, Reliability and Security. Proceedings, 2000. X, 432 pages. 2000.

Vol. 1944: K.R. Dittrich, G. Guerrini, I. Merlo, M. Oliva, M.E. Rodriguez (Eds.), Objects and Databases. Proceedings, 2000. X, 199 pages. 2001.

Vol. 1945: W. Grieskamp, T. Santen, B. Stoddart (Eds.), Integrated Formal Methods. Proceedings, 2000. X, 441 pages. 2000.

Vol. 1946: P. Palanque, F. Paternò (Eds.), Interactive Systems. Proceedings, 2000. X, 251 pages. 2001.

Vol. 1948: T. Tan, Y. Shi, W. Gao (Eds.), Advances in Multimodal Interfaces – ICMI 2000. Proceedings, 2000. XVI, 678 pages. 2000.

Vol. 1949: R. Connor, A. Mendelzon (Eds.), Research Issues in Structured and Semistructured Database Programming. Proceedings, 1999. XII, 325 pages. 2000.

Vol. 1950: D. van Melkebeek, Randomness and Completeness in Computational Complexity. XV, 196 pages. 2000.

Vol. 1951: F. van der Linden (Ed.), Software Architectures for Product Families. Proceedings, 2000. VIII, 255 pages. 2000.

Vol. 1952: M.C. Monard, J. Simão Sichman (Eds.), Advances in Artificial Intelligence. Proceedings, 2000. XV, 498 pages. 2000. (Subseries LNAI).

Vol. 1953: G. Borgefors, I. Nyström, G. Sanniti di Baja (Eds.), Discrete Geometry for Computer Imagery. Proceedings, 2000. XI, 544 pages. 2000.

Vol. 1954: W.A. Hunt, Jr., S.D. Johnson (Eds.), Formal Methods in Computer-Aided Design. Proceedings, 2000. XI, 539 pages. 2000.

Vol. 1955: M. Parigot, A. Voronkov (Eds.), Logic for Programming and Automated Reasoning. Proceedings, 2000. XIII, 487 pages. 2000. (Subseries LNAI).

Vol. 1956: T. Coquand, P. Dybjer, B. Nordström, J. Smith (Eds.), Types for Proofs and Programs. Proceedings, 1999. VII, 195 pages. 2000.

Vol. 1957: P. Ciancarini, M. Wooldridge (Eds.), Agent-Oriented Software Engineering. Proceedings, 2000. X, 323 pages. 2001.

Vol. 1960: A. Ambler, S.B. Calo, G. Kar (Eds.), Services Management in Intelligent Networks. Proceedings, 2000. X, 259 pages. 2000.

Vol. 1961: J. He, M. Sato (Eds.), Advances in Computing Science – ASIAN 2000. Proceedings, 2000. X, 299 pages. 2000.

Vol. 1963: V. Hlaváč, K.G. Jeffery, J. Wiedermann (Eds.), SOFSEM 2000: Theory and Practice of Informatics. Proceedings, 2000. XI, 460 pages. 2000.

Vol. 1964: J. Malenfant, S. Moisan, A. Moreira (Eds.), Object-Oriented Technology. Proceedings, 2000. XI, 309 pages. 2000.

Vol. 1965: Ç. K. Koç, C. Paar (Eds.), Cryptographic Hardware and Embedded Systems – CHES 2000. Proceedings, 2000. XI, 355 pages. 2000.

Vol. 1966: S. Bhalla (Ed.), Databases in Networked Information Systems. Proceedings, 2000. VIII, 247 pages. 2000.

Vol. 1967: S. Arikawa, S. Morishita (Eds.), Discovery Science. Proceedings, 2000. XII, 332 pages. 2000. (Subseries LNAI).

Vol. 1968: H. Arimura, S. Jain, A. Sharma (Eds.), Algorithmic Learning Theory. Proceedings, 2000. XI, 335 pages. 2000. (Subseries LNAI).

Vol. 1969: D.T. Lee, S.-H. Teng (Eds.), Algorithms and Computation. Proceedings, 2000. XIV, 578 pages. 2000.

Vol. 1970: M. Valero, V.K. Prasanna, S. Vajapeyam (Eds.), High Performance Computing – HiPC 2000. Proceedings, 2000. XVIII, 568 pages. 2000.

Vol. 1971: R. Buyya, M. Baker (Eds.), Grid Computing – GRID 2000. Proceedings, 2000. XIV, 229 pages. 2000.

Vol. 1972: A. Omicini, R. Tolksdorf, F. Zambonelli (Eds.), Engineering Societies in the Agents World. Proceedings, 2000. IX, 143 pages. 2000. (Subseries LNAI).

Vol. 1973: J. Van den Bussche, V. Vianu (Eds.), Database Theory – ICDT 2001. Proceedings, 2001. X, 451 pages. 2001.

Vol. 1974: S. Kapoor, S. Prasad (Eds.), FST TCS 2000: Foundations of Software Technology and Theoretical Computer Science. Proceedings, 2000. XIII, 532 pages. 2000.

Vol. 1975: J. Pieprzyk, E. Okamoto, J. Seberry (Eds.), Information Security. Proceedings, 2000. X, 323 pages. 2000.

Vol. 1976: T. Okamoto (Ed.), Advances in Cryptology – ASIACRYPT 2000. Proceedings, 2000. XII, 630 pages. 2000.

Vol. 1977: B. Roy, E. Okamoto (Eds.), Progress in Cryptology – INDOCRYPT 2000. Proceedings, 2000. X, 295 pages. 2000.

Vol. 1979: S. Moss, P. Davidsson (Eds.), Multi-Agent-Based Simulation. Proceedings, 2000. VIII, 267 pages. 2001. (Subseries LNAI).

Vol. 1983: K.S. Leung, L.-W. Chan, H. Meng (Eds.), Intelligent Data Engineering and Automated Learning – IDEAL 2000. Proceedings, 2000. XVI, 573 pages. 2000.

Vol. 1984: J. Marks (Ed.), Graph Drawing. Proceedings, 2001. XII, 419 pages. 2001.

Vol. 1987: K.-L. Tan, M.J. Franklin, J. C.-S. Lui (Eds.), Mobile Data Management. Proceedings, 2001. XIII, 289 pages. 2001.

Vol. 1989: M. Ajmone Marsan, A. Bianco (Eds.), Quality of Service in Multiservice IP Networks. Proceedings, 2001. XII, 440 pages. 2001.

Vol. 1991: F. Dignum, C. Sierra (Eds.), Agent Mediated Electronic Commerce. VIII, 241 pages. 2001. (Subseries LNAI).

Vol. 1992: K. Kim (Ed.), Public Key Cryptography. Proceedings, 2001. XI, 423 pages. 2001.

Vol. 1995: M. Sloman, J. Lobo, E.C. Lupu (Eds.), Policies for Distributed Systems and Networks. Proceedings, 2001. X, 263 pages. 2001.